DOING CULTURE
CROSS-CULTURAL COMMUNICATION IN ACTION

中西文化之鉴
——跨文化交际教程

Linell Davis（美）

外语教学与研究出版社

FOREIGN LANGUAGE TEACHING AND RESEARCH PRESS

北京 **BEIJING**

图书在版编目(CIP)数据

中西文化之鉴——跨文化交际教程/(美)戴维斯(Davis, L.)著 . — 北京:外语教学与研究出版社, 1999

ISBN 7 - 5600 - 1767 - 3

Ⅰ. 中… Ⅱ. 戴… Ⅲ. 英语—语言读物,比较文化 Ⅳ. H319.4

中国版本图书馆 CIP 数据核字 (1999) 第 73689 号

出 版 人:李朋义
责任编辑:刘相东
出版发行:外语教学与研究出版社
社　　址:北京市西三环北路 19 号 (100089)
网　　址:http://www.fltrp.com
印　　刷:北京市鑫霸印务有限公司
开　　本:850×1168　1/32
印　　张:11.125
字　　数:196 千字
版　　次:2001 年 9 月第 1 版　2005 年 12 月第 5 次印刷
书　　号:ISBN 7 - 5600 - 1767 - 3
定　　价:13.90 元
＊　　　＊　　　＊

Contents

LIST OF CASE STUDIES

LIST OF FIGURES

Preface

Many things happened during my sabbatical leave in 1998-1999. Among those of enduring significance is the completion of the book *Doing Culture: Cross-cultural Communication in Action* by my long-time friend, Professor Linell Davis. Few people, I think, can be as qualified as she is for writing a book on such a topic. She did her graduate study in sociology, social work, and anthropology at the University of Pittsburgh and American University in Cairo respectively. Before her first visit to China in 1987, Professor Davis had been an associate professor and chair of the Department of Sociology and Social Work at Seton Hill College in Pennsylvania for many years. She taught courses in intercultural communication and social work for over a decade and a half. Her education and teaching experience endowed her with a perspective rarely found in people trained in other fields.

China holds a special fascination for many Americans just as the United States does for many Chinese. Professor Davis' visit to Nanjing University on an exchange program that year turned out to be only one of many of her subsequent visits. Leaving her tenured position at Seton Hill, she spent nine years out of the past twelve in China, teaching at Nanjing University and Sichuan University as a "foreign expert". Her passion for Chinese culture, landscape, and most significantly, the Chinese students is genuine, profound and affecting. For her outstanding service, she received "Friendship Award for Foreign Experts" from Jiangsu Provincial Government in 1997. In Nanjing and Chengdu, she taught a variety of courses, among which were cross-cultural communication, American films and American culture to undergraduates and graduates alike. She also cooperated with her Chinese colleagues in Nanjing University in designing a cohesive 4-year English writing curriculum and editing four writing textbooks. To further expand her cross-cultural experience, Professor Davis undertook cross-cultural training and consultation, during holidays and vacation, for international and local organizations, such as Software Center Motorola China, Nanjing Ericsson Communication Co. She also did media consultation for various Chinese organizations such as Jiangsu TV, Yixing Special Development Zone, Jiangsu Tourism Agency, Jiangning Economic Development Area, etc. Her book *Doing Culture: Cross-cultural Communication in Action* undoubtedly draws heavily on all these teaching, training and consultation experiences in China.

I found the book title itself interesting. The phrase "Doing Culture" which is meant to be a contrast to learning "about" culture underscores the idea that communicating across cultures is a process of making meaning, of people understanding one another so they can get to know one another, build relationships, and solve problems together. It should not be words on paper, but ideas in practice.

The whole book is well designed. The first three chapters are concerned with attitudes. These chapters include opinion surveys and other activities to give the students a chance to explore and perhaps change attitudes so they are better prepared to communicate with people across cultures. The next three chapters are about what usually happens when Chinese and westerners first meet. It covers guest/host relationships, the fears and uncertainties that accompany the first contact, and some differences in the meaning of friendship.

The seventh, eighth and ninth chapters are about non-verbal aspects of communication such as cross-cultural differences in sensory perception, interaction distance differences, environmental design and basic cultural patterns of the grid, the star and the inside/outside contrast. Chapter Ten deals with the relationship between thinking, language and culture.

Chapters Eleven through Fifteen focus on cross-cultural communication in the work place. In Chapter Eleven students are encouraged to explore their home culture values and put them in comparative perspective. In Chapter Twelve the implications of value differences for work are covered. Chapter Thirteen covers the entirely new and important topic of teambuilding across cultures, which is a topic worth developing further and making it a book of its own. Chapter Fourteen looks at how national cultures influence the culture of organizations, and Chapter Fifteen considers how people need to alter their communication behavior in writing, interviewing and negotiating to be effective cross-culturally. The final chapter explores what occurs when people move from their home culture to another one. The focus is on adopting strategies that ease adjustment.

I am fully convinced that a wide range of readers both in China and abroad will benefit from this theoretically sound, experience laden, culturally rich and user-friendly book. For this we need to thank its author, Professor Davis, for her hard work and broad heart.

Liu Haiping
School of Foreign Studies
Nanjing University
June 28, 1999

Introduction

When I first came to China in 1987 on a faculty exchange program, I thought I would stay for a year. It would be exciting, I thought, to see something of China and get to know Chinese teachers and students. Maybe the experience would enrich my life and teaching back home. That was all I expected. What happened in the following years, however, was that I exchanged my life in the US for an extended period of teaching in China. It has been a most rewarding and challenging life.

This book is the fruit of that life. Even before I came to China I had spent my long summer holidays from university teaching traveling abroad. I had also extended my professional interest in sociology to include cultural anthropology and was already teaching a course in cross-cultural communication to my American students. In my travels and academic work, little by little, I moved beyond the usual tourist experiences and easy generalizations about cultural differences to a deeper curiosity about the ways in which the peoples of the world live their lives. An equally powerful motivation to learn about China has often come from the simple, practical need to understand my work situation, Chinese friends, and students better.

Learning about Chinese culture

In learning about China, Chinese people have been my best teachers. Sometimes I learn when students and friends answer my questions. Often I learn because I fail to understand something and end up confused or in the middle of a cross-cultural misunderstanding. Sometimes I learn when I completely fail in what I am trying to do and express my frustration by putting the blame on others. I appreciate the patience and kindness of many people who have forgiven me my outbursts and mistakes and, in

1

ways they did not even recognize, helped me to understand them better. Another way that I learn is to put forth an idea or principle to test it out. Again, my students and friends have been most helpful. They listen politely and then show their respect and affection by gently correcting my mistaken ideas.

Using this book in university English courses

Because I am a teacher and originally developed the materials that grew into this book for my course in cross-cultural communication, I wrote it as a textbook. Chinese English teachers are encouraged to use it for advanced English courses, specifically for courses they teach to students who have passed the Band Four English Examination. Students at this level in their English learning need to add cultural skills to their language skills. We are already living in an information age global village. In such a world, cultural skills are essential.

Some Chinese teachers of English may doubt that they are qualified to teach cultural skills. Please do not worry about that. Learning cultural skills is something like learning how to swim or how to ride a bicycle. After some brief instruction, the learner has to practice. The book is designed to give brief instruction and then give students an opportunity to practice. The teacher is expected to be a guide and helper rather than an expert. There are few experts in this field, and even if expert knowledge were more plentiful, we would still have to personalize our learning by applying it to our own lives. The assignments and student activities are called "Exploring Ideas", because I think at this stage of our cross-cultural understanding that is what we all need to do. I learn many new things every time I teach the course.

Using case studies to learn culture

Not many Chinese people have yet had much experience communicating directly with people from other cultures. At the same time personal experience is the best way to learn cultural skills. To bridge the gap between need and opportunity, I have included case studies to simulate, as far as possible, the cross-cultural experience in class. About half of these cases were written by two friends and former colleagues, Mary Knapp Wang and Wang Weizhong, when they were at the East West Center at the University of Hawaii. I also thank Dr. Richard Brislin of the University of Hawaii for his permission to use the case studies that were written there. Other case studies I wrote myself based on my own experience or on the experiences of people I know.

All of the case studies ask the question "what is going on here?" or "what went wrong?" Often there are several possible answers and one student's opinion may not be the same as another's. That uncertainty is realistic and it motivates students and teachers to discuss the cases further. This stimulates their active English learning and helps them to learn cultural skills at the same time.

Using this book to increase cross-cultural skills on the job

While writing this book I have had two additional audiences in mind:

- **Chinese professionals** in any field may want to read this book for what it can contribute to their professional work. As I teach my Chinese students I know they will live and work in an increasingly multi-cultural world in which they will need increasingly sophisticated cultural skills. As English majors they have a good start on learning those skills, but most Chinese learn English in addition to another specialty. They also need cross-cultural skills, and once they leave the university they have to learn on their own. I hope this book will help them.
- **Chinese and international companies** often face cultural problems in their work. I welcome training managers and staffs to use this book to increase the cross-cultural compe-

3

tence of their organizations as a whole. A wholly Chinese organization may not have any foreign employees, but it may have foreign customers. This book can help the staff become more knowledgeable about their customers' needs and expectations. It can also be used to prepare Chinese personnel for business trips abroad. I also invite training staffs to use the material in the book to increase the mutual understanding and effectiveness of expatriate and Chinese staff who work together.

Readers may think it unusual that a foreigner has written a book that in some sense describes Chinese culture for a Chinese audience. I can only say that I tried to write the book in a way that expresses my affection and respect for the people of China. It is my attempt to contribute something of value in appreciation for all that China has given to me. My understanding of Chinese culture is limited, so I have certainly misinterpreted or failed to recognize many things. I hope the readers of this book will let me know when they discover my errors, so that I can continue to learn.

Chapter 1: Thinking Globally

Thirty years ago the Canadian writer Marshall McLuhan introduced the term global village to express the idea that the world seems to be getting smaller. The planet Earth is not shrinking, but time and space are.

In a village residents communicate with other residents face to face. They usually meet formally from time to time to share information and make decisions, but most of the time information and opinions flow from person to person informally in talk between neighbors and family members. They know when other residents have suffered a disaster or are celebrating good fortune. They help one another, quarrel, work together and against one another as feelings and circumstances require them to do so. They share each other's lives for better or for worse. Now the whole world is like a village.

Trains, planes, telephones, televisions, the Internet, and other forms of modern transportation and communication reduce the time and distance that once kept the peoples of the world apart. Even people who do not travel far from home live in the global village. People who live in small towns watch television reports of wars and disasters half a world away and work in factories making goods for export to distant markets. Now a Chinese leader can meet with American students and journalists in a contemporary version of the village meeting, and the rest of the world will listen in by means of a television signal carried by a satellite orbiting the earth.

In the metaphor of the global village, nations are like families and continents are like neighborhoods. People feel most at home in their own families, but they go out of the house regularly to do some business and to buy what they need in the market. Now markets and businesses are global. If a neighbor's house burns down, it affects everyone. Others may be expected to give shelter to the victims. The smoke and flames may threaten someone else's home and family. If someone dumps garbage into the village well, the neighbors can't say it is his own business, because they also get their water from that well.

Residents want to stay on good terms with their neighbors. They may simply think that is the proper and civilized way to live. They may consider their neighbors to be a lot like them and therefore understand them and like them. They may remember that some neighbors helped them when they had some trouble. Perhaps they have just learned that life is better when people co-operate with one another. If some residents of the village have had trouble with their neighbors in the past or think they are strange or inferior, they may be suspicious and on guard to pro-tect themselves from harm in the future.

As in a village the nations (families) of the world are de-pendent on one another. Time and space no longer isolate or protect nations and groups from each other. As global environ-mental problems become more serious, people realize that the rivers of the world flow and the winds of the planet blow with-out regard to national boundaries. The economic, political and military actions of other nations are the actions of our neighbors. We might wish we could treat them as distant events that do not concern us, but in the global village that is not possi-ble.

Uneasiness with the global village image

Not everyone welcomes this image of the global village. To some it seems like an image of post-colonial dominance of the world by the West. They prefer to see the world in terms of their own family, their own nation. They may say, "We do not want to live in a village that someone else makes for us and con-trols." They worry that the global economy will force everyone to become like the families of the world that have the most eco-

6

nomic and political power. They do not want to be second class citizens in the village, and they do not want to give up their own treasured ways of life.

Others worry that conflict will increase as time and distance shrink. From news reports everyone can see that religious, ethnic, economic, and political differences continue to divide people. They rightly ask, "How can I and the members of my family get along with members of that other family who seem so different from me?" They see troubles in other families and wonder why they can't solve their problems. Above all, every family wants to protect itself. No one wants the problems of another family to spread to their family.

Whatever anxiety people have about the global village, they can see that contact among the peoples of the world is increasing. If the world is becoming more like a village, as its residents we want it to be a good place to live. Everyone wants to benefit from global trade and advanced technology, and they want to live among people who respect and appreciate one another. They want to protect themselves from danger and live at peace with their neighbors. But most people do not want peace imposed on them by the power of another family. They want to live in their own way.

These are some of the challenges of living in a global village. To meet those challenges people everywhere need to learn about other cultures. They need to know their neighbors. They need to do more than know about them. They need to know how to get along with them and how to solve problems that inevitably arise. To do this it is necessary to learn how to communicate across cultures, or in the words of the title of this book, how to do culture. That means residents of the global village need to learn to think, feel and behave in new ways. The reality of the global village challenges all its residents to develop a broader worldview, a more global psychology, and the cultural skills necessary for building relationships and solving problems across cultures.

Study the following list of developments that experts cite to convince us that the world is becoming a global village:

A. Satellite transmission of telephone, radio and television signals;

B. International computer networks such as the Internet;

C. Increased speed and availability of air travel;

D. International economic relationships such as multi-national corporations and foreign trade;

E. Economic cooperation through organizations such as the European Union and the Association of Southeast Asian Nations;

F. Economic regulation through global organizations such as the World Trade Organization;

G. The movement of people from rural areas to cities and from developing to developed countries;

H. More intense political, military, and diplomatic relationships among nations;

I. Environmental issues such as over-fishing of the oceans, global warming, deforestation, endangered species of plants and animals, waste disposal, and air and water pollution;

J. Higher standards of living that give more people the chance to travel and enjoy their leisure, thus stimulating the growth of the international tourism industry.

1. In small group discussions, describe how each development influences your personal life and the life of your nation. In what ways do these developments also effect people whose lives appear to be more traditional than your life? Think of specific changes these developments are creating in the lives

8

of people who live in remote areas as well as for people who live in modern cities.

2. In what ways are these developments causing fundamental changes in the relationships among the peoples of the world?

3. What benefits and problems do you expect from life in the global village?

New and old images of the world

Poets, scientists and artists have always given us images that help us make sense of our world. Marshall McLuhan's image of the global village is just one of the more recent ones. Another Canadian, Buckminster Fuller gave us another image "spaceship earth" that emphasizes that the planet Earth is like a finely tuned machine with limited resources. A short time later, astronauts took photographs of the earth from space and suddenly people around the world saw that the planet we call home is a delicate, beautiful, blue ball suspended in the vastness of space. We could see physical features of land, sea, winds and clouds but no political or cultural boundaries, no human activity at all.

Such images can and do change the way we see the world. The new ones compete with older images that come from local and national cultures. As an American I am familiar with several images about the meaning of the United States and its role in the world. The United States is a "melting pot" and it is a "city upon a hill", a phrase that comes from the Bible. Many younger Americans no longer accept the melting pot image, because it includes the idea that people lose their home cultural identities, traditions, and values when they become Americans. In recent years many people have proposed that Americans give up the melting pot image and replace it with the image of a "mosaic". A mosaic is made up of diverse materials or elements that keep their original character when they are combined to create a new design. This new image expresses the idea that part of the American way of life is respect for cultural diversity.

The "city upon a hill" image dates back to John Winthrop, the leader of the English Puritans who settled in North America in the seventeenth century. When their ship was about to land he told them that the new society they intended to build "shall be a City Upon a Hill, the eyes of all people are upon us." The Puritans expected their society to be better than the one they were leaving. Over time this image has come to represent the idea that somehow the United States is special and an example for other nations to follow. American politicians continue to use the phrase "city upon a hill" when they want to say that the United States needs to live up to its moral ideals and play a role of moral leadership in the world. No doubt that image gave generations of Americans confidence in their work of nation building, and certainly the American experience has inspired people around the world. On the other hand, when American officials or private citizens try to persuade people in other countries to do things the "better" American way, they can be most irritating.

My students tell me that as Chinese they are "descendents of the dragon". When I ask them to explain, they say that the dragon does not exist in nature (it is a mythical creature), it is powerful, and it is energetic. As descendents of the dragon they and Chinese people everywhere share these characteristics.

The Cheyenne, a Native American group, traditionally called themselves by a word that in English means "the human beings". This image suggests that they felt superior to other groups. It might also mean that they thought there was a "right", a human way to live. Maybe they saw outsiders as barbarians because they did not live in a "human" way.

While the people of some cultures are proud of the purity of their cultural heritage, the people of Mexico and the Philippines have an image of themselves as "mestizo," a Spanish word that means "mixed". They are proud that their cultures are a mixture of two or more great cultures.

Exploring Ideas

1. Make a list of images from your home culture and try to explain what they express about who the people of your culture are and what their relationship is to people from other cultures. For instance, does the image of the Middle Kingdom suggest that China is the center of the world or the center of civilization? What other meanings are parts of this image?

2. Compare older and newer images of your culture. Which do you prefer? Which do you think are the images that most truly express how people feel about themselves and the world? How compatible are these images with images of the global culture such as the global village and spaceship earth?

3. If you are in a class with people from different cultures and nations, explain your home culture images to one another.

4. Talk with someone from a different culture to find out what images they have of themselves and their culture. If no one is available, study the images on the national flags of other countries and do some research to find out what the images mean.

5. The images that people have of themselves are often quite different from the images people from other cultures have of them. When I ask my students for images of the United States they may produce a list like this: Michael Jordan, Oscar awards, Coca-Cola, White House, skyscrapers, eagle and the first man on the moon. Make a list of images of another culture and then discuss those images with someone from that culture to find out how accurate and complete they think your images of their culture are.

Surveying Opinions

What attitudes do residents of the global village have about

11

their neighbors? Conduct the following survey to find out. If possible, give the survey to someone you know from another country. This is a good way to start an interesting conversation.

AN EXPLORATION OF ATTITUDES FOR RESIDENTS OF THE GLOBAL VILLAGE

For each statement indicate whether you:

1. Strongly agree
2. Somewhat agree
3. Have no opinion
4. Somewhat disagree
5. Strongly disagree

A. ___The higher standard of material life in Western Europe and the US proves the superiority of western culture.

B. ___The fact that China has the longest continuous civilization proves its superiority.

C. ___Foreigners going to live in a new country should give up their foreign ways and adapt to the new country as quickly as possible.

D. ___Foreigners living in another country should behave as proper guests and avoid interfering in the affairs of the host country.

E. ___Much of the world's population does not take enough initiative to develop themselves, therefore they remain "underdeveloped".

F. ___The underdevelopment of much of the world is due to colonial and post-colonial exploitation by developed countries.

G. ___The sooner the people of the world learn to do things the right way, the sooner we will all understand each other better.

H. ___Countries may welcome outsiders for particular reasons but they should limit the influence of foreign ideas and ways of life.

I. ___The stress some societies place on individual freedom and rights contributes to the neglect of the well being of society as a whole.

J. ___The people in some societies do not place any value on human life. To them life is cheap.

K. ___People of every culture are entitled to the full use of their own language as an essential part of their culture.

L. ___One of the major languages should be adopted as the universal language of the world.

M. ___All people should be fluent in as many as three languages: their mother tongue, their national language and an international language such as English.

N. ___The cultures of primitive or native hunter and gathering peoples are inferior to the cultures of agricultural and industrial societies.

O. ___All cultures represent legitimate, fully human ways of being in the world.

Discussing the survey results

1. Collect the data from all the students in the class and compile it into a chart. List each question and then count how many strongly agree, somewhat agree, etc. Convert the numbers to percentages. For instance, 34% agree and 60% disagree and 6% have no opinion.

2. Form small groups to interpret the survey results. One group may discuss the three questions having to do with language (K, L and M) while another discusses the questions about cultural superiority and inferiority (A and B). What is the meaning of the responses your classmates gave? Is there strong agreement or disagreement or are attitudes very mixed? Would you expect Chinese of a different region, different ages, or a different educational level to have similar or different attitudes from those of your class?

   You may or may not agree with your classmates' opinions. Whether you agree or not, you should discuss the ways in which these differences of opinion might influence life in the global village. Will people have to change some of their attitudes if the village is to be a good place to live for everyone?

   Below is a list of the issues contained in the questions:

   A, B — inferiority or superiority of one culture in relation to another

   C, D — attitudes toward foreigners

   E, F — reasons for differences in level of economic development

   G, H — a measure of "ethnocentrism", the belief that the values and behaviors of one culture are "right"

   I, J — a measure of cultural values about individual rights and social rights

   K, L, M — attitudes toward language

   N, O — attitudes toward the relative value of different types of cultures

   If you conduct this survey with people from another

country, you may find differences in their attitudes as compared to those in your class. These differences can be traced back to differences in the histories of various nations. The United States, for instance, has a history of accepting immigrants, so Americans are more likely to strongly agree with question C than Chinese students are. On the other hand, Americans are notorious for being monolingual; most of them only speak English, so they are not very likely to strongly agree with question M.

3. What other national differences in attitudes do you expect to find? How do these different attitudes help or interfere with creating a global village in which everyone can live comfortably?

Competing Worldviews

Everyone would like to live in a peaceful and harmonious global village, but watching television and reading news reports reminds everyone that the global village is not free from conflict. Some conflicts are over territory or resources such as petroleum or water. Some are conflicts between groups and nations that began generations or centuries ago. Some are disputes over the terms and conditions of trade. All these are difficult to resolve, but there are even more serious conflicts than these.

Some of the major conflicts that are reported in the news involve competition about worldviews. This means that people are fighting and otherwise competing over what belief system will form the basis for the emerging global culture, the culture of the global village.

One author, Walter Truett Anderson, describes these different belief systems as stories. They are stories that people tell themselves not just about their own culture but about the whole world. (See "Culture is the story we tell ourselves about ourselves" page 19.) They are worldviews or images of what the world is like and how people should behave. Each of these

14

worldviews includes a claim that its truth is universal, that is, it is true for everyone, not just for the people from one culture. Some individuals and groups may combine two or more of these stories and there may be additional stories or worldviews that do not appear on Anderson's list.

Stories for the Global Village

1. the Western story of progress, with its enthusiasm for technological change and economic development and its image of a world in which the conditions of life keep getting better for everybody;
2. the Marxist story of revolution and international socialism;
3. the Christian fundamentalist story about a return to a society governed on the basis of Christian values and biblical belief;
4. the Islamic fundamentalist story about a return to a society governed on the basis of Islamic values and beliefs from the Koran; and
5. the Green story about rejecting the myth of progress in favor of living according to ecological values.

Anderson, Reality Isn't What it Used to Be Harper & Row, 1990, P.243

Each of these visions comes from a particular time in history and a particular set of circumstances. Both the Christian and Islamic fundamentalist stories were born in the premodern world and want to return us to a way of seeing the world that offers more moral certainty and security than the modern world provides. They want people to live according to laws and standards of good and evil that come from their sacred religious teachings. Not all followers of these religions want a society governed according to religious law, but the number and strength of movements advocating this has grown dramatically in the last twenty years. Chinese students sometimes think religious believers are poorly educated, but the truth is that many of the leaders of religious movements know the modern world well and have made a conscious choice to live by other values.

Both the capitalist/progress/development story and Marxist socialist story are products of modernism and have much in common even though followers of the two stories fought a cold war for nearly fifty years. Both stories include a confidence in materialism and scientific truth, perceive time as progressive, and see

15

history as an upward struggle out of ignorance and oppression. Both stories borrow from Charles Darwin's theory of evolution and try to apply ideas about survival of the fittest to the survival of civilizations.

The Green story comes from our own age and has become popular only since the 1960's. Greens in various countries protest against the building of new highways and oppose the use of new technologies they think will damage people's health or the environment. They think the idea of progress will one day be replaced by a belief that humans should cooperate with nature and with one another. They take ideas from twentieth century science just as the modernist stories borrow from nineteenth century science.

It is more difficult to resolve conflicts over worldviews than it is to resolve conflicts over territory and resources. What do people do when they realize that others have an entirely different worldview from their own? The first answer may be, "Let them live their way and I will live my way." Unfortunately it is not that simple, because each of these belief systems includes a claim that it is valid and true for everyone. Anderson says there are basically two choices.

1. The first is to take all stories lightly. Be ready to change them or get rid of them when they are not working.
2. The second choice is to deny the truths the other stories express, to argue for one story and against a competing one, or in some cases, to prevent the telling of other stories or living by other stories.

Exploring Ideas

1. Search your knowledge of the world for examples of each of the stories described above. You might include pro-abortion and anti-abortion advocates in the United States, conflicts over religious monuments in Israel and India, arguments be-

16

tween advocates for and against the use of nuclear power, efforts to save the rainforests and the drive to develop underdeveloped areas—among other issues.

2. What is your story for the emerging global culture? That is, which of the stories or worldviews listed above do you accept as the way the world really is or should be?

3. How should the people of the world solve problems of competing stories? For instance, how can the conflicts between Islamic fundamentalists in countries such as Afghanistan, Turkey and Algeria be resolved? How is it possible for peoples with different worldviews to live together in the global village?

4. Do you agree with Anderson that we only have two choices when faced with the reality of competing worldviews? If so, what is your choice? If not, what other choices do we have?

Chapter 2: Becoming Aware

The first step in learning to communicate across cultures, is to consider what people mean when they talk about culture. Most people assume that everyone knows what it means, so they do not define it. In fact people mean quite different things when they talk about culture. The most usual meaning is that culture refers to people's customs and behavior. People have no trouble recognizing that people in different cultures behave differently and have different customs, but they seldom try to figure out what the behavior and customs mean to the people who are following them. This is unfortunate, because culture is all about meanings.

What is culture?

Simply put, culture is a system of meaning. That is too abstract a definition to really understand, so consider the following images.

Culture is like an iceberg

Like an iceberg, only some of culture is visible. Aspects of culture that we can easily observe are often referred to as objective culture. This includes things such as history, literature, and customs. When we learn the facts about our own or other cultures, we are learning the objective culture. Most of culture is below the surface of our awareness. It is not easily observable. This is referred to as subjective culture. It includes feelings and attitudes about how things are and how they should be. When we only learn objective culture, we are missing the bigger part that is below the surface.

Culture is our software

Culture is the basic operating system that makes us human. Humans around the world are physically pretty much the same. There are variations in body size, shape and color, but the basic equipment is universal. We can think of our physical selves as the hardware, but we cannot be said to be human until we are programmed and each of us is programmed by our home culture. Humans are unique among all the animals on earth in that the infant is weak and incapable of survival for an exceptionally long period of time. At birth the infant is only a potential human. It must learn how to be human and it learns that in a culturally specific way. It is the culture that provides the software. As with any good software, we are only vaguely aware of it as we use it. It fades into the background and we just know that we can be, that the computer works, or perhaps sometimes does not work because it is incompatible with someone else's software.

Culture is like the water a fish swims in

Like any creature a fish scans its environment to find food, reproduce and protect itself from danger. It notices everything except the water it is swimming in. The fish takes the water for granted because it so totally surrounds the fish that it really cannot imagine another environment. The same is true for us. Our culture is so much a part of who we are and what the world is like for us that we do not notice it. We take it for granted. For most people for most of their lives, everything they see and do takes place in the same culture. Everyone is swimming in the same water. They couldn't describe the water even if they wanted to.

Culture is the story we tell ourselves about ourselves

Every cultural group has a story that provides a way for members of the group to understand who they are and what the world is like. People tell themselves their story in their folklore, arts, in politics and in intimate conversations among friends and family members. The stories may be very old and include legends of how the group was created, but stories also change to adapt to changing circumstances.

For instance, Chinese often say that China is an old country while the United States is very young. This seems to be true if American culture is assumed to begin with the European settlement of North America or American independence. In fact American culture is an extension of Western culture and that dates back to the ancient Greeks or even the ancient Egyptians. It can be argued that American culture is just as old as Chinese culture, but that is not what is important. What is significant is that Chinese tell this story and use it to define who they are as Chinese in comparison to other groups.

Similarly, Americans often say they are an immigrant nation. If you ask an American about his culture, he will probably tell you something about his ethnic or religious background. He may tell you where his ancestors came from and how they happened to go to America. He will tell you how his life and his family's life are unique. This story emphasizes the diversity within American culture. In fact many visitors comment that the United States is remarkably similar from coast to coast. It is recognizably American no matter what part of the country they visit. It can be argued that the United States is culturally rather uniform with the same language, and similar social attitudes and lifestyles throughout the country, while Chinese culture is remarkably diverse. People speak different languages or dialects in different areas and identify strongly with their local region or hometown. Again, it is not important whether the story is true or not. What is significant is that people tell the story to show themselves and others who they are.

Culture is the grammar of our behavior

Culture is what people need to know in order to behave

20

appropriately in any society. It includes all the rules that make actions meaningful to those acting and to the people around them. In learning to speak, everyone learns to use the grammar of their native language, but they use it automatically with little or no conscious awareness of the rules of grammar. Similarly people learn their cultural grammar unconsciously and apply its rules automatically. Just as native speakers of a language are usually unable to describe the grammatical rules of that language unless they have specifically studied grammar, most people find it difficult to describe the meaning system of their own culture. Like the grammar of a language, cultural grammars are repetitive. They are made up of basic patterns that occur again and again. For instance, an important pattern in Chinese culture is the distinction between inside and outside. This pattern shows up in the language, traditional architecture and in social relationships.

Learning about culture and learning to do culture

These images all point to the idea that culture is largely out-of-awareness. This is not obvious, because people often discuss culture, whether it is their own or the culture of another group or nation. Usually when people talk about culture, they mean some aspect of the objective culture, that part of the iceberg that can be seen above the water. The purpose of this book is to raise the hidden part of the iceberg so that more of it becomes visible.

Another purpose is to enable readers of this book to add new software to their basic operating systems. This means acquiring new cultural skills. No one should try to replace the software they already have; it is neither necessary nor advisable to try to change your culture for another one. It is possible and advisable, however, to add additional software to your operating system to increase its power and flexibility. Just as you want to keep your computer up-to-date by adding software as necessary, you want to add cultural software in order to be successful and

21

comfortable in the global village. Just as you need to know more than one language, you need to know more than one cultural grammar.

To do these things you need to look at your own culture as a system of meaning, as a grammar of your experience and behavior. You need to become a software engineer who can figure out how your own operating system works. Once you do that it is possible to add some new programming. Using another image, you need to become aware of the water you are swimming in. With greater awareness of your own culture, you will better understand the meaning systems of other cultures and will be better able to adapt to them.

English learners in China often take courses in American culture or Western civilization and feel confident that they know quite a bit about Western culture. In fact they do know much **about** the culture from which the language they are studying comes. They may have seen many Western films, may eat at KFC regularly, may know more about the National Basketball Association or about current popular music than many Americans, may speak quite fluent English, but that does not necessarily mean that they know American culture the way an American knows it. It doesn't mean they know the cultural grammar or can swim in those cultural waters. It doesn't mean that they can "do" American culture.

A fish in unfamiliar waters

A Chinese student, confident in her knowledge of American culture, prepares to give a speech in English appropriate for an international audience for an English speaking contest. In the speech she paraphrases Martin Luther King, jr. by using the phrase "I have a dream." She is confident that her intended international audience will understand the reference.

She is right. The audience will know that she is quoting Martin Luther King, jr. but they won't necessarily be impressed. King's speech was given thirty-five years ago and is so widely known that quoting it may be considered too simple, as saying what has already been said too many times. In the last years of the twenti-

---

eth century, it might be more appropriate to talk about visions than about dreams. Better yet, the speaker should invent a new and attractive metaphor to carry her meaning. An image from her home culture might be fresher to her audience than her borrowed phrase.

To most Americans and many other Westerners time flies by very quickly so using an out-of-date metaphor reveals you to be out of date. How much worse if you quote Abraham Lincoln or Thomas Jefferson. If you quote Ernest Hemingway to a literary audience your listeners will either think you are a sexist or that you haven't read anything in fifty years. If you quote him to an audience of young people who have technical rather than liberal arts training, they may not know who Hemingway is. Even if they do recognize the name, they probably will never have read anything Hemingway wrote.

In Chinese culture a writer or speaker shows her learning by quoting famous people from the past. It is not necessary to even say where the quote comes from. The audience will know and will respect your knowledge. In the United States people rarely quote famous people from the past unless it is an especially sentimental or patriotic occasion where it is understood that old and familiar images should be remembered. Many people attend such events with an attitude of amused nostalgia. It might be fun to hear those old cliches again.

If you quote a less well known person from the far past, you will be showing yourself to be very learned, which may or may not be appropriate for the situation. It might be all right at an academic conference, but even on that occasion, it might be more effective to quote a television commercial or make fun of the lyrics of a Madonna hit song.

Americans like to do something unexpected. An advertising executive may get his audience's attention by quoting the ancient Greek philosopher Plato, while a university professor might cleverly surprise an academic audience by using the famous Nike advertisement when he says, "Just do it."

If you quote Martin Luther King, jr. some listeners may suspect you of mocking him, as it is considered clever to quote a famous saying in an ironic or satirical way.

The cultural waters are treacherous indeed! Already we can see that the stories people tell themselves about culture, and especially about their own culture, are very different. To an American, culture is a fast moving train, and it is better for a speaker to stumble over his words than to fail to keep up with the train. To a Chinese, culture is a treasure of great works and cultural achievements. Speakers are expected to present themselves as cultured persons by speaking well and showing their knowledge of the appropriate cultural treasures.

Exploring Ideas

1. Form groups of three to five people to discuss the difference between knowing about a culture and being able to use the cultural grammar of a culture. To review, a cultural grammar is the collection of rules for behavior that make it meaningful. In your groups, select a particular culture (Great Britain, Japan, Brazil, Germany, Malaysia, etc.). Make two lists, one to show what members of the group know about that culture and the other to show what cultural grammar from that culture you can use. When you have finished, have a large group discussion to report the conclusions of each group.

2. From what you know of the cultural grammar of the United States or another English speaking country, give advice to a Chinese English speaker about how to make a speech to a Western or international audience.

Characteristics of culture

This is probably the most widely accepted definition of culture:

- *Culture is the total accumulation of beliefs, customs, values, behaviors, institutions and communication patterns that are shared, learned and passed down through the generations in an identifiable group of people.*

An important characteristic of culture is that it is shared. People with the same culture share ideas, ways of behaving, and a whole way of life. What members of a culture have in common includes values and beliefs, customs, perhaps gestures or certain foods and ways of eating. They may also share a distinctive his-

24

tory and artifacts as well as an artistic tradition including music, literature and folk stories. These shared aspects of culture are part of the objective culture, the part of the iceberg that is above the surface of the sea. But this definition does not go far enough. It leaves unanswered the important question of what causes members of a particular culture to agree that certain behaviors or historical events have certain meanings.

As participants in a culture, we are meaning makers

People often talk about the world as if it "has" meaning, as if the meaning of things were built into them. When people are living totally within their home cultures, meaning does, indeed, seem to be obvious, fixed, and mostly unchanging. As members of a particular culture, it is easy to believe that we are merely passively receiving meanings that are built into things. It takes some effort to realize that a gesture, a painting, or a contract has no meaning until someone assigns it. Humans are the meaning-making animals, and it is in making meanings that our human ancestors created culture and the particular cultures within which we all live. We ourselves continue this human activity of making meaning, of responding to and interpreting what goes on around us in such a way that we can make sense of it. We are constantly but unconsciously creating order and predictability out of the raw material of our day-to-day experience by assigning meaning to it. Sharing culture is sharing meanings.

It is the complex system of meanings that we merely accept from our culture without being aware that that is what we are doing that tells us how to interpret what is going on in any situation. It is what allows us to mold our actions and responses so that we behave in a way that others with whom we share culture can accept. It is what allows us to behave appropriately according to the meaning system of our culture.

25

Cultures are always changing

It is also necessary to recognize that cultures are not static. They are constantly changing and evolving under the impact of events and through contact with other cultures. Changes in behaviors and customs might occur rapidly while changes in basic patterns and values, in ways of looking at the world, in meaning systems, tend to occur more slowly.

Beginning to do culture

Learning to do culture rather than simply learning about culture is an ambitious undertaking. It is first necessary to raise your level of awareness. Reading this book and doing the suggested activities is a way to begin.

Another strategy you can use is to practice seeing your culture the way others who are not a part of it see it. Foreign observers are usually far from objective, but they often notice things that you have never noticed. Some of the most insightful writers about the American character and American culture have been Europeans. They were able to see things that the natives took for granted.

Another strategy is to gain some distance from your home culture by looking at it as if you were a scientist observing it systematically with no prejudgment as to what you will find. This is not easy, but we give you some tools for doing it in the later chapters of this book. By looking at your culture in comparison with other cultures you get some idea of how it may appear to others. The goal is to learn to approach your own culture more analytically and to encourage you to be cautious when interpreting another culture.

Exploring Ideas

1. Look for a book, article or film that describes a foreigner's experience with your culture. For instance, Mark Salzman's

book Iron and Silk and the film made from the book, describe his experiences with Chinese culture.

2. If possible, interview a foreign visitor to your country. Ask them what they noticed when they first arrived and what meaning they made out of what they observed. You may not agree with their analysis, but seeing your culture through other eyes will give you a new perspective. In a class discussion or in an essay give your own interpretations of the characteristics foreigners frequently attribute to Chinese culture.

3. Examine the popular images of your culture that appear in the mass media or literature of another country. To what extent do you agree or disagree with the images or stereotypes that foreigners have of your culture? How do you explain the reasons that these images have become accepted? What do these images tell you about the worldviews or meaning systems of the cultures that created them?

Contact between cultures

It is important to recognize how deeply culture influences us because when people come in contact with other cultures, they interpret the unfamiliar culture according to the meaning system of their home culture. A short fable told by Jean Brick in her book China: A Handbook in Intercultural Communication illustrates this point very well:

> Once upon a time a marmoset [monkey] decided to leave the forest and explore the great, wide world. He traveled to the city and saw many strange and wonderful things but finally he decided to return home. Back in the forest his friends and relatives gathered around. "Well," they cried, "what did you see?"
>
> "I saw buildings made of concrete and glass. Buildings so high that they touched the sky," said the marmoset. And all his friends and relatives imagined glass branches scratching the sky. "The buildings were full of people walking on two legs

27

and carrying briefcases," said the marmoset. And his friends and relatives could almost see the people running along the branches with their tails wrapped firmly around their briefcases.

When people first come in contact with another culture they are frequently like the marmosets. They interpret what they see or are told about the unfamiliar culture in terms of their own world and culture. The interpretations that people make about the meaning of events or behaviors of the new culture frequently do not match the interpretations members of that culture make for themselves.

Robert G. Hanvey in <u>An Attainable Global Perspective</u> (New York: Center for Global Perspectives, 1976) makes this point using an example from French contact with the Indians of North America in the seventeenth century:

> **The French in North America**
>
> When the French began to explore North America they came into contact with a number of aboriginal [native] groups. At various times they attempted to muster [organize] the males of these groups into fighting units. The Indians clearly had no aversion to fighting; they were warriors, skilled in the use of arms, proud of triumphs over an enemy. But they would not take orders. French commanders had no control and the so-called chiefs of these groups depended on persuasion, which might or might not be successful. Every Indian warrior made his own decision about whether to join a raid or war party, worked out his own battle strategy, and left the fray [fight] when he chose.
>
> This kind of contact between the French and the Indians provided the French with detailed information on the ways of their Indian allies—information they noted scornfully in their journals, sometimes sputtering in rage and frustration. But the behavior they described was incomprehensible to them. By virtue of the concrete experiences that the French had with the Indians, the French had rich data, but no understanding. The French were able to see Indian behavior only in the light of their own hierarchical social system, where it is natural for the few to command and the many to obey. Social systems that worked on other principles were literally unimaginable.

Four levels of cross-cultural awareness

Clearly something more than contact with other cultures is needed if people who do not share culture are to understand one another. In the fable of the marmosets and the reports of the French explorers, there was awareness of the other, but it was not an awareness that led to understanding. Hanvey in his book suggests that there are four distinct types or levels of cross-cultural awareness.

Level One: Cultural differences are exotic

The marmosets in hearing about life in the city interpreted what they heard as exotic and strange. They were aware that life away from their forest home was different and undoubtedly enjoyed the entertaining stories of a bizarre and unbelievable life. This is the level of awareness that people get from watching television programs of strange and exotic ways of life. They can only see very visible cultural traits that they most often respond to with a stereotyped view of the unfamiliar culture. This is also the level of awareness of tourists who visit a foreign country on a short trip and the level of awareness most students get from their study of foreign cultures in school. At this level of contact people learn about unfamiliar holiday celebrations, colorful heroes, exotic foods and unusual costumes, music and buildings. People entertain others and themselves with tales of the strangeness of others, but what is entertaining is how unbelievable the culture is.

Level Two: Cultural differences are frustrating

The next level of awareness comes with more substantial contact such as the French had with the natives of North America. The French recorded volumes of information about the Indians they met, and they knew in great detail about significant and subtle cultural traits that were very different from their own way of doing things. They found Indian life unbelievable in a most frustrating and irritating way. This is the level of awareness in which cultures are in conflict. People have knowledge of the other culture but it is still unbelievable. They find people from

29

the other culture to be arrogant, insensitive, dirty, superstitious, manipulative, or in some other ways not very human by their standards.

Level Three: The different culture is believable

At the next level of awareness people also have extensive knowledge of significant and subtle cultural traits and recognize that they are different from our own traits, but now they accept the other culture and its people as fully human. The culture of the other becomes believable; it makes sense as a legitimate way of life. People can accept it in their minds. What previously seemed strange now seems less strange. People at this level are able to look beyond the surface behavior of people in the unfamiliar culture to appreciate what motivates that behavior. They respect the values that people in that culture live by. This is the level of cultural awareness that people should attain with in-depth academic study of a culture as part of a foreign language curriculum. It is also the level of awareness that trainers preparing people for work or study abroad hope to achieve. This pre-contact intellectual awareness may change into Level Two awareness after contact with the new culture or may develop into Level Four awareness. (See "The adaptation process" page 315.)

Level Four: The different culture is believable as lived experience

At the highest level of cross-cultural awareness a person experiences how another culture feels from the standpoint of the insider. The culture is believable because the person accepts it emotionally. He or she participates in the culture by learning the language, making friends and accepting it on its own terms. The participant experiences the culture subjectively. It becomes familiar as lived experience. This is the kind of awareness that comes from cultural immersion, from living the culture.

Level	Information	Way of knowing	Interpretation
1	Awareness of superficial or very visible cultural traits; stereotypes	Tourism, textbooks, TV and films, popular opinion	Unbelievable, exotic or bizarre and possibly entertaining
2	Awareness of significant and subtle cultural traits quite different from your own	Culture conflict situations	Unbelievable in a frustrating way; it seems irrational
3	Awareness of significant and subtle cultural traits quite different from your own	Study about the culture; formal study in school	Believable but only at a thinking level
4	Awareness of how a culture feels to someone who is a member of it	Getting into and living the culture	Believable at an emotional level as it is lived experience

Figure 1   Levels of cross-cultural awareness

The goal for cross-cultural communicators is to reach Level Three or Level Four awareness. In the global village all cultures should be believable, at least intellectually, and ideally emotionally as well. To reach Level Four awareness it is necessary to go beyond objective knowledge to experience the unfamiliar culture on a feeling or emotional level. This requires imagination if you are not actually living in the culture, but you can start by reading the literature, appreciating the music and other arts of the culture you are interested in. A further step would be to have a personal relationship with someone from the culture. In the intimacy of friendship you may learn how the culture feels to a member of it.

Moving to higher levels of cultural awareness involves changing our emotional responses to our neighbors in the global village. To move from Level Two to Level Three people need to set their negative feelings aside to try to see the culture objectively. To move from Level Three to Level Four people need empathy, the ability to "feel with" someone who may be very different from them. One of the challenges of life in the global village is to develop a more global psychology. Part of this psychology is the ability to project ourselves emotionally into the minds and hearts of people with whom we do not share culture.

People often hold the naïve view that contact between cultures necessarily results in greater mutual understanding. Unfortunately the historical record does not support this belief. Achieving mutual understanding is not easy. It takes effort, desire and patience. It helps to realize that the more people are different from one another, the more they have to learn from each other. Part of the new global psychology is appreciating how rich humanity is by appreciating what each culture contributes to it. How much poorer we would all be if we were all alike.

Exploring Ideas

1. Watch a television program about another culture. Does the program show customs that seem exotic or bizarre to you? Is the purpose of the program to entertain the audience with pictures and stories of an unbelievable way of life? Are the producers of the program trying to show the culture from the point of view of Level Three or Level Four awareness?

2. Use the four levels of cultural awareness to evaluate your awareness of particular cultures. How did you get your knowledge or experience of each culture? What is your level of awareness with respect to each culture?

3. Have you ever changed your level of awareness of a culture? Have you moved from one level to another in your awareness of that culture? If so, what caused you to make the shift? Did you move to a higher or to a lower level of awareness?

4. Talk to someone who has traveled to a foreign country. From that person's talk, what level of cross-cultural awareness do you think the person has?

5. Do you think it is possible for people to achieve Level Four

awareness without actually living in the culture? Without knowing the language? Do you agree with the Native American saying, "You do not understand me until you walk a mile in my moccasins."?

Chapter 3: Making Generalizations

When people have little information about a group of people they are likely to think of them in a very general way. If the other people with whom they interact also lack information about that group, they are likely to share an overly simplified view of that group. The result of this process of over generalizing based on limited or inaccurate information is called **stereotyping**.

We all make generalizations

Everyone generalizes every day just to make sense of his experience. No one can respond to every situation as if it were entirely new and unique. A student anticipating a class taught by a teacher he has never met, generalizes from his experience that teachers have certain typical behaviors, opinions, and expectations. The student interacts with the new teacher he meets based on the generalizations he has made from his previous teachers. This is normal and sensible. The student may have a problem, however, if the generalization he makes is too broad or is based on inadequate or outdated information. Such an inappropriate generalization can get him into trouble.

Some generalizations are too broad, out-of-date, or inaccurate

When I was asked to give a lecture to a second year intensive reading class about the American character I was faced with a complex problem of generalization. First of all, are all Americans alike? Do they all have the same character? Of course not, but it is possible to say that Americans tend to have this or that attitude or speak in this or that way. People with a shared experience and shared history do have things in common.

The students had been reading an essay by the respected

American historian Henry Steele Commager. In my lecture I was supposed to expand on what Commager had said about the American character. The essay was written in the 1960's and I was lecturing in the 1990's. Surely much had changed in that time. Another problem was that Commager was comparing American culture to European cultures. While his generalizations may have been appropriate at the time the essay was written and for his intended audience, it was not as useful a generalization for Chinese university students reading it in the 1990's. A further problem was that Commager was describing what have come to be called dominant culture Americans. There was no mention of subcultures, regional or social class differences. I realized that Chinese students who formed their generalizations about Americans from Commager's essay would have many misconceptions.

A generalization that was too broad

When I first arrived in Hong Kong I was invited to a family home for dinner. I had read about leaving food in the bowl to indicate that you have had enough, so after having my fill I left about half an inch of rice at the bottom of my bowl. To my horror the lady of the house gave me a real mouthful, in Cantonese of course. Not speaking the language myself at that time, I had no idea what I had done wrong. I asked my new Chinese friend why his mother had shouted at me so angrily, and I was told that she was upset because I had left some rice in my bowl. Apparently leaving food in your bowl is not the correct thing to do in the South of China.

Some generalizations include positive or negative judgments

In my lecture I tried to point out these problems and caution the students about making generalizations, but usually that does not happen. Thousands, if not millions, of Chinese university students have read that essay and consider it a reliable source. It was reliable for its time and for its intended audience, but it isn't necessarily reliable for all time and for all audiences. Undoubtedly students in other cultures read similar essays about China.

Another problem with generalizations is that sometimes the

35

information we receive about other cultures contains biases. These can be positive biases or negative biases. A reader might think the information is purely factual, while in reality it is intended to encourage a particular attitude toward a specific group or culture. Sometimes even the authors are not aware of their own biases. A few years ago the prestigious Asia Society in the United States did a study of how Asian cultures were described in textbooks used in American schools. They found that American textbooks "often present Asian cultures negatively, regarding them as hindrances to progress or as primitive trappings that will become outmoded when change has taken place." Students using these textbooks are subtly learning that Western culture is superior to Asian cultures.

Such shortcomings in cross-cultural education on both sides of the Pacific should make us cautious about the generalizations we already have in our minds about other cultures and the sources we use when we attempt to refine and improve our generalizations.

Avoiding generalizations that are too broad

In a popular book Joel Garreau put forth the idea that the regions of North America are so different from one another that they can best be understood as separate cultures or nations.

The Nine Nations of North America

Consider the way North America really works. It is Nine Nations. Each has its capital and its distinctive web of power and influence. Several have readily acknowledged national poets, and many have characteristic dialects and mannerisms. Some are close to being raw frontiers; others have four centuries of history. Each has a peculiar economy; each commands a certain emotional allegiance from its citizens. These nations look different, feel different, and sound different from each other, and few of their boundaries match the political lines drawn on current maps. Some are clearly divided topographically by mountains, deserts, and rivers. Others are separated by architecture, music, language, and ways of making a living. Each nation has its own list of desires. Each nation knows how it plans to get what it needs from whoever's got it. Most important, each nation has a distinct prism through which it views the world.

It's valuable to recognize these divergent realities. San Francisco and Los Angeles are not just two cities. They represent two value structures. Indeed they are the capitals of two different nations—Los Angeles the capital of MexAmerica, and San Francisco that of Ecotopia. Chicago is not a capital city, because there is no such thing as the "Midwest." Chicago is properly an important border metropolis directing the trade in values and enterprise between the Foundry and the Breadbasket.

Yet the existence of interstate highways, dense air connections, cheap long-distance rates, ubiquitous television and the celebrated franchised hamburger has lulled many, incorrectly, into some sense that North America has become utterly homogenized, if not bland.

Joel Garreau, Houghton Mifflin, 1981

The excerpt from <u>Nine Nations of North America</u> reminds us that many **subcultures** exist within most national cultures. In this case cultural differences are described in terms of regional economies and characteristics of the populations living in those regions. This is a rather unconventional way of categorizing cultural differences in the U. S. People are more accustomed to thinking of American subcultures in terms of race and ethnic groups. In other countries language differences define the boundaries between subcultures as in the case of French speaking and English speaking Canada.

To avoid overgeneralizations, pay attention to levels of culture

In China people also define themselves as different from one another. Living in Jiangsu Province I have found that people make distinctions between people from the east and those from Nanjing on the basis of language (dialect difference) and those from south of the Yangtze River and those from the north (economic differences). People also define others as similar or different from themselves on the basis of urban or rural residence, occupation (professionals and workers), ethnicity (Han or one of the national minorities) and age.

37

Levels of Culture

As almost everyone belongs to a number of different groups and categories of people at the same time, people unavoidably carry several layers of mental programming within themselves, corresponding to different levels of culture. For example:

- A national level according to one's country (or countries for people who migrated during their lifetime);
- A regional and/or ethnic and/or religious and/or linguistic affiliation level, as most nations are composed of culturally different regions and/or ethnic and/or religious and/or language groups;
- A gender level, according to whether a person was born as a girl or as a boy;
- A generation level, which separates grandparents from parents from children;
- A social class level associated with educational opportunities and with a person's occupation or profession.

By Geert Hofstede, Culture and Organizations, 1991

Paying attention to the many levels of culture is one way to avoid overgeneralizing. People do not usually think of people who are different from them in age, gender or social class as belonging to different cultures. If, however, they remember that culture is a shared system of meaning, then they realize that people who are different in various ways experience the world somewhat differently from the way they experience it.

For instance, a Chinese urban dweller may be sympathetic to the problems of a farmer in the countryside. He or she may admire the farmer and advocate social policies that would benefit him and his family. At the same time the urban dweller might feel unable to fully understand the experience of that farmer, and it is likely that he would not want his daughter to marry the farmer's son. When differences in levels of culture involve age differences, people talk about the generation gap; when they involve differences between men's and women's attitudes or values, people refer to it as the gender gap. The use of the word "gap" is revealing, because it indicates that people in these different categories often have difficulty understanding each other. They do not fully share meanings with one another.

Surveying Opinions

Below is an opinion survey that should help you to discover which levels of culture are most important to you in deciding who you wish to associate with.

1. Before your class or training group takes the survey, add to or revise the descriptions of people in the survey to reflect the cross-cultural experience of your class. For instance, if you live close to a provincial or national border, include a description of your neighbors on the other side of the border. If you work for a company from another country, include a description of one or more people from that country.

2. Complete the survey. Gather the data from everyone in the class. Compile the results by computing an average score for each cultural group or person described.

3. In small groups discuss your perceptions of the groups that had the highest and lowest scores. What is it about members of that group that makes you relatively willing or unwilling to have contact with them? From your discussion you should be able to draw conclusions about how important national culture and the various levels of culture are to you.

How close are you willing to be?

For each "person" described, answer with the number that indicates the highest level of involvement that would be acceptable to you or people like you.

        0. No contact is desirable
        1. Work colleague
        2. Casual friend
        3. Intimate friend
        4. Marriage partner

A. ___ a PRC Han Chinese from the countryside with junior middle school education
B. ___ a Han Chinese professional from Hong Kong or Taiwan
C. ___ a Uighur university professor from Xinjiang
D. ___ a Tibetan shopkeeper from Xizang
E. ___ a Japanese professional working for a large company
F. ___ a Russian businessman or woman
G. ___ a middle class white American
H. ___ an African-American with a university education
I. ___ a technical expert from Nigeria

J. ___ a television actor or actress from Cairo, Egypt
K. ___ a socially and religiously conservative Moslem from Saudi Arabia
L. ___ a Mexican government official educated in the US

Negative stereotypes

When I conducted this survey in a class of third year English majors, I found that students gave quite low scores to people from Arab and Moslem cultures, so I told them this story.

I feel at home here

One day I met a man from Lebanon who was working for a foreign company in Nanjing. "How do you like living in China?" I asked.

"I like living in China very much. I feel comfortable here," he said, "because Chinese culture is so much like my home culture in the Middle East."

The students were very surprised and wanted to know what these similarities were, because their images of his culture did not include any similarities. The man told me that his culture and Chinese culture shared a strong emphasis on family values including respect for elders and unquestioning loyalty to family members. He also said that his culture and Chinese culture were alike in their conservative attitudes regarding relationships between men and women as compared to Western cultures. In China as at home, people understood his values including his obligations and feelings about family and respected them. This made him feel more at home in China than in America or Europe.

The students then told me the images they had of Moslem cultures. The people are fanatic religious believers; women are submissive and oppressed by men; they are sometimes featured in news reports of terrorism. It became clear that the students had little information about Middle Eastern cultures beyond what they knew from news reports and that this accounted for their negative bias or prejudice.

We want to be close to people who are like us

The survey results showed that most important for a perception of similarity was Chinese culture followed by education, residence in a developed country and ethnicity or race. In essays that explained their responses, many students explained their choices by saying that there is an "echo of the heart" when two people share culture. They felt there was something intangible and non-verbal about the intimacy that was possible only with those with whom one shares culture. For these people neither intimate friendship nor marriage is possible with a foreigner. Many students, however, rated educated foreigners higher than less educated members of their own culture.

Gender differences also proved to be important. Some students said that a Chinese man might marry a Japanese woman but a Chinese woman would not marry a Japanese man. Students who answered in this way believe that Chinese men treat women better than Japanese men do and that Chinese women are more independent than Japanese women. Many others did not feel that intimate friendships were possible with members of the opposite sex. (This is another similarity between Middle Eastern cultures and Chinese culture.)

Stereotypes and prejudices

A generalization that goes beyond the existing evidence, an inaccurate or overgeneralization, is a stereotype. We might have positive stereotypes (members of a certain group have good qualities) as well as negative stereotypes (members of the group have undesirable characteristics). In either case it is the inaccuracy or overgeneralization of the characteristics that we attribute to a group that is the problem. Stereotypes that include negative feelings and attitudes toward a group are prejudices. Strong prejudices are sometimes described as racism, sexism, ageism and extreme nationalism. A stereotype involves a person's thinking while a prejudice includes negative feelings as well as nega-

41

tive beliefs about members of a group. Prejudice takes many forms:

Severe prejudice

Some people believe that members of a particular group are inferior according to some standard. For instance, people who believe that women are inferior in mental ability to men are often called sexists, while people who believe that blacks are genetically inferior to whites are called racists. Such people deeply believe that members of the group are not worthy of equal or even decent treatment. This kind of severe prejudice was expressed by many Euro-Americans in their relationship to Native Americans when they agreed with the slogan, "The only good Indian is a dead Indian." Today we are repelled by such terrible feelings, but we all know that such severe prejudice still exists in the world. A number of recent regional wars have been accompanied by words and deeds described by horrified observers as genocide, the attempt to kill all members of the opposing group. Research on prejudice shows that this kind of severe prejudice decreases with education. More educated people are less likely to think that people from another group are inferior or in some way less than fully human.

Symbolic prejudice

Some people have negative feelings about a particular group because they feel that the group is a threat to them in some way. They do not dislike the group itself but feel that the group is a threat to a way of life that they value. For instance, in explaining their responses on the survey students often said that rural relatively uneducated Han Chinese have a "low cultural level". In discussing their opinions, it became clear that my educated students felt that uneducated people, especially those coming to the city from the countryside, threatened their way of life. They might become criminals, might cheat, might live in an un-

42

sanitary way or otherwise make the city less civilized. Those with symbolic prejudice may feel that members of a group (women, rural migrants, immigrants from a particular country, etc.) are making unreasonable demands on the society. They may feel the group is costing them money, driving down wages, putting too great a burden on the public schools or causing over-crowding, crime or a decline in family values. This type of prej-udice is more common among members of the educated middle class in various countries than the first type.

Tokenism

Some people have negative feelings about members of a par-ticular group but do not want to admit this, even to themselves. Such people do not view themselves as prejudiced and to prove this to themselves and others they often participate in unimpor-tant but positive behavior toward members of the group. For in-stance, a person can convince himself or herself that he or she is not prejudiced against members of a minority group by donating a small amount of money to a cause that benefits that group. At the same time the person is likely to pass up opportunities to en-gage in more important behaviors relative to the group, such as giving a significant amount of time and energy to a project that would benefit the group. We might show our lack of prejudice toward the disabled by helping someone in a wheelchair to cross the street, but we may be unwilling to work to make sure that city streets and public buildings are accessible to everyone who must use a wheelchair.

Subtle prejudice

Some people behave toward members of a group in a posi-tive and friendly way in relatively distant social situations but show their prejudice in more personal or intimate social situa-tions. For instance, at a banquet, in the office or at any public social event, the person will be polite and respectful, even

43

friendly, toward someone from the group he or she feels prejudice against. In more personal situations such as a dinner at someone's home or in a group of close friends, the person with subtle prejudice may be uneasy or unfriendly toward the person from the group he does not like. He or she is showing that they want to keep members of this group at a distance and not include them in more personal relationships.

Real likes and dislikes

Some people may have negative feelings about members of a group because they don't like some of the behavior of members of that group. For instance, someone may really be bothered by loud music and knows from experience that members of one group are more likely to play loud music. The person may respect the musical tradition of that group but still may not like it. If the older people in your area are very fond of Chinese opera and like to play tapes of it at loud volume, you may interact with the people who play their music in a disturbing way in a less than pleasant manner. Westerners visiting China sometimes comment on their dislike of spitting or the standard of cleanliness in public toilets. When they meet these conditions, their interactions with the local people involved will probably be negatively influenced by their dislike, even if they fully understand the reasons for the unpleasant situation they find themselves in.

Preference for the familiar

It is more relaxing and comfortable to interact with people with whom we share culture, language, level of education, beliefs, style of communication and experience. What looks like prejudice may, in fact, be a preference for non-stressful and enjoyable interactions. Lack of familiarity with a group or lack of fluency in a language can make it difficult for people to understand and accept one another. It just takes more effort to communicate and the risk of making a mistake is higher. If someone is unwilling to make the extra effort needed, he or she may appear to be insensitive to members of a particular group. It may be that it is only unfamiliarity that causes the insensitivity and misunderstanding. In these instances improved communication skill, help from someone else to bridge language and culture gaps and more familiarity with the group may help to improve the situation.

Exploring Ideas

It can be upsetting when someone calls what you consider a reasonable opinion a stereotype or prejudice. It is not helpful to accuse others of being prejudiced. A better way is to identify your own characteristics and then discuss the prejudices or stereotypes you have experienced because you fit into a particular category.

For instance, if you are a female, you may feel that people make unfair or inaccurate judgments about you based on that characteristic. If you are from a particular region of the country, others may think you have characteristics typical of that region that you do not have. If you are majoring in a particular department, others may think you are like others in that field in ways that you are not.

For this activity, form groups based on the personal characteristics of members of the class. Include gender, age, major field of study, hometown or region, ethnic group, family background, religion, favorite activities such as playing sports, music, dancing, writing poetry, driving a motorcycle, spending time on the Internet, singing Beijing opera, etc.

Form groups by letting one person begin by saying, "I am a girl." The others in the class who share that characteristic meet with her and identify any prejudices in the categories above that they may have experienced. Give concrete examples. As a group report your experience to the class.

Then another person may say, "I am from..." Others who share this characteristic meet and discuss the stereotypes or prejudices they have experienced. Continue this activity until you have discussed all the important categories that people respond to in stereotyped ways.

Attitudes of cultural superiority

Attitudes and opinions about another culture may be positive or negative, accurate or inaccurate, but what about our opinions about our own culture? It is normal and natural for each of us to be proud of our own culture's achievements, values and characteristics, but sometimes we go too far. We allow our pride to turn into an attitude that others are not as good as we are. Here are attitudes of superiority often associated with specific nationalities:

- Americans might think that America is the biggest and the best, the newest and the richest, and all others are a bit slow, old fashioned, rather poor and somewhat on the small side. Visitors to the US have commented that many Americans think all newcomers want to become Americans.
- Some Chinese think they have the highest civilization in the world, that their present relative poverty is the result of historical forces that will soon be corrected, and that the world will one day recognize the superiority of Chinese civilization.
- Spaniards may take pride in being especially brave.
- The French may believe that they are intellectually superior to everybody else.
- Germans may feel that they are the best in matters of efficiency, method, and organization and may be perfectly willing to share their expertise on these issues with non-Germans.

Both Asia and the West have traditions that rank cultures in hierarchies from the worst to the best, from the least civilized to the most civilized. In the West this idea was popular in the nineteenth century under the influence of Social Darwinism, a line of thinking that said that cultures evolve from a low level to higher levels. In Europe and America this thinking put Western society at the top, mostly because of its technological and scientific achievements. The American anthropologist Lewis Henry Morgan in his book <u>Ancient Societies</u> (1877) defined each level in the pyramid and classified all the cultures of the world according to this system.

Figure 2   A nineteenth century way of ranking cultures

Under the influence of Social Darwinism, some people still think that primitive cultures, what scientists now call hunter-gatherer societies, are simple and believe that members of those cultures are like children. Some of us are still burdened with attitudes from the nineteenth century that became popular because visitors to those cultures were unable to understand what they were seeing and hearing and were so proud of their own cultures that they could not appreciate a culture that was so different. Now researchers tell us that even the most primitive cultures have complex social patterns, valuable technology, wisdom lost to more "advanced" cultures and other achievements worthy of our respect.

In the survey you took earlier in the chapter, you may have found that cultures with lower levels of economic and technological development were rated lower than more developed countries. This is an example of the problem of attitudes of cultural

47

superiority we are talking about.

An Englishman living in Indonesia wrote the comments below when he got tired of hearing Westerners from highly developed countries criticizing his adopted country during the Asian economic crisis of 1998.

What is a developing country?

Our fast evolving western societies are quick to embrace faddish new values. Sitting in a Garuda [Indonesian national airline] domestic flight you hear the foreigners complaining about what a terrible country this is: people are allowed to smoke on the plane! But the last time I lived in a Western country, every flight allowed people to smoke. Now we have some new values, and we think everyone else should immediately be like us.

The same applies to corruption. Indonesia is a developing country. When our countries were at the same stage of development, we had similar shortcomings. As recently as the early part of this century, if you wanted to get your son a good job in the British army, or out in the colonies, you had to pay. (As recently as the 1950s I can remember that you had to pay if you wanted your son to get an apprenticeship.) Of course corruption is bad and should be eliminated. In due course, as it develops, Indonesia will move in that direction.

I can remember Jakarta when the side streets had garbage piled 20 feet high. When you kept two boys in the office, whose full time job was to get a dial tone on the phones. When thousands of people were living in cardboard boxes on the side of the road. When people were lucky to live past 50 and there were virtually no schools.

When you look at where Indonesia came from, the government has come a long way. They have taken 20,000 islands, which takes 7 hours to fly nonstop from one end to other, and over 300 ethnic groups and made a single nation with a single language. Little kids don't die like flies any more and they get to go to school. All those different ethnic groups are generally coexisting and coming to accept each other as Indonesians. Education and sense of nationhood has improved the reasoning powers of the people; neighbours don't solve disputes by killing each other, the way they used to.

But the IMF [International Monetary Fund], the US Congress and foreign correspondents don't seem to fully understand what the term "developing country" means. It means that almost everything is inadequate and in short supply. There are insufficient resources to fix the traffic lights, to draft new laws, to enforce the law, to make plans, to fix the roads and to implement plans. The high rise buildings and modern airports give an illusion of modernity. Behind this facade is the weakness and fragility of a developing nation.

Exploring Ideas

1. Think of words that you associate with the words "primitive" and "civilized". Make two lists. Now do the same with the words "developed" and "developing". Is there some overlap between the two sets of lists?
2. What are the factors you consider most when you judge one culture to be higher or better than another one?
3. Do you think that Westerners are prejudiced against people in developing countries? What evidence do you have to support your opinion? Are you prejudiced against people in countries that are less developed than China?
4. Review the responses from your class to the survey "How close are you willing to be?" Identify the sources of negative stereotypes that members of the class may have formed about specific groups. Discuss which of the six types of prejudice account for students' responses for each group.

Chapter 4: Using Codes to Communicate

When people communicate, they want their messages and meanings to be understood. The difficulty is that much of what people do when they communicate comes from their subjective culture. It is part of the cultural iceberg submerged beneath the sea of awareness.

In an earlier chapter culture was defined as a system of meaning. When people share culture, they share meanings, and when they communicate, they exchange meanings. These definitions are purposely abstract to direct attention to the fact that culture involves much more than the objective culture and that communication involves much more than the words people use when they speak and write. When people communicate within their home cultures they do not ordinarily need to pay attention to the many complexities involved. They just do it and it works, more or less.

When people prepare to communicate with people from other cultures, they usually begin by learning a language.

The importance of learning the code

The full success of a person is like a bird. The body of the bird is the solid professional knowledge in your respective areas. The head of the bird is your ideology and spirit, with creative ways in thinking and exploring into the unknown, which is the basis for any successful work. The two wings of the bird are computer knowledge and English. If you don't have them, no matter how much professional knowledge you have, no matter how daring and creative you are in your ideas, you cannot fly and be a true bird.

Chinese professor

Learning the language is a necessary but insufficient first step toward becoming an effective cross-cultural communicator. It is insufficient because not all meanings are exchanged through language. Furthermore, speakers of different languages use the language code in different ways. It is not just that words and grammar are different from one language to another, but people

50

from various cultures are doing different things when they use language.

Language codes

People pay attention to basic language codes in cross-cultural communication because of the essential role these codes play in communication. People also pay attention to language codes because they are part of objective culture. They readily understand that the speech and writing of people around the world is in different codes. Because of the pressing need to learn a basic code such as English, people sometimes fail to realize that communication involves much more than translating information from one basic code to another.

Even language codes have sub-codes, particular forms of the language that are used by various sub-cultures and in various situations. Most people are aware of the difference between British and American English, but may not be aware of the special styles and vocabulary of various professional groups.

A person who wants to talk business with an American will do better if he is knowledgeable about the sports of baseball, basketball and football, because American businessmen often encode their meanings in metaphors and images from these sports. A native English speaker who uses this code is not simply using a sub-code the meaning of which can be translated into the basic language code, but is probably also saying that he experiences his work as a game he is trying to win. The choice of code is meaningful in itself.

You have to keep your eye on the ball if you want to stay in the game
Sports metaphors in everyday American speech

Dropped the ball: failed to do what needed to be done
On the ball: alert, active, and smart
Drop back and punt: give up the present strategy and try something else
To score points: to make a favorable impression on someone
To play ball: to go along with, to cooperate
To throw a curve: to do something unexpected

> **To play hard ball**: to be tough and unscrupulous
> **To cover the bases**: to take everything into consideration
> **Can't get to first base**: unable to complete the first step toward a goal
> **To hold the line**: to be firm, to be uncompromising
> **To strike out**: to fail

A Chinese English speaker who is planning a career in business might try to memorize this vocabulary. That won't necessarily solve the problem. What the Chinese learner is missing is not vocabulary as much as context. He did not grow up in nor live in a world in which these particular sports provide the metaphors for work, and in some cases, for all of life. What the student lacks is cultural context. These sports may not be interesting or even understandable to a Chinese English learner. Even if he watches sports programs on television and pays attention to the language players and newscasters use, he will only get some of the context that someone who lives in a culture where these games are played has.

The student can certainly have a successful career without learning how to use sports metaphors appropriately. If he does master the code, however, he will be better able to participate in the life of the group that uses the code. He will also gain insights into the attitudes and strategies of the speakers of the code. Sharing a linguistic code with a group is an important way to gain entry into the group.

Exploring Ideas

1. To expand the lexicon of American sports metaphors, interview Americans you know. Ask them what other sports metaphors they know and use frequently. If no one is available, read articles in popular magazines rather than professional magazines to look for metaphors that may come from sports.
2. Investigate the special linguistic code of a professional field you are interested in. Some examples are journalism, televi-

sion and film, music, advertising, and computer science.
Read articles, view films, and interview people who are familiar with the field to question them about expressions they
commonly use.

3. In the American academic sub-culture there is a special linguistic code for recommending students for further study that
includes special meanings for phrases that include the word
recommend. In this code " recommend ", " highly
recommend", "my highest recommendation" and "recommend without reservation" all have different and widely understood meanings. Ask someone familiar with the American
academic sub-culture to explain the differences in meaning of
these phrases.

Behavioral codes

In addition to using basic and special language codes, people
also communicate through behavior. What does the blink of an
eye mean? What does the raising of an eyebrow mean? What
does it mean to be late for an appointment or early? What does
it mean when someone sends one low ranking person to meet a
visitor at the airport instead of a group of higher-ranking
people? There are codes for interpreting each of these messages
but the codes governing them vary from group to group, from
culture to culture and from situation to situation.

Without being aware of it, most of us act according to codes
that are as regular in meaning as the language codes we use.
While language codes are sent and received through reading,
writing, speaking and listening, behavioral codes are sent
through gestures, situations, physical settings, and objects. The
meanings that people exchange in ways other than language are
usually referred to as **context**. In many situations, there is little
meaning in the language people use and much meaning in the
context. Even messages sent through language codes are modi-
fied by the context, by the messages sent through non-language

53

channels.

When Chinese English teachers teach film courses they often emphasize listening comprehension. They want their students to increase their skill in receiving messages sent through the language code. When I teach film courses, I emphasize the context. I want students to understand the meanings in the film that are sent through the visual images, the behavior of the characters and all that I know about the historical and social background of the film. It is much easier for me to do this than it is for a Chinese teacher, because I share a national culture with the filmmakers. I know the context. I can decode meanings that are not sent through the language in the film.

Context in communication

Context is important in all communication, but it is relatively more important in some situations than in others. There are also significant differences across cultures in the ways and the extent to which people communicate through context.

The American anthropologist Edward T. Hall has described cultural differences in the use of language and context in communication. He calls communication that occurs mostly through language **low context** and communication that occurs in ways other than through language as **high context**. When he talks about the explicit code he is talking about what we have called language codes sent through speech and writing and received through listening and reading.

High and Low Context

A high-context (HC) communication or message is one in which most of the information is either in the physical context or internalized in the person, while very little is in the coded, explicit, transmitted part of the message. A low-context (LC) communication is just the opposite; i.e., the mass of information is vested in the explicit code.

Any transaction can be characterized as high, low or middle context. HC transactions feature preprogrammed information that is in the receiver and in the

---

Because people in the most highly developed countries of
the West communicate primarily through language codes using
language channels, some people assume that low context communication is characteristic of modern societies. This is only
partly true. In modern urban life many transactions that were
formerly high context become low context. More and more people look for and receive information from low context sources
such as newspapers, textbooks, lectures, roadmaps, announce-
ments and instruction sheets. In more traditional societies people
were more dependent on personal or relatively high context
sources of information. They got the news from their neighbors,
and they found their way to an unfamiliar place because someone they knew showed them the way. The move from a rural to
an urban area is a move from a smaller to a bigger world. In the
bigger world people communicate more frequently with people
they do not know. When people do not share context, when
they do not have a personal relationship, they do depend more
heavily on low context sources of information.

Even though modernization and urbanization are factors
that influence the amount of context people use when they communicate, they are not the only factors. Japanese culture, for
instance, is very high context even though it is highly modern-
ized and urbanized. In many social situations Japanese communicators continue to send and receive messages through context
that would be sent through language in another equally developed culture. To avoid overgeneralizing, it is wise to consider

level of development, national culture and the many layers or levels of culture when assessing the communication behavior of any individual or group.

Chinese people tend to be high-context communicators as compared to people from Western cultures, but they are not as high on the context scale as Japanese communicators are. As Hall points out, the use of context in Chinese communication extends even to the language.

Context and Chinese language

China, the possessor of a great and complex culture, is on the high-context end of the scale. One notices this particularly in the written language of China, which is thirty-five hundred years old and has changed very little in the past three thousand years. The need for context is experienced when looking up words in a Chinese dictionary. To use a Chinese dictionary, the reader must know the significance of 214 radicals (there are no counterparts for radicals in the Indo-European languages). For example, to find the word for star one must know that it appears under the sun radical. To be literate in Chinese, one has to be conversant with Chinese history. Another interesting sidelight on the Chinese orthography is that it is also an art form. To my knowledge, no low-context communication system has ever been an art form. Good art is always high-context; bad art, low-context.

Edward T. Hall Beyond Culture, Doubleday, 1976

In general, high context communication is economical, fast, and efficient. It works very well as long as the people communicating are looking for and understand the meanings in the context. Everyone, no matter what their culture, communicates in this way in some situations. The most common example is communication between close friends and family members. Husbands and wives, and parents and children in all cultures typically communicate in this way. They are so familiar with one another, that a glance, a turn of the head, or a slight change in facial expression carries more meaning than many words possibly could. In the intimacy of these relationships, people even discount what the other person is saying if what is said is not consistent with the context.

For instance, if you try to explain to your mother why you

56

did something, she will listen to you, but she will evaluate what you say by considering everything she knows about you. She will place your words in a context that includes her experience with you and your behavior while you are giving your explanation. You will probably not be able to convince her with words alone. If, on the other hand, you want to send her a message about how you feel, you will probably not need to explain it all in words. With one or two words, or with no words at all, she will get the message. In your relationship with your mother, most of the meaning is in the context. Relationships in which people have to do so little to understand one another are very satisfying.

While high-context communication is fast and efficient, it takes a long time to learn. You have a long history of communicating with your mother. A stranger coming into the house will not get the message, because the stranger does not know the context. If the stranger asks, "What is going on here?" you and your mother would find it difficult to explain. You would have to try to put all those meanings from the context into words. It would take a long time, if you could do it at all.

High-context communication brings people together. We feel close to others with whom we communicate in this way. When you and your mother try to explain what is going on, you are likely to be particularly aware of the distance that separates you and the stranger. Switching to low-context communication, that is putting the meaning into words, indicates that the people communicating do not share as much context with one another. Low-context communication is more impersonal, but it is an effective way of transmitting information among people who do not share the same experience. It is not necessary to have a relationship with the person who posts a notice on a bulletin board announcing a lecture. The message is delivered clearly and unemotionally, and anyone who reads it can act on it or not. Even in this situation, however, some context is necessary to understand the message. What groups typically announce lectures? What experience has the person reading the message had with similar notices and lectures? The meaning of every message depends to some extent on the context in which it is sent and received.

High-context	Low-context
Social roles	Language
Situation	Memos, letters, maps, manuals
Participants	What people say

Figure 3   Sources of meaning in high and low context communication

Culture and context

People in all cultures use both relatively high and relatively low-context communication. The problem for cross-cultural communicators is that speakers of different languages, members of different cultures, and people in various situations use language and non-language codes differently when they communicate. In one culture a situation may be understood to be high context (the message is in the situation), while in another culture a similar situation is one in which participants send and receive messages through language.

The difference between high and low-context communication is one of the major sources of confusion, frustration and misunderstandings in cross-cultural communication. When people move from one culture to another, they usually think about how they will manage differences in language. They study language codes and engage the assistance of interpreters and translators. They seldom pay attention to the significant cultural differences in the use of context in communication. As you work on the case studies in this book, you will encounter this communication problem again and again.

Observing cultural differences at the airport

If you are one of the residents of the global village who actually gets on airplanes and flies from country to country, you will notice an interesting phenomenon at the arrival gates of international airports. Usually there is a group of family members or a host waiting to meet the Chinese, Japanese, and other Asians who are getting off the airplane. Often there is no one waiting to meet the Westerners who are arriving. They just collect their baggage and then take a taxi or a bus to their destination.

Apparently the Asians think that no one arriving in an unfamiliar place should be left to find their way on their own. They need people at that time. Westerners are more likely to assume that certain predictable services will be available such as hotel booking counters and transportation services and that they can find these and use them without any assistance. The arriving Westerner may have a guidebook to the city and already learned a lot about the airport, hotels, tourist sites, what people he will need to contact for particular purposes once he gets there, where to get a good dinner, and more.

When I arrived in China for the first time, a young teacher from the university where I was going to teach met me. When I came out of the airport terminal, he was standing in the crowd holding up a sign with my name on it and smiling. At that moment there was no more beautiful sight in the world. It was also my young host's first trip to Shanghai, so he was as excited as I was. We had to wait a few days to meet another arriving foreign teacher, so we went sightseeing. Within a day, I was directing him to various tourist sites in Shanghai because I had brought a map of the city from home and he did not have one.

- Westerners, as low-context communicators, look for, trust and use impersonal sources of information while communicators from more high-context cultures prefer personal sources of information.

Think about the typical experience of a Chinese student going to the United States for study as compared to the typical experience of a student coming from the West to study in China. The Chinese student is likely to be met with lots of information, mostly in written form. There will be a handbook for international students, notices on the wall of the registration office

59

with information about what forms are required or what to do before and after registration, a handbook of dormitory regulations and printed information about different types of visas, how to renew them or how to change them — and much more. The Western student arriving in China will get some information of this type, but much less. In fact, Westerners often complain that they don't find out what the situation really is until after they arrive.

A cross-cultural dialogue

Foreign Affairs Officer: Foreign teachers ask me for lots of information before they come to China.

Foreign Teacher: What do you tell them?

FAO: I tell them they will find out everything that they need to know when they get here.

Foreign Teacher: Oh.

FAO: Yes, my office and the teaching departments arrange everything for them. Every foreign teacher has a contact person to help with problems of teaching and daily life.

Westerners appreciate the personal help they receive when they come to China, but they also want low-context information to help them plan, act and adjust to a new situation. High-context communicators need the low-context messages they receive, but without human helpers they experience their new cultural situation as cold and impersonal.

Exploring Ideas

1. Do you agree with Edward T. Hall that Chinese culture is high-context in comparison to Western culture? What further examples of this contrast can you think of?

2. Make a list of the communication situations you participate in. For each situation describe how much of the meaning is transferred through language and how much is transferred through context. Rank your list from high to low context. Compare your list and rankings with those of your

classmates.

3. Discuss the ways that hosts in high-context cultures can meet the needs of low-context culture visitors for low-context information.

4. Discuss the ways that hosts in low-context cultures can meet the needs of visitors from high-context cultures for high-context information.

How people use words

Low-context communicators pay little attention to messages sent non-verbally. They think communication is the exchange of verbal messages that are meaningful apart from the context in which they are said. They are aware of some non-verbal behavior such as facial expressions and tone of voice, but to them these only accent and modify what people say. When they respond, they respond to what people say rather than to how they are behaving. They pay little attention to the situation, the roles of participants and other factors that make up the context of the words. This means that they often fail to notice things such as the status of the people they are communicating with, what the other person is not saying, and any social expectations that are not expressed in words. Usually high-context communicators have no difficulty understanding the meaning of these contextual messages. When they see that low-context communicators cannot or do not respond to these messages, they think the low-context communicator is insensitive to other people and their feelings. Some high-context communicators may simply conclude that the low-context communicator is coarse and rude, because he talks too much, says things that are better left unsaid, and doesn't know how to behave in specific situations.

Low-context communicators have little experience with words that are used as part of social rituals. They do use a few formal phrases for greeting, expressing thanks, and saying goodbye, but the role of fixed phrases and speeches is much less than in high-context cultures. They expect what other people say to be informative, so they often misinterpret the meaning of formal or fixed phrases. For instance, if a Chinese host says, "We welcome you to come again," the low-context communicator may interpret this as an actual invitation rather than recognizing it as a polite phrase that a host says to a guest on departure. Low-context communicators are often frustrated when high-context communicators use fixed phrases in their speech. If a low-context communicator asks a question and gets a fixed phrase as an answer, he will probably consider the answer uninformative, and therefore meaningless. For instance, when I ask students about their English learning, they often say, "English is a tool." The second time I heard this, I realized it was a fixed phrase and from then on considered it uninformative. The high-context communicator is simply saying what should be said in the situation, but to the low-context communicator such an expected answer is no answer at all. (See "The Wrong Answer" in "Making mistakes" page 82.)

A cross-cultural dilemma

A Chinese thinks that the Westerner who does not use the correct speech formula is impolite.

A Westerner thinks that the Chinese who does use the correct speech formula is insincere.

When Westerners first arrive in China they are usually eager to understand what everyone is saying. They expect all the words to be meaningful, so they ask a Chinese to interpret the university vice president's speech at a welcoming party, introductory remarks of a municipal official who welcomes them, and the speeches given by leaders of any organization the newcomers visit. Soon the low-context communicator notices that these speeches are remarkably similar and include little if any specific information. The low-context communicator is not used to listening to so many words used in such a fixed way, and may be disappointed that the officials are not very informative. To the low-context communicator such speeches sound empty and are boring. What he does not understand is that the speakers are using words to behave in the proper way. They are saying what people in their positions should say in those situations. The meaning is in the roles of speakers and listeners and in the situation rather than in the words. In a culture that prefers low-context communication a speaker in a similar situation would say something specific to the audience and to the occasion. The speech might include some formally polite remarks, but it would probably also include an anecdote or a report of some new information of interest to the audience. The words would be informative apart from the context in which they were spoken.

Responsibility for successful communication

Low-context communicators think that the speakers and writers of words are responsible for the success of communication. They should make meanings clear and understandable with their words. Listeners and readers are supposed to ask for clarification or further information if the words do not fully or clearly explain the meaning. This is one reason why it is a custom in Western countries for a lecturer to answer questions at the end of a lecture. In more informal situations a speaker will specifically encourage listeners to interrupt to ask questions. In these cases the speaker is asking the listeners to help him make the meaning clear. Low-context listeners and speakers have similar expectations in informal conversations. The speaker attempts to be clear and the listener shows that he understands with brief comments and facial expressions. The listener is expected to politely interrupt with a question to encourage the speaker to give a further explanation. The speaker interprets this as positive behavior, because it shows that the listener does understand and wants to understand more fully. If the listener is silent it means that he or she understands and accepts the message. In **Case 4 Can We Talk About It?** Jiang Yumei does not raise any questions when Linda explains her expectations. Linda interprets this to mean that Jiang Yumei understands and accepts what she is saying.

High-context communicators expect listeners to take more responsibility for interpreting the meaning of messages. They assume that speakers do not always express their meaning fully or precisely in words. It is up to the listener to interpret the meaning of words by paying attention to the context in which they are said. From the point of view of a low-context communicator this sometimes causes high-context communicators to find too little meaning in words and too much meaning in the situation. For example, if a low-context manager gives instruction to an employee from a high-context culture, the manager may be frustrated if the employee keeps responding to the situation (the boss is telling me what to do) rather than paying attention to the exact meaning of the manager's words. In this situation the employee may even disregard the manager's words, if he interprets them as unreliable when interpreted according to the context. Like other high-context communicators he may have learned that words alone are unreliable because speakers frequently use speech formulas. He may think the manager is saying what he should say in that particular situation. He may think the manager is following a speech formula, when he is not. I have seen Western managers become angry when their Chinese workers respond to what they say by responding to the manager-worker relationship rather than to the manager's words. They struggle to express their meaning as clearly as possible with their words, but fail because the worker continues to find more meaning in the situation than in the words.

Differences in the significance and reliability of messages sent through language and through context are factors in almost all cross-cultural misunderstandings between people from high-context cultures and low-context cultures. The way people communicate is part of their basic cultural software, and it takes considerable effort to modify this cultural programming to adjust to communication situations that are culturally different. The first steps are to understand these differences and then to look for them in every cross-cultural communication situation. By doing this, high-context communicators can learn to use and respond to words differently and low-context communicators can learn to pay attention to context and learn to interpret meaning in terms of the context.

Exploring Ideas

1. Now that you have considered the difficulties in cross-cultural communication caused by differences in the ways people from various cultures use codes and channels, revise or add to the image a Chinese professor recently used to explain the importance of learning English. What other communication skills in addition to knowledge of a basic language code do you need in order to fly like a bird?

2. Ask everyone in the class to collect examples of misunderstandings in communication between Westerners and Chinese from their own experience, stories they have heard, or from reports in books and articles. Use the concepts of high-context and low-context to analyze the communication difficulties in each anecdote. What does this concept add to your understanding of cross-cultural communication difficulties?

3. Imagine that you are advising someone from China who is going on an extended trip to a low-context country. Explain to the person what changes he will need to make in his communication behavior in order to successfully communicate in a low-context culture. Then advise someone from a low-context culture on how he should change his communication behavior in order to communicate successfully in China.

Codes of etiquette

Behavior can be just as grammatical (or ungrammatical) as language. It can be either correct or incorrect according to a behavioral code. In all cultures, and especially in high-context cultures, some behavior is codified. When a person knows the code and behaves according to the code, he is behaving properly or grammatically. Others who know the code will be able to interpret the meaning and respond appropriately. A common problem in cross-cultural communication is that people from different cultures do not know each other's codes and therefore do not know how to behave properly. When one person is from a low-context culture and the other is from a high-context culture, the problem is even more difficult to solve, because the low-context communicator is probably not as experienced in using behavioral codes to send and receive messages.

Chinese Etiquette
Asia-Pacific Management Forum

Throughout most of China's long history, the relationships between people in all classes were based on carefully prescribed forms of behavior that covered virtually every aspect of conduct - so much so and to such a degree that learning and following proper etiquette was one of the major facets of life. The higher one was on the social ladder, the more meticulous and demanding were the rules of etiquette.

The Chinese word for etiquette, *li*, which originally meant, "to sacrifice," refers to the fact that following legally sanctioned etiquette required extraordinary sacrifices, not to mention detailed knowledge of hundreds of correct forms of behavior. Training in this highly prescribed way of living was so thorough, so pervasive, that people were judged first, last, and sometimes always on how closely they followed these rules of behavior. Etiquette came to be equated not only with learning in general, but also with culture and morality.

The Chinese eventually came to believe that their behavior was the only correct etiquette in the universe. The rules of etiquette in China today are no longer enforced by harsh feudal sanctions and they have been considerably relaxed, but they remain very important. There are still formalities that are ingrained in the behavior of the Chinese.

In Chinese etiquette, there are prescribed manners for everyone at mealtimes, when in the presence of superiors, and when greeting and seeing guests off. One always accompanies guests to the entrance or to the upper floor elevators if they are leaving your office building. The host normally pushes the elevator button, then waits until his guests are in the elevator and the door closes before returning to his office.

When offering an object such as a gift of a drink to someone, as well as when receiving something from someone, it is polite to use both hands. It is Chinese etiquette to say no when offered a drink, a meal, a gift, or a favor. It is up to the host to politely persist, without being crude or rude.

At hosted meals, it is the responsibility of the host - not waiters or servants - to see that the guests' drinking glasses are refilled. It is also mandatory in Chinese etiquette for the host to accompany each guest to the door when a meal or party ends. Ranking guests are normally accompanied all the way to their automobiles, and the host waits until they drive away before going back inside.

People in low-context cultures also follow codes of etiquette, but they are not nearly so elaborate as the Chinese codes. What often happens when Chinese are communicating with Westerners is that the Chinese person behaves especially well by the standards of Chinese codes of etiquette to show the Westerner his respect and welcome and to demonstrate his own high quality as a person. The Westerner may not fully understand the significance of his Chinese host's behavior, and even if he does, he may not respond appropriately according to the Chinese etiquette code.

Westerners may study the Chinese etiquette code in much the same way that Chinese study English. This does not guarantee that the Westerner will behave well, any more than learning English guarantees that Chinese will communicate well. It may be that according to the Westerner's behavioral grammar the situation calls for different behavior. Westerners sometimes think they should become less formally polite to show their regard at just the point when a Chinese thinks that he should show more formally polite behavior to emphasize his regard for the Westerner. Westerners as low-context communicators are often eager to do away with polite formalities as soon as possible so they can communicate more personally, which to them means using words in the low-context manner and behaving spontaneously. To them it is more sincere to say what they genuinely feel and to do away with formal codes of behavior in their actions.

Banquets and contracts

Two social situations that Westerners frequently participate in when they come to China for the first time are the banquet and the negotiation of a contract or agreement. The banquet is a high-context situation and the contract is a low-context document. While Westerners are becoming more skilled in managing Chinese banquets and Chinese are modifying what they expect from contracts, these two situations are still useful for demonstrating the contrast between high-context and low-context communication behavior.

The banquet is a very high context form of communication. The purpose of a banquet is to develop, strengthen and renew relationships. The meaning of a Chinese banquet is in the act of giving a banquet, the quality and quantity of food, the physical features of the round table and close seating, the status of guests and host, the relationships of participants, and the occasion being celebrated. If there are many dishes and the dishes are expensive, then the guest is supposed to know that he is being especially honored. Hosts may put food on guests' plates not just to encourage them to eat but to show that the host is devoting his full attention to the guests' pleasure. Those favored are encouraged to eat and drink as much as humanly possible. All these behaviors convey the meaning of the banquet.

At the banquet people often talk about the food and exchange words that formally demonstrate respect and friendship. From a low-context perspective, the things people say are not very personal or informative. People follow a code of etiquette more precisely than they do in other situations. This includes toasting one another and in using set phrases that are appropriate to the relationships and the situation. The meaning is not carried by these words so much as by the fact that the words are spoken in the right way at the right time. Talk is pleasant and light-hearted. No business is conducted, but the relationships that are developed or strengthened through the banquet may set the stage for a business negotiation. Possibly the high-context culture participants in the banquet interpret the situation as meaning that relationships have developed to the point where some business can begin or be concluded.

The contract is a low-context document, and for Westerners the meaning of the contract is in the words. Before signing a contract a Westerner will "read the fine print," which means he will pay careful attention to the details to make sure that there are no unfavorable provisions hidden in the legal language in which contracts are typically written. Once agreed to, a contract is binding on both parties, even if something neither party anticipates occurs after the contract is signed. For instance, if market conditions change and one party suffers a significant loss, low-context communicators who are parties to the contract do not think that is a reason to change the contract. This attitude may seem unfair to a high-context communicator who is more accustomed to taking situational factors into consideration. If a Westerner benefits more than he expected from the contract, he will just think he has been lucky; if he loses, he will think he has been unlucky. See **Case 22 Fair Price?**

What kind of help do you need?

In low-context cultures people turn to accountants, lawyers, and media advisors for help in managing low-context codes.

In high-context cultures people turn to go-betweens, matchmakers, and brokers for help in managing relationships and situations.

If the two parties to a contract have a dispute, low-context communicators will try to resolve the disagreement by referring to the terms of the contract. A high-context communicator will be more likely to consider relationship and situational factors in addition to the precise terms of the contract. In fact the situational factors may be more significant to high-context communicators than the exact terms of the contract. See **Case 18 Whose Car Is It?**

69

Because of these high-context/low-context differences, the meaning of a contract may be different for Chinese and Westerners who are parties to the same contract. For the Westerners the contract is usually the end of a process of negotiation, and for the Chinese it may be the beginning of a new stage of a relationship between the parties. For a high-context communicator a contract may be seen as a framework for the development of the relationship, while for the Westerners it is a firm commitment that each party will perform in agreed ways and benefit in agreed ways. Typically Westerners will want to include language in the contract to deal with problems that may occur in the future, while the Chinese will think this is unrealistic and unnecessary. They reason that if the relationship is good, people will cooperate in adjusting to new situations as they arise. After all, the contract is only words. It is the relationship that really matters.

Chinese practices in the use of contracts are changing, and most business firms now handle contracts in a more low-context way. When dealing with contracts involving organizations from more than one culture, it is important to consider the levels of culture (subcultures, age of participants, organizational cultures and region) as well as national culture to understand the meaning people attribute to a contract in a particular situation.

Exploring Ideas

The following case studies show people from Western and Chinese cultures using language in different ways. They also show the importance of the guest-host relationship in Chinese culture and how much this relationship is defined by codes of etiquette.

1. Before you read and discuss the cases, make a list of the responsibilities a host has toward a guest in Chinese culture. Make another list of expectations for guests. How should a

person behave when he or she is a host or a guest?

2. Read the cases and answer the questions that follow:

Case 1 Dinner with Friends

Dinner with Friends

Janice is a young American engineer working for a manufacturing joint venture near Nanjing. She and her husband George, who is teaching English at a university, are learning Chinese and enjoying their new life. They have been eager to get to know Chinese people better so were pleased when Liu Lingling, Janice's young co-worker invited them to her home for dinner.

When Janice and George arrived, Lingling introduced them to her husband Yang Feng, asked them to sit down at a table containing 8 plates of various cold dishes, served them tea and then disappeared with her husband into the kitchen. After a few minutes Lingling came back and added water to their tea. Janice offered to help in the kitchen but Lingling said she didn't need help. She invited the couple to look at their new CD player and their color TV and then disappeared again.

A half-hour later she came back and sat down and the three began to eat. Yang Feng came in from time to time to put dish after hot dish on the table. Most of the food was wonderful but neither George nor Janice could eat the fatty pork in pepper sauce or the sea cucumbers, and there was much more than they could eat. They kept wishing Yang Feng would sit down so they could talk to him. Finally he did sit down to eat a bit, but quickly turned on the TV to show them all its high tech features. Soon it was time to go home.

George and Janice felt slightly depressed by this experience, but returned the invitation two weeks later. They decided to make a nice American meal and felt lucky to find olives, tomato juice, crackers and even some cheese in the hotel shops. They put these out as appetizers. For the main course they prepared spaghetti and a salad with dressing made from oil, vinegar, and some spices they found in the market.

When Liu Lingling and Yang Feng arrived they were impressed by the apartment and asked the price of the TV, video player, vacuum cleaner and other things. Janice politely refused to answer their questions. They took small tastes of the appetizers and seemed surprised when both George and Janice sat down with them. They ate only a little spaghetti and did not finish the salad on their plates. George urged them to eat more but they refused and looked around expectantly. Janice and George talked about their families and jobs and asked the Chinese couple about theirs. After a while, George cleared the table and served coffee and pastries. Yang Feng and Lingling each put four spoons of sugar into their coffee but did not drink much of it and ate only a bite or two of pastry.

After they left, George said that at least they had a chance to talk, but Janice was upset. "We left their place so full that we couldn't walk and they're going to have to eat again when they get home. What went wrong?"

1. How are differences in objective culture, in this case food culture, contributing to the communication difficulties?
2. How do Chinese understandings of the host-guest relationships influence how Liu and Yang entertained Janice and George?
3. How are George and Janice relying on words to make friends with Liu and Yang?

4. Can you answer Janice's question?
5. In a role play in class explain the cross-cultural problems to each couple. For instance, explain to Janice and George what Liu and Yang will eat in the days after the dinner party. Try to explain to Janice and George why Liu Lingling and Yang Feng paid attention to their household appliances and asked how much they cost.
6. What advice can you give to both couples to help them further their friendship?

Case 2 Where's the Bus?

Where's the Bus?

It was National Day and everyone had a long weekend, so the Foreign Affairs Office of a large university in Shanghai arranged a trip for its foreign teachers to the city of Hangzhou. Almost all the foreign teachers decided to go. They were accompanied by a number of mostly monolingual Chinese guides from the Foreign Affairs Office as well as some young teachers from the English, German, French and Russian faculties who accompanied their colleagues to act as interpreters. Altogether about 50 teachers, guides, interpreters and Foreign Affairs Office staff traveled to Hangzhou on a university bus.

When they got to Hangzhou, they were unloaded at a hotel on the outskirts of the city, given a nice dinner, and told to meet in the lobby at 8 the next morning. In the morning, when they were ready to set off sightseeing, the teachers were told that they would be taking the city bus. They didn't understand why they should take the crowded, dirty, city bus when they had a comfortable touring bus, with a driver, in which they had driven to Hangzhou.

In fact, the Foreign Affairs Office had found out only

after they got there that the city of Hangzhou had passed an Emergency Traffic Control Regulation prohibiting buses without Hangzhou registrations from entering the city for the few days before, after, and including the holiday. The interpreters were told NOT to pass this information on to the foreigners, since non-Chinese "wouldn't be able to understand the reasons" for it. The interpreters were instructed simply to insist to the teachers that they had to take the city bus, or if necessary to make up a reason.

The foreign teachers demanded explanations from their interpreters, who tried to explain that they hadn't made the decision and didn't know the reason. When they could get no real answer, the foreigners resigned themselves to taking the city bus. The interpreters, who were also friends and colleagues, could see that not knowing what was going on was affecting their foreign friends' enjoyment of the trip, so one by one they revealed the reason to the foreign teachers. The teachers were then annoyed with the Foreign Affairs Office staff for trying to deceive them. "Why couldn't they just have told us the truth in the first place?" they asked.

The Foreign Affairs Office was annoyed with the interpreters for not following directions. They blamed the interpreters for the fact that the foreigners were annoyed. By evening, everyone was annoyed with someone, and the holiday was turning out to be no fun at all.

In this case low-context Western communicators rely on information sent through the language channel to understand meaning, while the Chinese participants are relying on situational factors such as the etiquette code governing guest-host relationships and the social roles of university staff to make their meanings clear.

1. What is the social context as the staff of the Foreign Af-

74

fairs Office understands it? Try to explain their behavior to the foreign teachers.

2. What is the situation, as the foreign teachers understand it? Try to explain their reactions to the Foreign Affairs Office staff.

3. Why did the Foreign Affairs Office staff expect the foreign teachers and interpreters to cooperate with their plan?

4. How might the FAO see conditions in developed countries compared to conditions in China? Does this help to explain why they did not tell the foreign teachers the real reason they had to take the public bus?

5. As newcomers the foreign teachers neither understand the language code nor are they able to understand the behavioral code. What can Chinese hosts do to help make similar newcomers more comfortable?

6. What advice would you give to foreign teachers in China about how to deal with Chinese communication situations?

Several years after first reading **Where's the Bus**? I went on a Foreign Affairs Office holiday trip during which the bus broke down. From the first sign of trouble the Foreign Affairs Office staff kept the foreign teachers fully informed of the situation. The teachers, most of whom had been in China for several years, knew that their hosts were doing everything possible to solve the problem. As a result, the teachers were relaxed and expressed sympathy for the driver and the FAO staff. They cooperated with the necessary changes in the tour schedule. Everyone had a good time and the bus problem was just part of the adventure.

Chapter 5: Starting to Talk

As we have seen, codes of etiquette often determine much of what we do and say when we are in the early stages of a relationship with someone. Often we see such a situation as a communication between a host and a guest. In that case, social rules from each person's home culture about how guests and hosts should behave in relation to one another guide the behavior of conversation partners. Even though etiquette codes vary from culture to culture, we often simply assume that our meanings are shared with those with whom we are communicating. If two people are speaking the same language, each of them may not realize that the other is following a different and unknown behavioral code.

Making contact

One way to begin unraveling etiquette codes is to describe how important they are when two people from different cultures meet for the first time. In some cultures and in some groups and social situations within cultures, behaving in a formally polite way is more important than in other cultures, groups and situations. In general:

- Asians are more formal than Westerners.
- Older people are more formal than younger people.
- People in larger organizations are more formal than people in smaller organizations.
- People in older, established organizations are more formal than people in younger, entrepreneurial organizations.
- People in older industries (for example, mining) are more formal than people in newer industries (for example, computer technology).

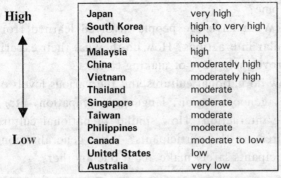

High	Japan	very high
---	South Korea	high to very high
↑	Indonesia	high
	Malaysia	high
	China	moderately high
	Vietnam	moderately high
	Thailand	moderate
	Singapore	moderate
↓	Taiwan	moderate
	Philippines	moderate
Low	Canada	moderate to low
	United States	low
	Australia	very low

Figure 4　Formality rankings for countries and Asia-Pacific regions

If a businessman wants to meet a senior executive of a Japanese organization, he will need to find someone to arrange an introduction. In this situation the requirements for formal politeness are very high. If, however, a Chinese student wants to meet an Australian student who is studying Chinese at his university, he is likely to receive a friendly response if he telephones the Australian student to suggest a meeting, or even if he simply walks up to him on the street and introduces himself.

Among the factors that influence how people make first contacts are these:

- **Status**: What are the social positions of the people involved? Is this a conversation between an adult and a child, or a teacher and a student or one between two students? Is one person a host while the other is a guest? What groups or organizations do the people involved represent? What are their statuses and roles in those organizations?

- **Activity**: What is the purpose of the meeting? Is it to make friends, conduct business, arrange for a service, exchange information, or something else?

- **Setting**: Where is the conversation being held? Is it in a classroom, on the street, in a business office, dormitory room, formal dinner party, on the telephone, or in

77

someone's home?

- **Experience**: What have the people involved learned from previous similar interactions? How do they use their experience to improve their ways of making contact?
- **Culture**: How do national cultures and the various levels of culture (age, gender, region, language, occupation, etc.) influence the interaction? How similar in national culture and subcultures are the participants? What generalizations can the participants safely make about one another?

Meeting foreigners

It is my experience that Chinese tend to approach all foreigners in a similar way regardless of the differences listed above. It seems to me that most Chinese students, especially, have a limited range of formality responses to foreigners they meet. Their approach is often too formal for someone whose social status is similar to theirs and too informal for someone of a higher status. Apparently in their minds the critical characteristic of the person is that he or she is a foreigner. I suspect that they have learned that there is one right way to go about meeting **all** foreigners. The result is that many Chinese ask me the same friendly questions when they first meet me. Where am I from? How long have I been in China? Even when I tell someone how many years I have been in China, the person may still ask me if I know how to use chopsticks! It is as if they have learned a ritual that must be followed regardless of how appropriate it is to the specific situation.

Questions for foreigners

Chinese English learners have learned an array of common questions to ask a foreigner questions soon known to foreigners. These questions serve as a barrier rather than a means of communication. There is no direct route beyond the barrier to an area where one is exchanging ideas and information.

Joanne White in <u>TESOL Matters</u>. Aug/Sept 1998

There is nothing harmful about the Chinese meeting-a-foreigner ritual. It is an expression of friendliness and welcome.

78

The only problem is that it is too limited and inflexible. I suspect that many Chinese have missed opportunities to develop more substantial relationships with people from other cultures because of their over-dependence on this ritual. That is because the ritual emphasizes the ways in which the two people are different from one another. The ritual does not provide ways for conversation partners to discover what they have in common.

I encourage my students to use a more flexible approach to meeting people from other cultures. Instead of asking a fixed set of questions, I suggest that they tell their conversation partner something concrete and significant about themselves. In this way they and their partners can look for and possibly discover common interests and shared opinions that provide a more solid basis for a relationship than the general friendliness that Chinese typically show to foreigners. If you want to ask questions, you should ask more interesting questions than the ones the foreigner has probably answered many times if he has been in China more than a few weeks. Remember that relationships are based on shared meanings. If your conversation is only about the ways in which you and your partner are different, there is nowhere for your relationship to go.

The meeting-a-foreigner ritual is based on an overgeneralization that foreigners are mostly alike and have similar interests, purposes, and experiences in China. In addition to individualizing yourself when meeting a foreigner, you should also try to individualize the foreigners you meet.

Exploring Ideas

1. Individually or in pairs write dialogues for a first meeting between you (or someone like you) and someone who is culturally different. For each dialogue change one of the factors you should consider in making a first contact. Change the status of one or both, change the activity or change the set-

ting. How does each change, change the way you make contact?

2. Write a dialogue for a meeting between you and a foreigner from a particular country, someone of a particular status, and in a situation in which you have a specific purpose. How would you change the frequently used meeting-a-foreigner ritual for your meeting? Try to individualize both yourself and the foreigner.

3. In class act out the dialogues people have written. Members of the class should give further advice about how to improve the way of making contact in each situation.

4. Chinese students studying English often approach foreign students suggesting that they become language partners. They propose that they spend one hour speaking Chinese and one hour speaking English. In what situations is this a good way to approach a foreign student? What are some other ways to approach a foreign English speaker if your goal is to make a friend and improve your language skills? (Remember, if you like to play basketball, you probably have a better chance of making a friend if you suggest meeting on the basketball court.)

5. Chinese English speakers sometimes meet foreigners at an English Corner. Foreigners often expect this to be a good way to meet Chinese people, but they usually decide after one visit that it is not. They find it tiring and not very enjoyable to "perform" English for a large group of people who ask them the same questions several times and do not seem to listen to or respond to the answers. How can you converse with a foreigner you meet at an English Corner to avoid this problem?

Making mistakes

Even when people consider all the factors they should keep in mind when they initiate contact, they might still make mis-

80

takes. It is one of the unavoidable risks of cross-cultural communication. There are simple ways to deal with the risk of making mistakes, so no one should allow fear of making mistakes prevent them from making contact across cultures. Making mistakes and getting involved in misunderstandings shows that people are reaching out beyond their home cultures and learning how to live in the global village.

- Some mistakes are funny.

Experienced cross-cultural communicators take it for granted that they will make mistakes. They cope with mistakes by enjoying the unexpected and somewhat crazy conversations that sometimes occur when people misunderstand one another. Some of them like to collect and tell funny stories.

A story to tell the folks back home

I was running at a good clip on my usual route down a narrow street in Nanjing. Cars were passing so I stayed over to the side. Behind me a bicycle bell rang and I motioned for the person to pass—there was plenty of room. Again the bell rang and again I motioned. Then a man's voice rang out a two-syllable phrase. He didn't pass though and kept ringing his bell nonstop.

Now, I do run fast and in China faster than most bike riders, but to my mind this guy obviously wanted to cause a hassle. He could have passed easily. Instead, he yelled his two-syllable phrase over and over. The tone of it sounded to me like what we Americans say when someone cuts us off in traffic. So, I decided to return the sentiment and gave him one of our best two syllable invectives — the one referring to body parts. He immediately followed with his one, and we were off speeding down the street both of us yelling back and forth to one another.

Later I learned that the phrase he used was *jiayou*, which is used to cheer someone on. It's like saying, "Go for it." I wonder what he thought I was saying?

Greg Brock

- Some mistakes are more serious.

Once a young Chinese woman asked me for advice about how to deal with an American who was visiting her company on business. When I heard the man's name and listened to her description of his speech and behavior, I realized that he was not an American even though he lived in the United States and worked for an American company. She had made a mistaken assumption, and it wouldn't help to give her advice about communicating with Americans. Nowadays Western companies often operate multi-nationally or globally. Representatives of these companies can actually be from anywhere in the world.

- Other mistakes are embarrassing.

Looking back the person may realize that the mistake was the first step in learning something important.

The Wrong Answer
Chen Xiaoyuan, student

When I was a freshman I had an American teacher. One day when we were on the subject of poetry, he wrote a sonnet by Shakespeare on the blackboard and asked the students what it meant. To tell the truth I would have had difficulty in understanding it even if it had been translated into Chinese. There was a long silence during which everyone, afraid of answering, lowered their heads. Unfortunately the teacher chose me to answer the question. I mustered up all my courage and said, "Sorry, I don't know." That was always my reply to difficult questions in my Chinese classes. I expected him to go on and ask one of my classmates as my Chinese teachers would do.

To my surprise he spent the rest of the class (a nightmare for me) explaining how childish my answer was. "As an adult, you should at least have some idea about a question, no matter how difficult it is. Even though your answer is totally wrong, it is much better than 'I don't know.'"

I did not know why I could not say "I don't know." It was always safe for me to say that in my Chinese classes. After I had several more American teachers I began to realize that Chinese teachers concentrate on the results of learning and teaching, while American teachers generally emphasize the process. Chinese teachers expect students' answers to be correct, while American teachers welcome any answer because all answers are the fruit of the student's thinking. That is why a Chinese teacher prefers the decent "I don't know" to a wrong answer, while an American teacher feels annoyed by it.

- Even mistakes we do not notice can cause harm.

The American teacher also made a mistake by criticizing his Chinese student so severely, so publicly, and for such a long time for her innocent reply. This situation could have had another result. If Chen Xiaoyuan were not so strong and determined, she might have retreated into silence in future classes with this or other foreign teachers. The teacher's criticism might have made the student more afraid than ever of making a mistake.

- A few mistakes are potentially dangerous.

> **Is the invitation proper**?
> A Chinese student saw a foreign man at a busy traffic circle who looked like he was having trouble finding his way to his destination. She approached him and, speaking in English, offered to help him. He was most appreciative and they had a friendly conversation and exchanged telephone numbers. He called her the next day and invited her to go to his apartment at 9 p.m. that evening. She was unsure about what to do. A Chinese man would not do such a thing, but she thought that perhaps this was simply a cultural difference and the invitation was proper.

This student is so open-minded that she risks putting herself in an unpleasant or even dangerous situation. If the man sincerely wanted to develop a friendship, he would invite her to meet him at a restaurant or some other public place at an earlier hour. His invitation is not proper and the student should say "No." The problem is that the student has learned to be polite, especially to foreigners, so she may find it hard to give a firm, direct reply when she should. In this case the student asked for advice from her foreign teacher and avoided the mistake.

The risk of making mistakes in cross-cultural communication is real. It is not possible to avoid them entirely. What we can do is to keep a sense of humor, pay attention to the reactions of others in order to identify our mistakes, ask people to point them out, learn from the mistakes we do make, and minimize them by asking for advice from people who have more experience.

Exploring Ideas

In the following case both George Hall and Mr. Li make mistakes. As a result both may have missed a promising business opportunity.

Finding an Interested Buyer

George Hall was in Beijing attending a trade fair and looking for an opportunity to do business in China. He had been very successful in his business dealings in the US and prided himself on his ability "to get things moving." His first day was going well. He looked around at the displays of sporting equipment to get some idea of whom he might approach. He was sure that his products, tennis rackets with an unusual new design, would arouse some interest. On the second day he approached the company which he felt would be most responsive to his products. He introduced himself to the general manager, a Mr. Li. Since he had read that Chinese find getting down to business immediately too abrupt and rude, he began a casual conversation, eventually leading up to the topic of his products and suggesting how Mr. Li's company might benefit from using them. George then suggested that he could arrange to get together with Mr. Li and provide more specifics and documentation on his products.

Mr. Li responded in fairly good English, "That would be interesting."

Knowing that he had only a few days left in Beijing, George wanted to nail down a time. "When can we meet?" asked George.

"Ah. This week is very busy," replied Mr. Li.

"It sure is," said George, "How about 10 o'clock? Meet you here."

"Tomorrow at 10 o'clock?" asked Mr. Li thoughtfully.

"Right," said George, "I'll see you then?"

"Hmm, yes; why don't you come by tomorrow," was the reply.

"OK," responded George, "It was nice meeting you."

The next day at 10 o'clock he approached Mr. Li's company's exhibit only to find that Mr. Li had some important business and was not able to meet with George. He called back later in the day and was told that Mr. Li was not available.

1. What expectations do each of these men have about the formality of a first busiesess contact?
2. What should George have noticed about Mr. Li's responses to his suggestion for a meeting? Use the concept of high and low context communication in your explanation.
3. What advice would you give to each of the two men about how to avoid making the same mistakes the next time one of them is in a similar situation?
4. In class role-play another dialogue between Mr. Li and George Hall in which they avoid some of the mistakes they made.

Direct and indirect communication

One of the problems in the case study is that George Hall is being direct in his proposal while Mr. Li is being indirect in his refusal. Like the student who was reluctant to say "no" directly to a foreign man's improper invitation, Mr. Li wants to be polite. Undoubtedly George Hall would have preferred to save the time he wasted in fruitlessly returning to Mr. Li's company's exhibit. Westerners tend to assume that communication is better when everyone involved knows exactly what is going on, and they assume that the best way to know that is to say it in words. It is not that Westerners are not polite and sensitive to other people's feelings. They are generally polite according to their own standards, but they also value directness and think the best way to handle a sensitive situation is to give complete information in a direct (and hopefully gentle) way.

Westerners also tend to assume that everyone else in the world is equally committed to directness. When Westerners encounter Chinese indirection, they may feel that they are being deliberately lied to. This was the interpretation the foreign teachers made in **Case 2 Where's the Bus?** Often in China when someone answers, "We must give it more thought" to a request, he is refusing a request that cannot be met. He does not want to disrupt the relationship with the person making the request and expects the other person to interpret his answer for what it is, a polite refusal. In a similar situation many Westerners would not hesitate to say, "Sorry, it can't be done."

An important difference between indirect and direct communication is that with indirect communication, the burden of interpreting the meaning falls on the listener, while with direct communication the speaker has the responsibility for making the meaning clear.

A polite request

The first year I taught in China students occasionally visited me in the evening for friendly conversation. They also used these visits to give me polite (indirect) advice for improving my teaching. One evening when someone mentioned grades, the class monitor quickly commented, "We all look forward to getting better grades." Several weeks later I realized that she was telling me that the grades I was giving on student essays were too low.

It has taken me a long time to learn how to interpret indirect messages and a longer time to learn how to communicate indirectly myself. My students often say that they find managing human relationships very complicated. Now I think I know what they mean. As listeners they have the burden of interpreting meanings without being able to easily check to find out if their interpretations are correct. As speakers they have to figure out how to communicate their opinions and feelings without offending anyone. Sometimes I find the uncertainty this produces uncomfortable, and would rather get a message directly. At the same time I appreciate how sensitive to human feelings indirect communicators can be. I am starting to understand that the purpose of indirect communication is to maintain social harmony and to protect the dignity of all the participants in a communication situation.

> **We do not agree**
>
> After I had been teaching in China for several years a student came alone to visit me one evening. She brought a small gift from her hometown. In class that day one of her roommates had criticized the topic I had chosen to teach the class. In our evening conversation the student made some comments about how she and her other roommates did not always see things the same way as the roommate who had criticized me. I think I correctly interpreted her message as saying that she and her roommates did not agree with what the student had said in class. I never told her, but I was very touched by her kindness.

Sometimes Westerners find Chinese communication more direct than it would be in a similar situation at home. This can be the case when students suddenly announce their intention to leave when visiting a foreign teacher or friend. In less than a minute they will be out the door. What probably happened is that the host failed to signal (by offering tea or commenting on how enjoyable the visit has been) that it is time to leave. In the West it is not usually the host's responsibility to decide when a guest should leave. Lacking this signal, the students simply say, "We are leaving now." In the West guests decide when they will leave but explain, perhaps by making a comment about enjoying the visit or giving a reason for leaving such as the late hour or pressing business elsewhere.

In Chinese guest-host relationships, it is the duty of the host to plan and direct the guest's activities. Westerners are not used to this. As a result they may not recognize a host's signal that it is time to leave and then be surprised when the host makes a direct statement clarifying the matter. This is the kind of mistake that people find amusing. Westerner guests normally do not expect their hosts to make as many decisions for them as Chinese guests do. They are more comfortable when a host suggests an activity or gives the guest a choice of activities. When a Chinese host says, "Now we will do this," the Western guest may think he is being too direct. He would rather hear, "We have planned an activity we hope you will like. If you would rather not do it, please say so."

Similarly senior members of Chinese organizations can direct the activities of other members, so Westerners sometimes feel they have been directed to do some work or attend an event when they think they should have been asked instead of ordered to do so.

The concept of face

Sometimes Westerners interacting with Asians refer to Asian communicators' high regard for human feelings and their need to protect the dignity of others as face or face-saving. When I hear them use these words I sense that they are trivializing if not criticizing the priority some communicators place on human dignity. I often notice that Chinese are confused when Westerners talk about face. Often the Westerner will then clarify that it is a translation of the Chinese word *mianzi*. As so often happens, the translation of the name of a concept from one language to another does not mean that the speakers understand the concept in the same way. See page 175 "**What do you really mean?**"

In fact concern about dignity (what Westerners call face) is universal. What is different from culture to culture are the personal characteristics on which one's dignity depends and the social priority given to preserving one's own dignity, the dignity of others, and the dignity of important groups to which the person belongs.

Behaving in a dignified way

In a business negotiation a Westerner might readily change his bargaining position in order to reach an agreement. He does not experience a loss of dignity in doing so. His personal dignity is likely to rest on his effectiveness as a businessman. He might be very insulted and "lose face" if his boss accused him of being too inflexible, rigid, or even too stupid to do what needed to be done to complete the business deal.

A Chinese businessman in a similar situation might think that he would lose face if he changed his position in the middle of a bargaining session. His dignity is more likely to depend on being loyal to his principles and strong and firm when facing opposition.

Another difference is the social significance of dignity. In the last example, the Chinese man would probably try to protect the dignity of his social role as well as his personal dignity. He may be concerned about protecting the dignity of his company, his rank in that company, and his nationality. In the West concern about dignity is more often only an individual matter. People do not feel the need to protect their status, the good reputation of their profession or country to the same extent as is common in China and other Asian countries. They may not feel the need to protect the dignity of groups they belong to unless they are specifically acting as a representative of a particular group. This explains why some Westerners feel no embarrassment when discussing the shortcomings of their company, their relatives, and their country.

In China concern about dignity extends to protecting others from loss of dignity, embarrassment or troubling feelings of any kind. I have learned that in China, people are often very considerate of others even when they are in distress themselves. A few years ago, a Chinese colleague with whom I have a close working relationship thought of my feelings even when one of his family members died. He never told me this himself, even though we saw each other several times. A few days later, another colleague gave me the news and invited me to the funeral ceremony. When I asked why he hadn't told me himself, my colleague said, "He did not want to trouble you."

Westerners sometimes comment that the Chinese people they know laugh when they are told that someone has experienced trouble or even when they learn that someone is seriously ill. In the West laughter usually means that the person laughing is amused, but sometimes in China it is a sign of embarrassment.

It is probably because Chinese are less used to receiving embarrassing or unpleasant information directly. When they do get such information from a Westerner, who thinks giving information directly is always a good idea, they may cover their embarrassment with laughter. The Westerner is likely to interpret this as amusement and think the Chinese person is terribly insensitive to someone else's misfortune.

Fake Smiles

Asia-Pacific Management Forum

An uncomplimentary story that Westerners used to tell about the Japanese, and about other Asians as well, was that they had so little respect for human life that when a member of their family or someone else close to them suffered tragedy or died, they would laugh instead of cry. In reality, when faced with tragedy and death, the Japanese suffered the pangs of sorrow just as much as anyone else, but they had been conditioned by their culture to repress their emotions in public in order not to upset or embarrass other people. The smile that they showed to the outside world was their way of both hiding their own feelings and protecting others.

Expressing sincerity

In Chinese culture being sincere usually means doing the right thing. It means being especially careful about following rules of politeness and showing high regard for the dignity of the other person. If someone has caused another person to be embarrassed by behaving badly, then a sincere apology is needed to restore the relationship. In this case a sincere apology is some recognizable behavior, not necessarily words, that conveys especially high regard for the other person's dignity, which the offending person damaged with his careless or inconsiderate behavior.

The meaning of sincerity is quite different in most Western countries. It means doing away with social rules of politeness in favor of more honest, more spontaneous, more open expressions of feeling than is usual. It sometimes happens that a Westerner in China will give a sincere apology for having offended someone. To the Westerner this means that he says that he honestly and truly regrets what he did. A Chinese receiving the apology might not think it is sincere enough. This will be very confusing to the Westerner who gave a genuine and heart-felt apology. What the Chinese person means is that the Westerner did not follow the proper social forms to restore the wronged person's dignity. To do this the Westerner would need to do something to show his humility and the respect he felt for the person he had wronged. Words alone, no matter how genuinely felt, are not enough.

Silence, questions, and topics

To most Westerners silence is the absence of communication. It makes them uncomfortable. If a conversational partner does not respond quickly to what the Westerner is saying, he is likely to continue talking himself. This is a problem for Chinese English speakers for two reasons. First, Chinese communicators consider silence a message. They may remain silent or allow a significant pause before responding to what a speaker has said to indicate that the question is sensitive or unwelcome. A Westerner may not receive the message the silence is meant to convey. The other problem is that because English is a second language, it often takes Chinese English speakers longer than native English speakers to form a reply. Native English speakers without much experience with second language English speakers may not take this into consideration and may rush to fill up the silence with more words.

English speakers are likely to ask relevant questions of a speaker to show their interest. Some Chinese speakers may consider such polite questioning to be rude interrupting. They more often consider it polite to listen attentively and allow the person time to finish what he wants to say.

Western communicators usually expect an answer to questions they ask. In many situations, it is permissible to give a vague or evasive answer, but you must answer. Chinese speakers sometimes give evasive answers to avoid answering sensitive questions, but often they respond to questions with information that is more personal than a Westerner would give.

I didn't want you to tell me that!

A foreign teacher once asked a Chinese student a polite question about his parents. The student's answer revealed serious difficulties the family was experiencing. The answer embarrassed the foreign teacher. She did not want such personal information and regretted that her question had caused the student to reveal it.

A Western student would have answered her question in a way that protected the privacy of his family. In most situations in the West a person answers the questions he is asked, whether he considers them appropriate or not, but the answers to personal questions need not be very personal. Chinese speakers are more likely to remain silent when asked questions they consider rude or otherwise inappropriate. Most Western speakers think remaining silent when asked a question is rude.

Questions that are sensitive or inappropriate in one culture are often considered appropriate in another. Chinese speakers frequently ask new acquaintances their age, marital status and income, and have been known to ask foreigners these questions. Most Westerners consider these questions sensitive or, in the case of income, entirely inappropriate. If another American wants to know my salary, perhaps to determine whether his employer is treating him fairly, he will first consider whether or not he knows me well enough to ask. If he thinks he does, he will tell me why he is asking, then he will apologize for asking such an inappropriate question, and he will surely say that I do not need to answer the question if I do not want to.

Foreigners sometimes make mistakes by following the example of Chinese speakers and ask those same sensitive questions they have been asked by Chinese they meet. This can cause embarrassment, if the foreigner is making an inappropriate generalization based on his experience with these social rules. Questions about age and marital status can be as sensitive in China as in the West. For example, middle aged Chinese women may be sensitive about their age and women in their late twenties might be embarrassed about being single.

The answers Westerners give to questions new Chinese acquaintances ask can also cause embarrassment. A Western woman over thirty who answers a question with the information that she is unmarried, divorced or has no children could embarrass her Chinese conversational partner. The Chinese asking the question should keep in mind that the Western woman is not likely to answer such questions by revealing personal information that she considers unpleasant or embarrassing. These conditions are not necessarily regrettable to the Western woman who gives these answers, and these answers do not mean that the woman's life is unhappy.

There are similar cultural differences about what topics are suitable for a conversation between two people who do not know each other well. Some conversational topics such as the weather, jobs and hobbies and local and national events are acceptable almost everywhere in the world. Westerners do not normally discuss their political opinions, sex life or religious beliefs with strangers in their home countries. Most will follow the same social rules when they are in China. If a foreigner you do not know well introduces one of these topics, you should question their motives for talking about such a sensitive topic with a stranger. For instance, sexual matters are more sensitive in China than in the West. Westerners who start a conversation on this topic invariably make a bad impression.

While Westerners do not usually reveal their political opinions to strangers, they may joke about political leaders. This may surprise a Chinese conversational partner if the joke is at the expense of a politician from the foreigner's home country, but it may be embarrassing or offensive if the foreigner makes a joke about a Chinese politician. Chinese conversational partners can also be embarrassed by or misinterpret personal compliments a foreigner makes. In the West a man can casually compliment a woman on her appearance or clothing without meaning much by it. In China similar comments usually indicates a special personal interest. In some Western social situations, it may be acceptable for a man or a woman to tell a member of the opposite sex that he or she is sexy or in some other way indicate that the person is attractive. Again this can be embarrassing or offensive to a Chinese conversational partner. The best response is to tell your foreign partner that such comments are inappropriate.

Unfortunately some people are not as careful about following conversational rules when they are in a foreign country as they are at home. It may be that they realize that their home culture rules do not apply in the new situation, but they are poorly informed about or insensitive to the social rules in the foreign country. It may be that they simply make mistakes and need your patience and explanation.

Exploring Ideas

In this case a Westerner relies on talk to make an agreement and resolve a conflict, while her Chinese partner uses indirection and silence.

Case 4 Can We Talk About It?

Can We Talk About It?

Linda Carmichael lives in a Canadian city with her two-year-old adopted Chinese daughter Ming. Linda is a busy professional woman and a single parent who wants her daughter to speak Chinese and know the culture she was born into. For this reason Linda invites new Chinese immigrants to live in a spare bedroom in her house. She always interviews prospective housemates before they move in. She

---

wants to avoid any misunderstandings by making her expectations clear, and she wants everyone who lives in the house to benefit. Among other things, she wants to see how Ming likes any new person who might live with them. She expects a new resident in her home to agree to share housework and to speak Chinese to Ming. In exchange Linda agrees to help with English and any other problems the newly arrived immigrant might face in adapting to life in Canada.

Linda liked 32-year-old Jiang Yumei, an engineer from northeast China, immediately when she came for her interview, and so did Ming. Jiang Yumei thought this would be an ideal place to spend the six months she had to wait until her husband and 4-year-old son could join her. They lived with Jiang Yumei's parents, where she and her husband had lived since they married. She had never lived apart from her parents except when she lived in a university dormitory, so she was pleased to be able to live with a family. She readily agreed to everything Linda said during the interview.

After a few weeks Linda noticed that Jiang Yumei seldom did any housework. She did not even clean up after herself, so Linda had more housework than before Jiang Yumei moved in. Linda helped Jiang Yumei with English and job applications, and practiced job interviews with her. At the same time Jiang Yumei did not seem to spend much time with Ming.

Linda gave Jiang Yumei some lighthearted reminders such as joking about how she hates housework or saying, "Ming, tell me what you and aiyee did this afternoon."

This did not produce any positive results, so Linda decided to discuss the problem directly. One evening at the kitchen table Linda said, "I think we have some crossed lines of communication. I understood that we had a certain

agreement between us, but you obviously understood something different. Can we talk about it?"

Jiang Yumei was silent and stared at the table.

Linda tried again: "I hoped you would spend more time
with Ming. You two got along so well at first. She likes you
and is disappointed that you don't play with her."

Jiang Yumei did not say anything. She did not look at
Linda. Her body stiffened, her face turned red, and she
stared at the floor.

Linda tried again. "I'm not angry, just confused, tell
me what you're thinking, I want to understand your point of
view."

More silence.

Finally Linda could not tolerate Jiang Yumei's silence
any longer. She was angry when she said, "You know, in
this culture it's very rude to stay silent when someone is trying very hard to resolve a misunderstanding."

The next day Linda went to see her friend Liu Qian,
who had lived in Canada for over a year. Liu listened to
Linda's story and said, "She's angry!" This was a surprise to
Linda.

"What is she angry about? Why won't she talk to me?"

Linda never found out. Jiang Yumei moved out soon after.

1. Why did Jiang Yumei agree to Linda's proposal about how
   they would live together? Why didn't she fulfill her part of
   the agreement?
2. What was Jiang Yumei angry about? Why didn't she explain
   her feelings to Linda?
3. What false assumptions did Linda make?
4. How do you think Jiang Yumei's family life in China was different from Linda's family life in Canada? How might these

differences have contributed to their misunderstanding?
5. What advice would you give to each of these women to help them avoid similar misunderstandings in the future?

Chapter 6: Building Relationships

Starting to talk is only the beginning. Most people want more from their cross-cultural contacts than a pleasant conversation. They want to move from a first conversation to more substantial personal and working relationships. This can be a problem because people generally carry expectations about relationships from their home culture to a new cultural situation. They expect that people everywhere develop relationships in similar ways and expect similar things from those with whom they have relationships, but of course, this is not the case.

While people from all cultures have friends, neighbors, co-workers and relatives, it is not true that everyone behaves in the same way towards them. Like almost everything else, relationships follow cultural rules. While we all have to learn how to get along with others, we do it in different ways.

What is a good neighbor?

In "Out of House and Home" by John C. Condon and Fathi Yousef (An Introduction to Intercultural Communication, 1975) the authors describe homes and family life in various cultures. This is part of what they say about leases or rental agreements in Germany:

A lease will often specify who may use the garden or the yard in the back of the house, if there is one, and at which hours. It will probably require the tenant to sweep and wash the stairwell outside of the apartment, and quite possibly the front steps and the sidewalk, too.

After reading this in class I said that in the United States neighbors might have a meeting to make a plan for cleaning the shared areas in an apartment building. They make some rules and then expect everyone to follow the rules. If someone breaks the rules, they complain to the owner or to the tenant committee in charge of maintaining the building. Another way would be for the owner to give each tenant a written description of the rules. Often the owner hires a person to clean stairways and halls and to do routine repair work. I asked the students how this issue would be handled in a Chinese apartment building.

One student said that if you want your neighbor to clean the stairway, you communicate this by cleaning the stairway yourself and then waiting to see if the neighbor responds by taking their turn to clean. If you have a good neighbor they

---

will do that. Some of the students looked a little shy and embarrassed. Maybe they lived in apartment buildings where there was no good way to solve this problem. All they could do was take care of their own apartment and not pay too much attention to what the shared areas looked like.

We can understand these differences in terms of high and low context communication. In the German example duties and responsibilities are defined very precisely in a formal written contract or lease agreement. The result is that neighbors do not have to talk about these matters, but they also have little choice about how to handle this aspect of their lives. The apartment buildings are probably very clean, but relationships with neighbors may tend to be formal and distant.

As an American I would find it difficult to follow so many rules and to arrange my life according to the time schedule specified in such a lease. Like many of my countrymen I think a small group of residents could talk together and make a reasonable plan. In a bigger building I would gladly pay a little more money to have the owner take care of cleaning. So I do not expect such a low context solution as a German might, but I also would not be comfortable with the high context solution proposed by my student. What if my neighbor does not clean? What do I do then?

We can also understand these differences by looking at the obligations or duty neighbors owe to one another. In our example, the answer might be that a German's duty is to follow the rules that create order. For an American a neighbor's duty might be to solve problems by talking about them and finding a solution acceptable to everyone or else to pay for a service. In the Chinese case, the obligations may come from the fact that residents are all members of one work unit, so have duties to one another from that relationship. Another possibility is that you encourage your neighbor to behave in a certain way by acting that way yourself. In that case you are asking your neighbor to

99

live by a certain social code that you have in common. If neither of these define your duties to each other, you may have to close your eyes to things that do not concern you.

Friendship obligations

In writing assignments in English classes, my students frequently raise the topic of friendship. Reading what they write, I start to understand Chinese friendship obligations. For instance, once a student wrote that she understood that her friend wanted to go shopping. My student was busy and really had no time to do that, but she kept silent, put her work aside and went shopping with her friend. Sometimes they write about middle school friends and describe the closeness they feel when they are together. Sometimes they write with great sadness when they feel they are no longer close to someone they considered a friend. All this is quite different from what American young people would say about friendship.

In the United States you can certainly ask a friend to do something with you, but you would not expect a friend to recognize and respond to your wishes without stating them. Nor would you expect a friend to drop everything to respond to a non-urgent need such as going shopping. In fact an American friend would feel that they had imposed too much if the friend gave up a real need to study to go shopping. There are limits to what you can expect from a friend. In the US you feel free to ask your friend for help, but you recognize that the friend may say no, if they give you a reason. A friend in China is someone who, sensing that you are in need in some way, offers to assist you without waiting to be asked. In China there are few limits on what you can ask or expect of a friend. You can feel free to tell your friend what he or she can or should do to help you or please you.

Chinese expect friendships to be more lasting

Another difference is that my Chinese students seem to expect their friendships to stay the same over a long period of time, maybe for a lifetime. A true friendship is a relationship that endures through changes in the lives of the friends. In the United States a person is likely to change even "best friends" several times over the years. Even this relationship in which people feel close emotionally and tell each other their secrets and personal problems may not survive life changes such as a move to another city, graduation from a university, a significant change in economic circumstances, or the marriage of one of the friends. I think the reason is that friendship, like so many other relationships in the United States including marriage, depends on frequent interaction with the other person. If the people involved do not see each other and interact regularly, the relationship is likely to wither and die.

In the West people often have many friends at one time, but the friendships are usually tied to specific circumstances or activities. When a person changes circumstances and activities, he or she changes friends. A person may have work friends, leisure activity friends and neighborhood friends. Also two people who are friends usually have similar financial circumstances. This is because friendships in the West are based on equality. Friends should exchange similar activities and give similar things to one another. If one can afford to treat the other to a meal at an expensive restaurant and the other does not have enough money to do the same, it will cause a problem in the relationship.

Americans expect friends to be independent

As with so many other things in the West, people prefer to be independent rather than dependent, so they do not feel comfortable in a relationship in which one person is giving more and the other person is dependent on what is being given. For West-

101

erners friendship is mostly a matter of providing emotional support and spending time together. Chinese friends give each other much more concrete help and assistance than Western friends do. A Chinese friend will use personal connections to help a friend get something hard to obtain such as a job, an appointment with a good doctor, an easier path through an official procedure, or an introduction to another person who might also be able to give concrete help. Chinese friends give each other money and might help each other out financially over a long period of time. This is rarely part of Western friendships, because it creates dependence of one person on the other and it goes against the principle of equality.

American friends like Chinese friends give each other emotional support in times of trouble, but they do it differently. A Westerner will respond to a friend's trouble by asking, "What do you want to do?" The idea is to help the friend think out the problem and discover the solution he or she really prefers and then to support that solution. A Chinese friend is more likely to give specific advice to a friend. For instance, if in a friendship between two Chinese women, one woman is arguing with her husband, the friend might advise her to forgive him. She wants her friend to choose the solution that is in her best interests and she says so directly. An American friend in a similar situation may want her friend to choose wise actions too, but she will be very cautious about giving direct advice. Instead she may raise questions to encourage her friend to consider carefully what may happen if she does one thing instead of another.

Chinese can usually expect more from their friends than Americans can
In the last chapter we noted that Chinese people often communicate indirectly while Westerners tend to be more direct. In close personal relationships such as friendship, the opposite is often the case. Talk between Chinese friends would probably sound too direct to Western ears. As we have seen Chinese codes

102

of etiquette require more formal and polite interactions with strangers or guests than is typical in the West, but in China relationships with friends are much more informal than similar Western relationships.

Americans apologize to their friends for minor inconveniences such as telephoning late at night or asking for some specific help. Even in close friendships Americans use polite forms such as "could you. . ." and "would you mind. . .". Because Chinese do not use these polite forms in their close relationships, they probably do not use them when speaking English with Westerners they know well. As a result they may seem to be too direct or demanding to their Western friends. At the same time a Chinese person who is friends with an American may be confused when the American continues to be formally polite after the two have established their relationship.

<hr>

Exploring Ideas

Read the following cases and answer the questions.

Case 5 What is True Friendship?

What is True Friendship?

Yang Ruifang worked as a secretary in an Australian company in Melbourne. She became friendly with one of the Australian secretaries, a woman named Cathy Lane. The two usually ate lunch together and Yang Ruifang often asked Cathy for advice on problems she faced adjusting to Australian society. Cathy gave her a lot of advice and helped her move from one apartment to another. Cathy went with Yang Ruifang to the Immigration Bureau several times to help sort out some problems. Yang Ruifang visited Cathy several times at home but did not invite Cathy to her apartment because she shared it with four other people. If they did not see each other over the weekend, they usually talked on the telephone. As Yang Ruifang was also preparing to take an English test, she was able to get a lot of help with English in this way.

However, something seemed to be going wrong. Cathy seemed to be getting impatient, even a little cold. She started going out by herself at lunchtime instead of eating with Yang, and seemed reluctant to answer questions. Yang Ruifang was puzzled. She couldn't imagine what the problem was.

1. What was Yang Ruifang doing that made Cathy decide that the relationship was not a true friendship?
2. Why did Yang Ruifang think the relationship was developing well?
3. From this case what do you think Australians and other Westerners expect from their friends?
4. Give advice to Cathy and to Yang Ruifang to help them restore their friendship.

Case 6 Are You Mad at Me?

Are You Mad at Me?

Jeff was pleased to have been assigned an international student as his roommate in his second year at a small liberal arts college in the US. Ji Bing was an easy-going guy, a good listener, warm-hearted, and always ready for a new experience. He appreciated Jeff's explanations of American life and unfamiliar language. Jeff didn't think Ji Bing was any more difficult to get along with than the American roommate he had the year before, except that he seemed to want to study more than Jeff was used to and he sometimes borrowed Jeff's things without asking first.

One night Jeff was working on a project that required some artwork. Ji Bing was at his desk studying for a test. Jeff's scissors were just too dull to do the job, so he asked Ji Bing, "Sorry to bother you while you're studying, but could I use your scissors for a while?"

Ji Bing said, "Sure," opened his desk drawer and handed Jeff the scissors. "Thanks, thanks a lot," Jeff said. A few minutes later Jeff decided that his crayons were not going to do the trick. He addressed his roommate again; "Sorry to bug you again, but these crayons make this look like kindergarten. You know those colored pencils you have? Would it be OK if I used them for my project?"

Ji Bing got up and got them off the shelf and said, "Help yourself," and went back to reading as Jeff thanked him.

After another few minutes, Jeff said, "I must be driving you crazy, but have you got any glue or tape? Promise I'll buy you another roll."

Ji Bing handed Jeff a role of tape that was on his desk saying, "Use as much as you want. I don't need it." "Appreciate it," mumbled Jeff as he went back to his project.

Ji Bing went back to his reading. As Jeff was finishing his project he noticed that Ji Bing was watching him. He looked up and was surprised to hear his Chinese roommate ask him in a plaintive tone, "Are you angry at me?"

"Of course not," Jeff replied, "what makes you think that?"

1. Why does Ji Bing suspect that Jeff is angry?
2. What answer will Ji Bing give to Jeff's question?
3. What are the differences in what American and Chinese young people expect from their friends?
4. Give advice to both Jeff and Ji Bing on how to handle their

relationship.

A question of love

As contact between cultures increases in our global village, it is inevitable that people will not only form business and friendship relationships, but will also fall in love. People everywhere like to hear stories of lovers overcoming obstacles to realize their dream of a life together. The appeal of romance is universal, but the attitudes that people have about romantic relationships between men and women of different cultures are not always positive. Parents may be afraid that a son or daughter will live far from home if he or she chooses a mate from another country. More important, they may fear that a cross-cultural marriage may not be as happy or harmonious as a marriage between two people who share culture. As we have seen relationships are built on the basis of similarities, but we have also seen that people often judge similarities in age, educational level and economic status as more important than similarity of national cultures(See page 41, "We want to be close to people who are like us"). While the cultural barrier can be difficult to overcome, it may not be any more of a challenge to lovers than other differences.

The problem is not true love, but how and why people get involved in romantic relationships. For instance, American young people are sometimes very practical and not very romantic about their dating relationships but expect to marry someone they truly love. In contrast Chinese young people might be more romantic about their youthful love affairs and be very practical when they choose a marriage partner. These cultural differences in expectations cause many misunderstandings. Added to this are the misunderstandings that result from inaccurate or overly generalized stereotypes about the dating behavior and sexual attitudes of people from specific cultures.

106

What does a kiss mean?

Ge Jizhi, student

In Chinese culture, we consider kissing as a somewhat sacred behavior. In doing so, one declares a commitment to the other person. For that reason we are always quite cautious in giving kisses, especially between a man and a woman. When two people are dating, they will know each other for a long time before their first kiss, and if they do kiss, it means their relationship is strong and stable.

Most Westerners, however, do not regard a single kiss as so important. I once had an American friend. When she came to China to study Chinese she already had an intimate boyfriend at home and they were about to be engaged. During her stay here, however, she often went out with other boys and I saw her kiss some of them. When I asked her about this, she explained to me that she regarded kissing as a casual physical touch, which most of the time was a way of greeting and showing amity. It had nothing to do with commitment or anything further. She also told me that for two people in love, a more significant stage is the period of understanding each other, which usually comes much later than kissing.

Exploring Ideas

In small groups study the following anecdotes. For each one identify the expectation or stereotype that is causing the misunderstanding.

1. A young Canadian man who returned home after teaching for a year at a teacher training college in rural China was disturbed when he started receiving letters from some of his former students declaring their love for him. He had treated his young students in a friendly but professional way, and had not intended to give any of them the idea that he was interested in finding a girlfriend. He was shocked to discover that the girls he had complimented on their appearance or behavior had interpreted his personal attention as a sign that he had a romantic interest in them.

2. A young Chinese woman who teaches English occasionally meets Chinese men who expect her to be more liberal in her sexual attitudes than other Chinese women. They believe that Western women satisfy their sexual hunger as casually as they satisfy their thirst with a drink of water. Because as an Eng-

lish major and English teacher she has been influenced by Western thinking, some men think or hope that her attitudes about sex are similar to those they believe are common among Western women.

3. A young Chinese man was assigned to be the interpreter for an American woman on a lecture tour of several universities in a Chinese province. The two got along very well and the American woman often invited her interpreter to have dinner with her, sat with him on the bus that took the group from place to place, and praised his work to his superiors. One day she was told that her interpreter had been reassigned and she would have a new interpreter, a woman.

4. A young Russian man who speaks excellent in English has been studying Chinese in China for three years. He is a tall, good-looking and kind-hearted man who has friends from several different countries. He reports that quite a few Chinese girls have been interested in him, but they lose interest as soon as they discover that he does not have a passport from a Western country.

The importance of connections

When an American who was teaching in China had to go to a hospital, she was surprised to find that the hospital had gone to a lot of trouble to find a nurse for her with whom she had a connection. The nurse's husband, she was told, worked for the same university as the American teacher. The hospital staff thought she would feel better and have more confidence in the care she received if she had a personal connection with her nurse.

The way in which Chinese people personalize their lives through connections is unfamiliar to most Westerners. They would expect good care from the hospital if it had a good reputation and met all the regulations for hospitals whether or not the patient had ever met or had a personal connection with someone on the staff. In the West people rely on one another to meet their professional obligations without regard to personal relationships.

Permission to use the library

A Chinese professor needed to do some research. She knew that she could find the books she wanted in the library of another university in her city. She was afraid she would not be allowed to use that library. She went there and discovered that a classmate from her own university days worked at the library. She was relieved. Because she had a connection, she would have no trouble getting the books she needed.

An American professor needed to do some research at another university's library. He telephoned ahead to find out if there were any special procedures he should follow to use that library. Once he got the information, he went to the library. He did not know anyone there but was given the same service as a professor from that university.

Hospitals and universities are typically large professional organizations. Members of the staff may have an especially kind word for someone they know who uses their services, but in general services are provided impersonally according to accepted standards. Most staff members get their jobs based on their technical skills and professional qualifications without regard for background or connections. This is the ideal in the West. Organizations should operate according to the rules and services should be provided on the same basis to everyone who is entitled to them.

The ideal is not always achieved. Like many Americans I have had many different jobs in my life. For most I was hired based on my qualifications, but when I moved to a small city I failed to get one job because I was new in town. I got another job because I was a member of the sponsoring organization and because the people doing the hiring knew a member of my family. In the West people do use personal connections to get resources but not to the same extent as in China. As in so many issues of cross-cultural communication, it is necessary to look at the differences within cultures as well as those between cultures.

In general, resources such as services and jobs are distributed more impersonally, that is without regard to background and connections:

- In urban areas
- In large organizations
- When the service relies on special technical and professional skills
- When government or professional standards are well-established
- When operating in this way is good for business

In fact, in some Western organizations someone with a personal connection could be at a disadvantage, because the leaders do not want anyone to think that they are making decisions based on personal relationships rather than professional qualifications. Some organizations have rules against hiring someone who is a relative of a person who already works for the organization.

Social obligations

One of the most troublesome difficulties Westerners have in their personal and business relationships in China is the matter of social obligations. Most Westerners do not realize that relationships in China ordinarily involve a system of social debts and credits. Even when they know the concept in general, they are frequently unaware of how it works in practice. This causes many mistakes and misunderstandings. Westerners often do not know when they are incurring a social debt in China, and they often do not know what they need to do to earn social credits. They are simply unfamiliar with this form of social exchange.

Buying vegetables

When she does her marketing a Chinese woman establishes a relationship with a particular vegetable seller. She knows that is the best way to get a good price and good quality when she shops for her family. The vegetable seller likes doing business with someone he knows . He gives her a good price and gives her the

---

best quality. He knows that treating the woman well is a social investment. She understands the social obligation she is incurring. When the vegetable seller needs a resource, he may ask the woman for help. The woman will assess the extent of her obligation and use her social network to help the vegetable seller in a way appropriate to the obligation she has incurred.

An American housewife reads the supermarket ads in the newspaper before she does her weekly vegetable shopping. There are several supermarkets close to her home and she decides which one to go to by considering her family's likes and dislikes, the level of service and quality of vegetables she has learned from experience each store offers, and the special offers at each store that week. Sometimes she goes to one and sometimes another. She recognizes the workers in the supermarkets but she has no special relationship with any of them.

Often Chinese people can see that some Westerners who come to China are respected professionals with good jobs. From that they might assume that a Westerner has enough influence back in their home country to get a student a scholarship at a university or arrange for a difficult-to-get visa. Usually this is not the case. The Westerner has valuable relationships at home, but usually those relationships do not include social obligations to do what is requested. The Westerner can write a letter of recommendation and will be willing to do so, if the student is qualified. If the Westerner is someone whose opinions and recommendations are respected, then his recommendation will be influential to that extent. His influence, however, is usually limited to his professional reputation and the persuasiveness of the arguments he makes on the applicant's behalf. He cannot get the resource he desires because a decision-maker has a social obligation to him. Chinese students applying to foreign universities need to recognize that foreign professors can influence the decisions of officials of foreign universities, not because they have others have obligations to them but because their opinions are credible and their arguments are persuasive.

Social obligations in China
Asia-Pacific Management Forum
Westerners generally base their personal and business relationships on imper-

sonal rules that apply to everyone—friends and acquaintances as well as strangers. These rules, in turn, are founded on the principles of frankness, fairness, and equality. In principle, we can approach anyone, anytime, and expect to be treated fairly and courteously.

Chinese, on the other hand, are accustomed to dealing with people on the basis of social debts built up through a variety of personal relationships in the past — with family members, relatives, teachers, friends, business associates, and employers. In accepting help, of whatever kind, from various people, the Chinese build up a reservoir of debt that they owe to these people. By the same token, they also build up a bank of "receivables" from people they help along the way.

Paying and collecting these social debts serves as the primary means of interpersonal relationships in China, from purely social to business and political affairs, and is controlled by the concept of social reciprocity.

Failure to properly discharge social debts that are owed is regarded as one of the most dishonorable things a Chinese person can do. People who ignore it are regarded as uncivilized.

As more Chinese are involved with outsiders, many make some attempt to establish new types of relationships that are not based on social obligations. Even so, virtually all Chinese automatically make a strenuous effort to very quickly establish the kind of obligatory social debts they are used to because that is the only way they know how to react.

Giving and receiving gifts

Students often give me small gifts such as a souvenir from their hometown, something they have made themselves, or a card with kind words written on it. I certainly appreciate each person's thoughtfulness, but I worry when someone gives me a more expensive gift. In that case I am afraid that the person giving me the gift will expect a favor. It sometimes happens, so now I try to anticipate what favor the gift-giver is seeking, and I refuse gifts that I suspect carry social obligations with them. I would be angry and embarrassed if someone treated me most respectfully, gave me a nice gift, and then showed up some time later asking me to edit pages and pages of English translation. For me such editing is hard, time-consuming, professional work. Anyone can hire me to do it, whether they know me or not, but I would only do it as a favor for someone with whom I had a long and cooperative professional relationship.

112

In general Westerners do not use gifts to incur or repay social obligations. According to the usual social rules in the West, a person repays like with like. He responds to a dinner invitation with a dinner invitation and a birthday gift with a birthday gift. Westerners do give gifts as a way of thanking someone for their hospitality. A dinner guest will usually take a bottle of wine, bouquet of flowers or box of chocolates to his host. This social custom is sometimes misunderstood in China. I was once invited to spend a few days at the home of a Chinese friend. As is the custom in the United States, I took along a gift for the family. My gift created a small crisis. They hurriedly went out to buy gifts for me. Somehow I had violated the rules of giving and receiving appropriate to my relationship with them and they had to restore the balance.

Most Westerners accept gifts after they have done something, if the gift cannot be interpreted as payment for what was done. In that situation the gift is a welcome way to say "Thank you." The same gift given before someone acts might be interpreted as a bribe, an unfair attempt to influence the person's behavior. If a student gives me a gift before I have given grades for a course, that is a bribe. If the same student gives me a small gift after the course is over and the grades have been recorded, then that is a gift of appreciation. The gift should not be too valuable, otherwise I might think the student was trying to repay me for special favors. I do not want anyone to think that I perform my professional work on the basis of social relationships. If colleagues suspected that I could be influenced in my professional behavior by gifts and personal obligations, it would ruin my professional reputation.

Exploring Ideas

Read the case and answer the questions that follow.

Who Are You Trying to Fool?

Larry Wilder was enjoying his sabbatical year teaching English literature at a university in central China. He was quite favorably impressed with the quality of the Chinese faculty, many of whom had studied abroad and seemed dedicated to quality teaching and research. He also enjoyed his graduate students and occasionally visited them in their dormitories.

On one such visit to Qiu Gang, a second year Ph. D. candidate, a visitor interrupted their conversation. After a brief exchange in Chinese, Qiu Gang handed the visitor an audiocassette tape, and the visitor departed.

Larry asked what the exchange had been about, and Qiu Gang casually explained that the visitor had been Qiu Gang's roommate's cousin. The cousin had been accepted to a very good graduate program in chemistry in the US and had been offered a teaching assistantship contingent upon receipt of a tape of him speaking English. "He doesn't really speak English very well," Qiu Gang explained, "though he reads it all the time, and he did spectacularly well on the Graduate Record Exam, so to make sure that he wouldn't lose his chance to study in the US, I made the tape for him."

Larry was horrified. "Don't you realize that the purpose of that tape is to make sure that he speaks English well enough so that the undergraduates he is teaching can understand him? It isn't fair to them to have a T. A. that can't speak English."

Qiu Gang seemed untroubled. "He's a smart guy. He'll learn to speak English really fast. And besides, I had to do this. His cousin is my roommate; how could I say no to my roommate? What's more, when my mother was sick last year, my roommate's other aunt, the sister of the chemistry student's mother, got my mother into a really good hospital."

Larry was baffled and embarrassed. He thought Qiu Gang was a really nice guy, a conscientious and creative scholar, but now he didn't know what to think. Larry made an excuse to leave and made a point of avoiding Qiu Gang in the future.

1. What differences in the importance of connections can explain the misunderstanding between Larry and Qiu Gang?
2. How do you explain why Larry judges Qiu Gang so severely for making the tape?
3. Does Qiu Gang think there is anything ethically wrong with making the tape?
4. Is there any way for the two to save their friendship?

Chapter 7: Perceiving Culturally

No matter who we are or where we live, no matter what our language or our culture is, we have many things in common with all other human beings. We can all feel the breeze on our skin, hear a child's cry, enjoy the smell of flowers, see the stars in the night sky, feel the pain of a knife cut on a finger, experience heat and cold, thirst and hunger and tense and relax our muscles. To use our computer image, we all have the same hardware, the same equipment. We all have similar eyes, ears, muscles and nerve endings that enable us to sense the world.

We can also all think and as a result of thinking, we all know that the physical world exists apart from our ability to sense it. We know that the moon exists even though we have never been there or talked to anyone who has been there. It may look like a shining flat round disk when we look at it, but others tell us that it is more like a big round ball with rocks and soil. We believe them even though that is not what we see when we look at the moon. We know many things that we have not directly experienced and we accept the idea that others know these things too. There is a physical reality that is "out there" quite separate from our experience of it.

How we interpret the information we receive through our senses is molded by culture

Our senses and the world beyond our bodies are physical realities that have nothing to do with culture, yet we interpret the information we receive from our senses and this process of interpretation is molded by culture. We interpret a flash of red color as the rising sun or a sharp cry as a hungry baby. It is in our culture that we learn how to interpret our sensations. We learn what to pay attention to and what to ignore.

116

Years ago when some groups living in the rainforest of Central Africa had little contact with people outside their group, a Westerner made contact with one group. He showed them a photograph and reported that the people did not see the image in the photograph but described it as a dark square surrounded by a white square. In their culture they did not learn to "see" images of people and places on a flat piece of paper. As soon as the man showed them how to "see" the image, they could see it. It is the same for a person from a tropical country who travels to the far north for the first time. He can only see "snow" until a native points out the differences among the various types of snow. In time he learns to see, feel and even smell different types of snow. As he walks, he can feel which type of snow is under his feet.

A European coming to China for the first time may think that everyone looks alike because he sees people with black hair and dark eyes everywhere. After a time, if the newcomer is paying attention, he or she will start to see differences in the blackness of hair. It is the same with the taste of food, the sounds of voices and the sounds of music. For someone unfamiliar with Asia, at first all rice will just taste like rice. They may not notice differences in types and quality until someone points out their characteristics. In learning Chinese it is especially difficult for speakers of Western languages to hear the tones of Chinese words because words in their languages do not have tones.

I hope these examples convince you that how we experience the world through our senses is molded by our home culture. One of the least recognized difficulties that people have when they move from a familiar to an unfamiliar culture, is the difficulty in perceiving things as the local people do. Travelers might prepare for a journey by taking language lessons, but they seldom realize they also need lessons about the perceptual world they are going to. Even if they do know it, who will teach

117

them?

Moving to an unfamiliar culture often means moving to an unfamiliar perceptual world

When I first arrived in China a student took me to a shop so I could buy something I needed. I don't remember what we bought, but I do remember that she taught me how to cross the street. Where you look, how you move and when you move to cross a street is entirely different in China from how it is done in the United States. She didn't know I needed to learn that or that she was teaching me until I told her. I also had to learn how to ride a bicycle, how to ride a bus, how to climb a mountain and how to read the non-verbal behavior of my students even though I knew how to do all these things before I came to China. I also had to learn how to get to a service window when there is no queue, how to separate the meat from the bones when eating fish with chopsticks, how to use an Asian toilet, how to look at a Chinese painting, as well as many other things. Before I knew how to do these and other things, life in China was sometimes troublesome and irritating. Now that I am able to live and move in the Chinese perceptual world, I feel comfortable and enjoy many things I could not enjoy before.

Different Perceptual Worlds

The concept that no two people see exactly the same thing when actively using their eyes in a natural situation is shocking to some people because it implies that not all men relate to the world around them in the same way. Without recognizing these differences, however, the process of translating from one perceptual world to another cannot take place. Significant evidence that people brought up in different cultures live in different perceptual worlds is to be found in the way they orient themselves in space, how they get around and move from one place to the next.

From Edward T. Hall The Hidden Dimension

The American anthropologist Edward T. Hall brings the concept of different perceptual worlds to life with detailed descriptions of cultural differences in how people use all their sens-

118

es — vision, hearing, smell, touch, kinesthetics or movement, and perception of heat and cold. He points out that some cultures use one sensory system, vision for example, more than another, touch for example, to orient themselves in physical space. If a particular culture relies more on sight than touch, then people from that culture are likely to stand and sit apart from others. If the culture uses touch for orienting then people have to be close enough to other people and things to touch them.

High contact and low contact cultures

Hall shows how people from different cultures combine information from several senses to orient themselves in space and then classifies some cultures as **high contact** and others as **low contact**. In high contact cultures what people sense when they are close to a person or object is most important. The information from touch, from the skin generally and from muscles as well as what people see using the inner part of the eye (the part you use to thread a needle) is used a lot. In high contact cultures people want to get close enough to one another and to objects to sense them in these ways. In a low contact cultures the middle third of the eye plays a greater role, because to see someone's whole face without distortion, we must stand a certain distance away. At that distance we do not sense the other person's body heat or subtle smell but we can see a frown or a smile. This far away we probably cannot see the widening of the pupil of the other person's eyes.

These ideas may be new to you. For most of us the cultural aspects of sensory perception are part of subjective culture. It comes from that part of the cultural iceberg that is hidden below the sea of our awareness. People going from a familiar to an unfamiliar culture are not aware of the reasons, but they often have strong emotional reactions to these differences. When a person from a high contact culture goes to a low contact culture, he or she is likely to feel that people are cold, lack human warmth, and are indifferent and pay no attention to them. The person is reacting to differences in the way people in the new culture use their senses.

I once spent two months in Egypt, which is much more high contact than the middle class American culture I am used to. When I was there I felt that everyone was staring at me very intensely. It made me feel they were intruding, getting too close and personal with me. The streets seemed full of smells, noise and people pressing up against me in a way that tired me out. When I arrived back at the airport in New York, I immediately noticed that the service people did not really look at me when they helped me. Their eyes moved quickly away from mine. Everything was clean, orderly (no strong smells) and impersonal. I felt ignored and alone until I again adjusted myself to the American perceptual world.

Exploring Ideas

1. Observe people in different situations such as standing in line in the dining hall, getting on a bus, buying snacks from a street vendor, and strolling in a park on the weekend. Observe eye movements, sounds of speaking, touching, moving and other senses. From these observations do you think Chinese culture is high contact or low contact? Are there differences according to age, gender, social situation or some other category?

2. Try to describe the contact behavior of your culture. Do some social situations require high contact behavior while others require low contact? How do people use their senses differently to orient themselves in high contact and low contact situations?

The world of sensory perception

Hall takes his readers on a journey through the senses starting with the distance senses of sight, hearing and smell and then to the closer senses of movement, touch and perception of heat. He begins the journey with the sense of sight and tells us that vision is a synthesis, a combination of what is recorded on the retina of the eye and information from other senses. In our home cultures we learn how to synthesize our various senses, and we learn what to pay attention to and what to ignore.

The Visual Field and the Visual World

It is necessary to distinguish between the retinal image and what man perceives. The former is called the visual field while the latter is the visual world. The visual field is made up of constantly shifting light patterns-recorded by the retina—which man uses to construct his visual world. The fact that man differentiates (without knowing that he does so) between the sense impressions that stimulate the retina and what he sees suggests that sensory data from other sources are used to correct the visual field. As he moves through space, man depends on the messages received from his body to stabilize his visual world. The feat of being able to recognize as stationary that which is recorded on the retina as constantly moving is accomplished by synthesis within the brain.

From Edward T. Hall The Hidden Dimension

Because this process is out of our awareness, a good way to raise our awareness is to look at and compare the visual arts of various cultures. I discovered this when I was teaching English writing. I asked the students to write descriptions of a place and I was not satisfied with the results. One student essay in particular reminded me of a Chinese landscape painting but other essays also had what I thought was a vague, dreamy and sentimental quality that was not familiar to Western readers. One student described her home in Sichuan. I had lived in Sichuan and had seen houses like the one she was describing, yet I could not recognize it from her essay. It made me think that the students were paying attention to different things and trying to communicate something quite unlike what Westerners do in their descriptive writing. This idea started me off on a journey of my own.

121

Visual Worlds in Art

Everything that is known of man's art in all his various cultures indicates that there are great differences in the visual worlds of those cultures. Since the time of the Renaissance, Western artists have used a form of spatial representation based on the so-called laws of linear perspective where the perspective lines are made to converge on a single point. In holding space static and organizing the elements of space so as to be viewed from a single point, we treat three dimensional space in a two dimensional manner.

Chinese and Japanese artists, on the other hand, symbolize depth in quite a different way. Oriental art shifts the viewing point while maintaining the scene as constant. Much of Western art does just the opposite. A significant difference between the East and the West, reflected in the art but far transcending it, is that space itself is perceived entirely differently. In the West, man perceives the objects but not the spaces between. In Japan, the spaces are perceived, named and revered as the ma, or intervening interval.

From Edward T. Hall, The Hidden Dimension

Visual Perception in Chinese landscape painting
Guo Xi, Linquan Gaozhi

Real hills and streams are like smoke and vapor; they differ from season to season. In spring the hills are light and seductive as if smiling; in summer they are green and moist as if dripping; in autumn they are clear and bright as if dressed up; in winter they are barren and silent as if slumbering. The painting gives the general idea but does not sharply delineate the details.

Some hills and streams are for passing through; some are to be viewed; some are to tour and enjoy; some to live in. The last two are to be preferred over the others.

Quoted in Li Zehou, The Path of Beauty Oxford University Press, 1994

Of course, all great civilizations have many arts and various painting styles, but I think it is fair to say that landscape painting has been particularly influential in defining for viewers what they expect to see in a painting in China. Similarly the realistic style using linear perspective has been especially influential in the West in defining what viewers expect to see. It could be that these two defining styles from the two cultures show us something about the visual worlds of the two cultures.

These culturally different visual worlds also carry over into other forms of communication. I decided to experiment with this idea by showing my writing class two paintings, one a Chinese landscape and one an American painting in the realistic style. I started by asking them to tell me what they saw in each painting. Then we compared them. I certainly learned a lot in that class. When we had a list of similarities and differences, I suggested to my students that they were writing Chinese landscapes and I wanted them to write Western realism. We looked at the list of characteristics of the Western painting and discussed how they could translate those characteristics into their English writing. (See "Painting pictures with English" page 291)

We had a genuine breakthrough in the writing course. Just as I had to learn to adapt to the Chinese perceptual world to live comfortably in China, my students had to adapt to a Western perceptual world in order to write well in English. This is an example of adding software to our basic operating systems. The students can still write in the "landscape" style when it is appropriate, but now they can also write in a Western realistic style.

Exploring Ideas

1. Describe what you see in each of the two paintings. If possible, invite someone from another culture to do this with you. You will probably find that people from various cultures see different things in the paintings.

2. Compare the two paintings. Check your observations with the list below.

Chinese painting: **Tugged Away from the Bustling City** by Bi Baoxiang	American painting: **Tables for Ladies** by Edward Hopper
Does not imitate objective reality	Imitates objective reality
Includes white space that suggests clouds and a stream	The canvas is completely covered
Forms seem to be "impermanent"	Forms are very solid
No specific light source	Light is shown "scientifically"
Nature dominates human structures	The man-made environment is shown
The viewer is expected to move eyes	The viewer's eye is held constant
The viewer uses imagination to fill in	The artist provides a complete picture

Neutral colors	Wide range of colors
An idealized view of a general scene that makes the viewer feel peaceful and happy	Details make it seem real even if the artist invented it.

Figure 5 Tables for Ladies

Edward Hopper (1882-1967) Tables for Ladies, 1930
The Metropolitan Museum of Art, New York

Figure 6 Tugged Away from the Bustling City

Bi Baoxiang
Tugged Away from the Bustling City

Finding meaning in visual worlds

My class had no trouble understanding the meaning of the Chinese painting. It is, they say, a product of the imagination. It does not show a specific mountain, valley, house, river or trees. It is a picture of a peaceful place where one can enjoy tranquill'ty and be close to nature. It is an ideal picture, perhaps expressing the desire of the artist. What the students described as a stream or a river in the painting is actually white space with brushstrokes suggesting a riverbank. The bridge is a few brush strokes that suggest a bridge over the river. The mountain is not a specific mountain but brushstrokes applied in a way that means mountain to viewers who are accustomed to this form of visual representation. Some said that the white space was a mist or fog that gives the painting a spiritual quality that set the scene apart

126

from ordinary daily reality.

My students were eager for me to tell them what the Western painting "means". Some suggested that it describes the material richness of modern life, because it is a picture of a restaurant with richly detailed wooden walls and a display of colorful fruit in the foreground. The picture has four human figures, two women toward the front and a couple sitting at a table farther back. As an American viewing the picture I felt that the artist intended to express the loneliness and impersonality of modern life. This interpretation came as a complete surprise to my students. I pointed out that even though all four people are in the same room they are not interacting with one another. They appear to be lost in their own thoughts. The painting shows a materially rich setting, but the human quality of the painting is distant and remote.

Visual space is not as "friendly" as tactile space

Hall says that we do tend to experience the space we take in with our eyes as separate and distant from us. We feel connected to the space and things we experience through touch. Hall goes so far as to say that visual space is unfriendly while tactile (touching) space is friendly. You may or may not agree, but the idea does become important when we realize that people in some cultures rely more on sight, and especially sight at far distances, than people in other cultures do. He argues that European cultures and especially those of the north emphasize vision at a distance. As always, this is a generalization and it is best to check it against some actual experience such as looking at art, traveling in the culture, or discussing the topic with someone from a particular culture. Let me just say that Americans like to live in houses with big windows, not windows aligned to capture the heat of the sun, but windows for looking out. European architects have long designed public buildings and monuments that are meant to be impressive when viewed from afar.

127

Other Chinese viewers may make somewhat different interpretations of the Chinese painting, and other Westerners will undoubtedly offer different interpretations of the American painting. The point is that we can "read" a painting that comes from a cultural tradition that is familiar to us but may not be able to find any meaning or find an entirely different meaning from a painting that comes from an unfamiliar artistic tradition.

Sensing through movement

Earlier I told you that I had to learn to cross the street, ride a bike and climb a mountain when I came to China. I also had to learn how to appreciate a garden. At first the Chinese gardens seemed colorless as they do not have as many bright flowers as Western gardens usually do. I kept hurrying through, looking for that place where I could see the whole thing before me. It took me a long time to learn to hear, smell and move in this new space.

Japanese Gardens

Lacking wide open spaces, and living close together as they do, the Japanese learned to make the most of small spaces. They were particularly ingenious in stretching visual space by exaggerating kinesthetic involvement. Not only are their gardens designed to be viewed with the eyes, but more than the usual number of muscular sensations are built into the experience of walking through a Japanese garden. The visitor is periodically forced to watch his step as he picks his way along irregularly spaced stepping stones set in a pool. At each rock he must pause and look down to see where to step next. Looking up, he is arrested for a moment by a view that is broken as soon as he moves his foot to take up a new perch. Olfaction, shifts in temperature, humidity, light, shade, and color are worked together in such a way as to enhance the use of the whole body as a sensing organ. Unlike the western garden, which like the Western painting is often designed to be viewed from one point, the Japanese garden is designed to be enjoyed from many points of view. The study of Japanese spaces illustrates their habit of leading the individual to a spot where he can discover something for himself.

From Edward T. Hall The Hidden Dimension

Japanese gardens are modeled after classical Chinese gardens such as those of Suzhou.

The Chinese art of landscape design incorporates all the senses in a way that is unfamiliar to westerners like me. Americans in particular tend to orient themselves by using sight. To appreciate a skyscraper you need to view it from afar. This is also true of traditional sculpture and most public monuments.

A Chinese-American Monument

When the young Chinese-American architect Maya Lin submitted her design for the Vietnam War Memorial in Washington D. C., it was something new for the United States. At first her design was controversial. Some people did not like it at all. Now that Americans have lived with her creation for several years, it is very popular. The visitor does not view her monument from a distance but walks through it. It consists of a series of stone tablets inscribed with the names of the soldiers who died in the war set low to the ground. The more typical American or European monument is raised above ground level on a pedestal. Her design incorporates the experience of movement she learned from Chinese culture. It is a wonderful example of how combining cultures enriches us all.

129

Have you figured out yet how climbing a mountain in the US is different from climbing a mountain in China? I think there are two basic reasons why Americans climb mountains. The most important reason is to get to the top. This is a matter of meeting the challenge of the mountain. Can I do it? Do I have the physical fitness, strength and endurance to meet the challenge? Can I conquer nature by conquering the mountain? How fast can I do it? The second reason is to see the view from the top.

Chinese mountains

Westerners find Chinese mountains confusing as they do not provide an experience of wild untamed nature. They expect mountains to be natural rather than paved with steps from bottom to top. They don't expect to see very old people and very young children climbing mountains. I have also noticed that each local area in China has a "mountain" even if it is quite small and even if people had to build it themselves. After a few experiences of finding there was nothing to see from the top or that the view was lost in clouds and mist (Emei and Huangshan, for instance), I started trying to figure out what people are really doing when they are climbing mountains. My conclusion is that in China people climb mountains because the experience of doing it is enjoyable. I think they also do it to experience the mountain by moving into it and up and down it. In climbing the mountain they realize their connection with nature rather than their power over it. We will return to this topic again in the chapter on cultural values.

Why did I find it hard to cross the street or ride a bicycle when I first came to China? One reason is that the "rules of the road" are quite different. Westerns tend to take a low context approach to keeping the flow of traffic safe and orderly. They pass many laws that define the rights of everyone involved, walkers, drivers, drivers of emergency vehicles, and anyone else who might be in the streets. In China people put more emphasis on responding to the immediate situation. I have noticed that cyclists must pay attention to what is happening in front of them but do not have to worry about what is going on behind them. This means that you can enter the flow of traffic more freely. The cyclists behind you will change direction to keep from running into you. In the US you cannot enter the traffic unless you know there is enough space without requiring the people coming behind you to change direction or slow down.

Exploring Ideas

1. Ask someone who has come to China from another country what new skills they needed to learn in China. Give them my list above and ask them if these skills are performed differently in China from the ways they do them in their home culture. Ask them if there are other similar skills they had to learn to live comfortably in China. If everyone in class shares

their reports, you can make a long list of specifically Chinese sensory experiences. Once you have your list offer to teach a newcomer one of these skills.

2. Maya Lin's Vietnam War Memorial is not the only example of the wonderful things that can be created when the sensory experiences of two different cultures are brought together. Look for additional examples from your knowledge of Chinese people who have taken their cultural experience to the West and Westerners who have brought their perceptions to China. For a start I think of the Taiwan filmmaker Ang Lee who began by making Chinese films and now directs Western films in Hollywood. If you are familiar with his films, consider how he contributes his Chinese perceptions to world filmmaking.

Auditory space

The next stop in our journey through the senses is sound. Hall observes that people from different cultures have much different tolerances for particular sounds and for the loudness of sounds. For instance, in the US parents try to provide quiet and darkness when their children are sleeping. The result is that many Americans cannot sleep unless they are in a quiet place. In other cultures people may have a more relaxed attitude that allows them to sleep almost anywhere.

The sound of the human voice also varies by culture as well as by situation, gender, social position and age. Americans do not learn to focus their voices as many British people do, so they are often thought to be loud. Even though my students like American accents, I find that often films with British actors are easier for them to understand. British actors like educated British speakers are trained in the use of the voice while Americans tend to make all talk sound like casual conversation.

The technology of sound is also handled differently in different cultures. In some countries people are asked to hand in their cellular telephones when they enter a restaurant or café as the sound of the ringing and talking into the phone is disturbing to other diners. In other countries noisy restaurants are considered friendly and warm. The loud noise is a sign that everyone is having a good time. In some American cities it is against the law to use the horn on a car except in an emergency. In China I imagine that I know how important a driver thinks his passenger is by how often and how strongly he leans on the horn.

Screening Sounds

Space perception is not only a matter of what can be perceived but what can be screened out. People brought up in different cultures, learn as children, without ever knowing that they have done so, to screen out one type of information while paying close attention to another. Once set, these perceptual patterns apparently remain quite stable throughout life. The Japanese, for example, screen visually in a variety of ways but are perfectly content with paper walls as acoustic [sound] screens.

In contrast, the Germans and the Dutch depend on thick walls and double-doors to screen sound, and have difficulty if they must rely on their own powers of concentration to screen out sound. If two rooms are the same size and one screens out sound but the other one doesn't, the sensitive German who is trying to concentrate will feel less crowded in the former because he feels less intruded on.

From Edward T. Hall The Hidden Dimension

In the building where I live we have a German professor and a Japanese professor. They are almost the same age and both are considerate, patient and generous men. The motor for the heating system is close to the apartments where these two professors live. The noise from the motor almost ruined the year for the German professor. He finally asked to be moved to another room. The Japanese professor, as far as I know, never mentioned the noise from the heating system to anyone.

The world of smells

Smell is the most powerful sense for recalling our memories and arousing emotions. When we first notice the smell of spring, perhaps we remember the springs of our childhood.

When we first taste a new food, maybe we feel very attracted or disgusted by the unfamiliar smell. The power of smell to remind us of the past probably plays a part in people's emotional attachment to a local place and their childhood homes. If as Hall claims, American society has few smells, then it is not surprising that Americans are more mobile than people in some other societies. They have few smells in their surroundings to stimulate memories and emotions and therefore, they feel less attached. Of course, this is not the only or most important explanation for American mobility, but it does show that culture does repeat itself and does follow recognizable patterns. If a feature of a culture is important it will show up in language, art and architecture, sensory perception, basic values, attitudes and behaviors.

The Lack of Smells in American Society

In the use of [smell] Americans are culturally underdeveloped. The extensive use of deodorants and the suppression of odor in public places results in a land of olfactory blandness and sameness that would be difficult to duplicate anywhere else in the world. This blandness makes for undifferentiated spaces and deprives us of richness and variety in our life. It also obscures memories, because smell evokes much deeper memories than either vision or sound.

By banishing all but a few odors from our public life, what have Americans done to themselves and what effect does this have on life in our cities? In the northern European tradition most Americans cut themselves off from a powerful communication channel, olfaction. Our cities lack both olfactory and visual variety. Anyone who has walked along the streets of almost any European village or town knows what is nearby. What smells do we have in the US that can compare to those in the typical French town where one may savor the smell of coffee, spices, vegetables, freshly plucked fowl, clean laundry and the characteristic odor of outdoor cafes? Olfaction of this type can provide a sense of life; the shifts and the transitions not only help to locate one in space but add zest to daily living.

From Edward T. Hall The Hidden Dimension

Once I was walking down the street of an American city with a Japanese friend. We found that we were walking behind two Japanese students who were talking to each other in Japanese. I asked my friend what they were talking about. She told me they were complaining about how bad Americans smell.

134

The Importance of Smells in Arab Societies

Americans traveling abroad are apt to comment on the smell of strong colognes used by men living in Mediterranean Arab countries. Entering a taxicab, they are overwhelmed by the inescapable presence of the driver, whose olfactory aura fills the cab. Arabs apparently recognize a relationship between disposition and smell. The intermediaries who arrange an Arab marriage may even on occasion ask to smell the girl and will reject her if she "does not smell nice," not so much on esthetic grounds but possibly because of a residual smell of anger or discontent.

The olfactory boundary performs two roles in Arab life. It enfolds those who want to relate and separates those who don't. The Arab finds it essential to stay inside the olfactory zone as a means of keeping tabs on changes in emotion. Bathing the other person in one's breath is a common practice in Arab countries.

To smell one's friend is not only nice but desirable, for to deny him your breath is to act ashamed. The American is taught not to breathe on people. He experiences difficulty when he is within olfactory range of another person with whom he is not on close terms, particularly in public settings. He finds the intensity and sensuality overwhelming and has trouble paying attention to what is being said and at the same time coping with his feelings. Americans automatically communicate shame in trying to be polite. Who would expect that when our highest diplomats are putting on their best manners they are also communicating shame?

From Edward T. Hall, The Hidden Dimension

Exploring Ideas

Become more familiar with your own perceptual world and those of people from other cultures by trying one of these activities.

1. Buy a roll of film for your class. Go around your campus and take photos as you like. Then buy a roll of film for some people you know from another country and ask them to take their own photos of the same campus. Develop the film and compare the two sets of prints. What did each group choose to photograph? How are people shown?

2. Find someone who knows something about Western music and Chinese music. Ask them to tell you about the differences in

135

musical traditions. What does this discussion tell you about the differences in the auditory spaces of different cultures?

3. Take someone from a Western country to the vegetable market. Try to figure out what part of the experience they find attractive and what part is difficult for them. What senses are involved?

Chapter 8: Moving to the Rhythms of Culture

If you have ever seen a foreign film originally produced in another language and dubbed in your local language, then you know something about the role gesture and movement plays in communication. The words may be perfectly coordinated with the mouth movements of the actors, but often the actors do not seem to use the appropriate body posture to match the words or their gestures and facial expressions seem somehow not right. The gestures do not match the words in the dubbed language as well as they did in the original language.

The language of gesture and movement

When individuals talk, their bodies keep time to the rhythm of their speech. Movements of the fingers, eyelids and brows, head, and other body parts provide a rhythmic punctuation to the rise and fall of the voice and the flow of words. When people who share culture talk, their body movements gradually fall into rhythmic harmony with each other. Sometimes they will use the same posture, almost as if they were mirror images of one another. When two people are interacting and do not show this harmony of posture and movement, it is a sign that while the two may understand each other's words, they are not in tune with each other non-verbally or kinesthetically. If this is the case, there may be some misunderstanding or tension between them.

Because human bodies are jointed and hinged in the same fashion, we tend to think of all people around the globe as sitting, standing and lying down in similar postures. In fact there are hundreds of different body postures that humans can comfortably adopt and the popularity of one posture over another is largely determined by culture. Most people have learned to expect differences in gestures, but too often they only notice the more obvious sign language such as the Chinese finger signs for numbers or the hand gestures people use in different countries to indicate come here. By paying attention to only the most obvious behavioral codes, people miss more subtle differences in how people use their bodies to communicate.

Dances are catalogues of the movements of a culture

Researchers have found that the movements that people use in daily life are reflected in the movements of their dances. One way to compare the cultural aspects of movement is to compare dance styles from different countries. For instance, most dancers from Europe, the Americas and East Asia move the middle part of the body as if it were one unit. They tend to use rigid energetic movements that are different from the movements we find in dances from Southeast Asia, Polynesia and South Asia. In these cultures, dancers move the body as if the trunk (mid section) were two (or more) units—bending and swaying the upper and lower sections independently of each other. These movements are very fluid, as if the muscles and spine were moving in waves. The flowing movements of a Polynesian hula dance contrast sharply with the tension and bodily control of a Spanish flamenco. Further, flamenco is often danced by one man and one woman with each answering the other with their movements. In other cultures it is more common for a group of male dancers to coordinate their movements with a group of female dancers.

I was always considered a good dancer at home, but in China I am not. I have difficulty following the intricate and highly practiced steps of Chinese social dancing. In the United States social dancing does require mastering the forms but they are usually fairly simple. Beyond that dancing is a matter of following the rhythm of the music, being relaxed and free and expressing your feelings with movement. It is not surprising that rock dancing, which emphasizes separateness and "doing your own thing," evolved in individualistic cultures such as those of England and the United States.

Eye behavior across cultures

An important part of the language of movement is the way people use their eyes. Eye behavior is different from one culture to another and also varies within cultures by gender, age and social status. In the United States high status and socially confident individuals have more eye contact than do submissive or anxious persons. For Americans the speaker who uses more eye contact seems more relaxed, more informal, and yet more authoritative. Teachers and others who do a lot of public speaking receive special instructions on how to establish and maintain eye contact with an audience. They are usually told to meet one person's eyes, rest there for a moment and then to move their gaze to another person in another part of the audience. In this way the audience feels that the speaker is speaking directly to each individual.

I have noticed that well-educated Chinese show their anger almost entirely with their eyes. When angry the person may stiffen slightly and may stare more than usual, but their anger appears mostly in the widening of their eyes. It took me a long time to recognize this as widening of the eyes in the West usually indicates surprise or excitement. Until I learned how to recognize subtle signs, especially in the eyes, I thought Chinese friends rarely felt or expressed anger. When interacting with people from the West, keep in mind that they are unlikely to notice what to them are subtle signs of changes in how you feel in response to what they are saying or doing.

In many cultures averting the eyes is a sign of humility and respect. White middle class Americans have a problem accepting this, as for them looking down or away from the speaker means that the person is ignoring or rejecting what the speaker is saying. For them it is a sign of disrespect as it indicates the other person is not listening. This has caused many misunderstandings in relationships between white middle class teachers and African-American students in schools. You should be conscious of eye behavior and other body movements that you use to convey humility and respect as these may be misunderstood by Westerners.

Exploring Ideas

1. Go to a street, your university dining hall or some other place where people gather and from a respectful distance observe people in conversation. Notice the interaction of the participants' body movements and gestures. Then view a film or television program from another culture in which people are talking together. With the sound off, can you tell when people are in tune with one another? What body movements indicate that the people talking are having a misunderstanding or conflict?

2. Make a list of body movements from each culture you observe and translate the movement into the message the movement conveys. For instance, stretching the body upward and toward the other person may mean that the speaker wants to say that he is in control or he is the dominant one in this conversation. Moving back may mean that the person does not want to listen to what the speaker is saying.

3. Observe styles of dancing from different countries. From the dances try to guess how people in each culture use their bodies. If possible, ask someone from another culture to teach you how to do a dance from that culture.

4. North Americans and Northern Europeans usually do not use postures that communicate humility and they do not squat. What difficulties might this cause when they visit China?

5. Observe the eye contact behavior of Chinese public speakers and compare it to the eye contact behavior of Americans or

140

other Westerners. What differences do you notice?

The world of touch

Everyone is programmed with his home culture software from the moment of birth. In some cultures a baby is carried on the mother's back, in others on her chest, stomach, or hip. In some cultures babies spend much time in playpens, baby seats, or baby carriages. In some places children are picked up when they cry; in others they are not for fear of "spoiling" them. Some babies sleep in beds of their own from birth while babies in other countries sleep in their parents' bed for years. In these ways infants learn to experience the warmth of human contact, or they learn to live with little of it.

In the United States many families and individuals, especially the young and the old, have pet cats or pet dogs. Various explanations have been offered to account for this phenomenon, but it is at least partly because the rules of touching in the United States are so restrictive that people turn to animals to satisfy their need for touch. A dog usually welcomes its owners touch and likes to be petted and stroked. It is not so simple in their relationships with people, even their closest family members. In Chinese families pets are not necessary to satisfy the human need for touch. Family members give one another rubs and use other forms of soothing and comforting touch.

Touching has culturally specific meanings

Cultures can be categorized as high contact or low contact depending on which senses a particular culture emphasizes. American culture can be classified as low contact, which means that perceiving at a distance as with sight is emphasized over perceiving close up as with touch. We must be cautious, however, with our generalizations. You may have concluded from watching Hollywood films that there is a lot of touching in Western cultures. I suggest that most touching in American cul-

141

ture is either aggressive or sexual. There is little touching to express non-sexual affection among friends and family members except with young children. A hug that expresses emotional closeness between people who are not lovers is relatively rare outside the rituals of greeting and saying good-bye. Another exception is in same sex groups such as sports teams. When you watch a game on TV you often see players hugging their teammates. In this case we see the role of touching in creating bonds among the members of a group.

In the past it was true that relatively high status people (men, supervisors, adults) could touch lower status people (women, workers, children), but the rules about this are changing. Now there is much public concern about sexual harassment in the workplace and about the possibility of sexual abuse of children by caregivers such as teachers and activity leaders. This has resulted in further restrictions on touching in American society. Touching of lower status people by higher status people has become suspect as it could indicate a sexual intention. Americans still talk a lot about touching and especially honor the hug as expressing emotional warmth, affection and care.

The touch of friendship

A Canadian woman who tutors Chinese immigrants in English writes:

As soon as my favorite student and I left the building, she linked her arm tightly in mine and walked right up against my side, matching my steps as we joked and laughed all the way to my car. I had to control my stiffening; it was such a strange feeling for me.

I know that in China, and also in many Latin countries, this kind of physical intimacy between women friends is standard—It's not here, and I found it uncomfortable. On the other hand, when I greet or leave my female friends we almost always hug and kiss each other on the cheek, something Chinese women have told me feels uncomfortable to them.

In general Chinese people are more deeply involved with people with whom they have an intimate or very personal relationship, such as family members and close friends, than is typically true of people from Northern European cultures. It is also true that Chinese people tend to be more distant with people with whom they have no connection or only a weak connection. These cultural differences are expressed in the cultural rules of touching. Once we realize this we become more sensitive to the details of the cultural rules of touching and can modify behavior to fit the cultural situation we are in.

Adding new cultural software to your present home culture software, especially in international work situations, means learning to use touch to communicate as members of that emerging global culture do. A good place to begin is with the handshake. After years of exchanging weak handshakes with Chinese people, especially professional women, I wrote this essay for my Chinese students.

Have you hugged a foreigner today?

Probably not.

If you are typical Chinese you do not hug anyone in public. (Well, maybe you put your arm around your sweetheart's waist as you stroll down the street.) Go to any airport or train station and you will see scenes of greeting and good-bye with all the feelings expressed in the face and the eyes and in the practical things loved ones do for one another. It is unlikely that someone will put their arms around the returning or departing dear one and squeeze.

How much more unlikely that you would hug a foreigner. A foreigner is a *wai guo ren*, a person outside the wall. Not much hugging goes on inside the wall, inside the intimacy of the family home, and people outside are dealt with much more formally than people inside. Sure, you might welcome a guest to your home or office and that guest would be given the best hospitality you can offer. You would show the sincerity of your welcome by performing many rituals such as giving the guest your undivided attention and paying compliments that carry the message that the guest is great and you are humble. Most foreigners are treated as honored guests. You don't hug an honored guest.

But you should.

The question "Have you hugged a foreigner today?" is not really a question. It is a suggestion, a play on the popular American slogan "Have you hugged your kids today?" That was never meant to be a question but a reminder to parents to physically demonstrate their affection for their children every day. Parents should get closer to their children. They should let them know in a very concrete way that they are loved.

143

So when I say, "Have you hugged a foreigner today?" I am not asking you a question. I am advising you to reduce the social distance between you and the Westerners you meet. I am not suggesting that you put your arms around the Westerners you know, but I am suggesting that you put aside your home culture rules of politeness that say you should show your sincerity by being humble and deferential. Instead show your sincerity by standing tall, looking the person in the eye, saying your name in a clear strong voice and giving the person a firm handshake. Don't ruin it by being tentative with your grasp. Reach out and hug that hand. Take as much of the hand as you can get hold of and squeeze.

By doing this you show that you consider yourself equal to the person you are meeting.

In the West people of different social statuses communicate in a way that tries to reduce the status differences. A high-ranking person will convey the message "I am just like you." Similarly, a lower ranking person will communicate in a way that sends the message "I am just as capable as you are."

In China it is considered polite to stress your low position and the other person's higher status, greater accomplishments or finer virtue. A Westerner on the receiving end of such behavior is likely to interpret this as a lack of self-confidence, as a sign that you are unsure of yourself and probably inexperienced in the present social or business situation. They are likely to take your word for it that you are unworthy, that your humility is a reliable message about your self-confidence or ability. Your sincere effort to be polite can backfire if the Westerner interprets your weak handshake as meaning that you are not worth paying attention to.

So, hug a foreigner today.

I hope you understand my meaning. I am not recommending that you actually hug Westerners when you first meet them. I only mean that if you want to send a message about who you are to someone from a Western culture, you need to use a behavioral code that is understandable to that person. To send the message you want to send, you have to encode it in a strong firm handshake with the right kind of eye contact and the right quality of voice. This is an aspect of cultural grammar that is worthwhile for you to master.

Exploring Ideas

1. In class practice giving and receiving the type of handshake described above.

144

2. Write an essay of your own giving advice to Westerners coming to China about how and when to touch others. You can also advise them against touching in situations where touching would be acceptable in their home cultures but is not acceptable in China. Explain what meaning touch conveys in the situation you are writing about.
3. Read and discuss the following case.

Case 8 Too Close for Comfort

Too Close for Comfort

Bill had just arrived from the United States to study engineering at a Chinese university. He studied Chinese back at his home university and was confident that doing his graduate study at a Chinese university would give him an edge in taking advantage of future opportunities in the growing Chinese economy.

In the first few days he met and moved in with his roommate Zemin and met several of the students who lived in nearby dormitory rooms. Most of them were also studying engineering but had little experience with Americans. He usually went to the student cafeteria with them and they were very helpful in showing him around and in gently correcting his classroom Chinese.

One evening he settled in for his first study session in his room. After a time Zemin left to visit another room where friends were listening to a radio broadcast. Bill said he would join him later. When Bill decided to take a break and see what the "guys" were up to, he found Zemin and two other boys huddled over the radio. Bill found it quite odd, however, that Zemin was draped over the back of the boy seated in front of the radio. Moreover, that boy had his feet propped up on his roommate who was seated nearby. It seemed to Bill that he had startled them, since they jumped up and welcomed him and even offered him tea. After Bill had a cup of tea and a chair to sit in, the group returned to the radio.

Bill shrugged the incident off, but over the next few days noticed that female students on campus frequently walked arm-in-arm or even holding hands. He noticed, too, that students of both sexes, but especially the boys, would huddle around newspaper displays in a fashion of close contact similar to Zemin and others around the radio. Bill felt rather uncomfortable and wondered how he would respond if one of his classmates were to put his arms around him.

Answer the following questions:
1. Why is Bill uncomfortable with this kind of touching?
2. What advice would you give him?
3. Explain touching in Chinese friendship groups to Bill.
4. Study the following excerpts from a handbook for international students at an American university. Is the advice helpful? Should it be more precise by taking into consideration age, gender and situation? If possible show it to an American and ask for more details about the cultural aspects of movement, gesture and touch.
5. Write a similar list of observations for students from other countries studying in China.

International Students Handbook

Gestures and movements

✓Direct eye contact is given and expected in return by Americans talking with other people.
✓A smile is the universal sign of greeting and Americans give it freely.
✓People who have good posture usually appear more self-confident.

✓Some Americans tell stories or talk in a dramatic manner, using a lot of hand and body gesturing. These people are considered popular, attractive, and of high social status.

✓Men take up more space than women in their use of gestures, body posture and movements:

Legs spread apart when standing

Wide use of arms when speaking

And legs crossed at the ankles when sitting

✓Imitating the posture of the persons with whom you are communicating shows you are probably agreeing with them.

✓Some people use a lot of nodding and smiling as they listen.

✓Others choose to communicate by leaning forward, touching, or use of a conversational style.

To touch or not to touch

✓Researchers classify Americans as low touchers in relation to other people of the world. However, touch in a multicultural society is very individual.

✓You will meet some people who will never touch you, even though they highly prize your friendship. And you will meet others who will touch you often, usually on the shoulders and arms, but such touches will not really express a meaning.

✓Because US society is very aware of the potential for people to use negative touch to intimidate or threaten, people are careful in how they touch.

✓In the US, touch is used mainly as a greeting or to say goodbye.

✓Americans can give the feeling of touch (without touching) by allowing others to move in close when talking.

✓Good friends may exchange hugs, friendly punches, kisses, and may touch frequently when talking to each other.

✓For acquaintances and superiors, like professors or interviewers, a simple handshake is all that is expected.

✓Some people are high touchers and give friendly arm, back and shoulder touches even to new acquaintances.

✓You will find that some students feel free to show in public what might be considered "private" expressions of affection in your culture. An example might be kissing outside classrooms.

Space is jealously guarded

Privacy is the key to understanding the use of space and territory in the US.

✓Americans claim, use, and will defend what is their chair, their television, their stereo, or their kitchen.

✓Most interpersonal disagreements between roommates focus around the use of space and the idea of ownership. For instance:

> "He drank my milk from my side of the refrigerator!"
>
> "She used my stapler and kept it on her desk."
>
> "They just walked in and turned on my stereo without asking."
>
> "He took five drawers for his clothes and left me just two!"
>
> ✓US students feel free to decorate their environments if they have "paid" for them through rent or dorm fees.
>
> ✓In general, Americans are generous people who will lend and give freely of possessions, but only to those who ask first.
>
> ✓Even in public places (library or large dorm lounge), people often "mark" their space by putting down a piece of clothing (coat), books or food to show that, "This place is mine and I'll be right back. Don't come here."
>
> ✓Doors send messages. In almost all cases, the open door says "I'm friendly," and the closed door suggests "I'd rather be alone." You might shut your door only because you want to study, but you should be aware that others may see that shut door and, fairly or not, assume it represents your whole attitude or personality.
>
> ✓68 to 72 degrees Fahrenheit is considered a comfortable room temperature.
>
> ✓Americans are very aware of scents and smells, judging others and their dwellings by the type and intensity of scents detected. Windows and doors are usually kept wide open to let in "the fresh air."

Interaction distances

Most of the time we are not touching others, but we are constantly positioning ourselves in relation to others. As the handbook above says, people often give the feeling of touch by allowing others to move close while talking. This raises the question of what various distances mean in face-to-face interactions. As with all the cultural characteristics we have been discussing, we have to pay attention to the layers of culture, to differences within national cultures based on social class, region, ethnic group, gender and age. Even with that caution, I will take the risk of giving you some observations from middle class dominant-culture professional white Americans' behavior. This is the culture you might encounter if you meet a manager from a company that has its origin in the United States. To a lesser extent, it might also be a guide to the behavior of other professionals from the West. Whatever national or subculture we are talking about, moving closer or moving away frequently carries a specific meaning. You will have to do your own observations to discover the meaning in a specific cultural context.

Your classroom English may be too formal for work situations

People in all cultures behave somewhat differently depending on the distance from which they are communicating. The quality of the voice, gestures, and even the style of the language people use varies according to the interaction distance they are using. This is important for Chinese English speakers to remember because they usually learn English in a classroom where the interaction distances between students and teachers are greater than the typical distances used by co-workers cooperating on a task. They may find that their English, like Bill's Chinese in **Too Close for Comfort**, sounds like a classroom language. One reason for this is that the tone and style people use when responding to a teacher is probably too formal and distant for the usual work or social situation. This is one reason why small group discussions are so valuable in English learning. By speaking English with their peers, Chinese English learners are more likely to learn to speak and respond in a way that is appropriate for the closer interaction distances they are likely to experience in their future work.

A distance of one meter and in more formal situations up to two meters is the typical distance people maintain in business and social relationships. Two meters is the distance a salesman or an employment interviewer is likely to use. It might also be the distance a Western manager will use when formally discussing work with a Chinese worker. In the most formal meetings with a manager or supervisor he or she may sit behind a desk while the worker stands or sits in front, far, far away, listening to the voice of authority. A manager or teacher who wants to communicate that the relationship is more collaborative rather than authoritative will use the friendlier distance of one

149

meter or a little more and will not rely on a desk or other physical device to increase distance between him and the worker. Perhaps you have noticed that foreign teachers often leave the podium in front of the class and move closer to the students. This reflects the more collaborative form of some Western educational systems.

How to establish and avoid interaction at intermediate distances

If you are in a hallway or some other rather public place and you see someone you know, you must acknowledge that fact with a friendly greeting if the person comes within two meters of you. If you are further distant you can ignore one another by avoiding eye contact, but if you make eye contact you must speak or in some way acknowledge the other person. You can keep the conversation brief by breaking eye contact. If you keep eye contact, the other person is likely to keep talking and will expect you to respond. This hidden rule of culture probably accounts for conversations between Americans that are perceived as loud and too public by people from other cultures, including European cultures. In many other cultures people remain silent while working side by side or across a desk and the silence simply indicates the person has his own work to do or wants to be left alone. It is not unfriendly in that context, but in the United States a physical screen would be necessary to remove the social expectation that two people sitting two meters apart should talk to one another.

The usual rules do not apply under conditions of crowding

The rules are different in crowded spaces like buses and elevators where people are often very close to strangers. In this situation, Americans typically tense their muscles and avoid eye contact as a way of showing that the physical contact is involuntary and does not mean intimacy. This could be one reason why Americans and other non-contact people find crowded streets

150

and shops in China stressful. They are uncomfortable with the close distances and even being touched by strangers. They convey through muscle tension that the closeness and touching carries no meaning about a relationship with the people involved. I have enjoyed my life in China much more since I learned to relax in a crowd.

At very large communication distances the rules are different

At distances over six meters it is not possible to have two way communication. At that distance speakers have to use microphones to make their voices heard and so do not expect a verbal response from the audience unless microphones are provided for individuals to ask questions. Western performers and speakers are sometimes dismayed by the habit of some Chinese of talking during a performance or lecture. Westerners interpret this as a sign of the Chinese audience's lack of interest or even disapproval. Applause, cheers, standing, and throwing flowers are the typical ways an audience communicates its approval of messages received from distances common in lecture halls, concert halls, theaters, and sports stadiums. At this distance a speaker or performer docs not perceive individuals but an audience, a mass.

Exploring Ideas

1. Observe the interaction distances used by people from various cultures by watching films and television programs. Be sure to notice differences based on age, gender, social class, ethnic group and situation for the culture you are observing. From your viewing, attempt to interpret the meaning of someone moving closer to or away from another person.
2. Describe interaction distances as they are used in Chinese culture. Note variations for age, gender, social class, ethnic group and situation. To do this you might need to systemati-

cally observe people's behavior in a classroom, dormitory, business office, department store or restaurant.

3. Getting the right distance between people occurs more easily when the people interacting are from the same culture. When people from different cultures are interacting, there is often a lot of moving about and uneasiness as each person tries to find the correct distance. Have you had such an experience when interacting with someone from another culture?

Chapter 9: Building Culture into the Landscape

People usually look at language, customs, history, values, and behaviors to find the influence of culture in their lives. They accumulate a great deal of specific information. The act of accumulating is important, both in creating culture and in learning about another culture. This reminds us of one of the most widely accepted definitions of culture:

- *Culture is the total accumulation of beliefs, customs, values, behaviors, institutions and communication patterns that are shared, learned and passed down through the generations in an identifiable group of people.*

Now we turn our attention to another characteristic of culture and that is the patterns. Instead of looking at the individual trees, we look at the forest as a whole. What are the basic patterns according to which all the details are organized? What are the basic structures or forms that give meaning to the details? We can find basic structures, forms or patterns almost anywhere, because if a pattern is basic to a culture, it will show up in many places, including in the physical world that is part of our daily life. Human beings build not only to provide shelter but also to provide structures for ordering relationships and activities. Our cultures are built into the layout of cities, villages and farmland, and in the design of buildings. These physical forms both reflect and are reflected in social patterns and in the languages we speak.

Nature and Culture

The earth is our home — we have no other — yet we do not feel at home in it. Alterations have to be made. These may be small and imperceptible such as naming the parts of nature. In the mere process of naming, strange plants, animals and rocks are subtly altered to become suitable denizens of the human world. Large, tangible changes occur when we apply physical force to clear bushes and trees and convert wild nature into orderly fields and houses. All these changes — tangible and intangible — are works of culture.

Yi-Fu Tuan "Strangers and Strangeness" The Geographic Review

The grid

Most of the cities and towns of the United States are arranged in a grid pattern of right-angled streets. A map of New York City shows that the streets running east and west are numbered in sequence. Thirty-fourth Street (famous for its large department stores) is south of Forty-second Street (famous for its movie theaters). The north-south streets are also numbered in sequence but are called avenues. Fifth Avenue with its fashionable shops is east of Seventh Avenue, home of the fashion industry. On the southern tip of Manhattan Island streets do not follow this pattern but continue to reveal the decisions made by the earliest Western settlers. Here we find the origin of the one street that breaks the overall pattern, Broadway. It runs diagonally across the grid, causing trouble for taxi drivers, visitors and residents who have come to expect that they can easily find any point on the logical grid of the city.

The naming and numbering system varies from city to city, but the basic grid pattern is the same. Some small towns name their streets after trees and name them in alphabetical order, so that Maple Street follows Locust Street and comes before Oak Street and Pine Street. With a pattern like this it is difficult to get lost, because the address of any building locates it in a specific place on the grid. This is a pattern that provides easy access even to strangers and is low context in that the visitor does not need to rely on a knowledgeable insider to find his way. My brother's address is 46040 125th Street East in a small city in southern California. In fact he does not live in a city at all, but far out in the desert. The grid pattern has been extended endlessly into the desert, so anyone can find him. Just follow the grid east to the intersection of 46th Street and 125th Street and there he is.

The same pattern can be seen in the interstate highway system that covers the country with a grid of regularly numbered highways. The odd numbered roads run north and south and the even numbered roads run east and west. Highway 95 will take you from Maine to Florida and Highway 3 will take you north or south along the West Coast. Physical features such as rivers and mountains seldom interfere with the grid pattern, because engineers construct bridges and tunnels to keep people going straight on their way. Anyone can go where they like with the aid of a map and the distinguishing features of local areas are only barely visible from the highways.

The large farms of the Midwest are arranged in a similar way. After the War of Independence the United States acquired large tracts of unsettled land from England and promptly divided it into regularly shaped states, counties, townships, and farms. Notice that the boundaries of many states are straight lines. Each farm is a regular rectangle and one plot in each township and a larger tract in each state were set aside to meet the educational needs of the area. This pattern encouraged settlers to move west, because the grid provided a path for them to follow. It ordered and civilized the wilderness.

Farmers live on their individual farms rather than in towns and villages. Probably you have seen photographs of single American farmhouses surrounded by large rectangular fields. What is not obvious in the photograph is that the family that lives there is connected to other similar families and to urban areas and markets through a grid of roads. They are not nearly as isolated as they appear, because their lives are ordered by a pattern first used by the ancient Romans to connect the far-flung corners of their empire. You can find the same pattern in the characteristic American suburban sprawl. People who rise in social class and income move out from the city into newer and newer and more expensive housing areas far from the city. Older areas in the inner city are taken over by new arrivals. They live there until their fortunes improve at which time they follow the grid out to more desirable housing on the outskirts.

In grid cultures there is no fixed center

This pattern does not have a fixed center. Any point on the grid can become important depending on what is located there. It can just as easily disappear into obscurity if economic development or public taste favors another location. New cities grow up at the intersections of the interstate highway system while the centers of older towns die from neglect. I am often asked questions like, "What is the best university in the US?" or "What is the greatest city in the US?" I can only answer that there are many good universities and that I appreciate various cities for their particular characteristics. I am the product of a grid culture. I am not looking for the center. Like other Americans I want to know what opportunities I will find as I move out across the grid. Any corner can become a center. Bill Gates' Microsoft has its headquarters in Redmond, Washington. Ted Turner's CNN network is located in Atlanta, Georgia. Their activities have created centers, at least for now.

The radiating star

The grid pattern has many advantages, but for a wonderful holiday trip, I would choose to go to France. Once I traveled there with friends. We started in Paris and then rented a car and went out to the edges of the country. We traveled around the periphery stopping in local areas, each one delighting us with its own flavor, its own wines and cheeses, its own unique style of cooking. Traveling by car is fairly easy but quite different from moving across the American grid. In France we had to look for signs to *centre ville*, the city center. We followed those signs, found the center, and oriented ourselves from there. In the star pattern important things are at the center and everything else radiates out from the center. In France all major roads lead to Paris and most mileage signs tell you how far you are from Paris. Since we were moving around the edge of the country, we had to travel by minor roads. The treasures we found were the treasures typical of the forgotten corners of a society where the center sets the standard. If you look at a map of France that shows the highway system, the radiating star is clearly visible. The star pattern is also visible in the social and political life of the country.

In France people live in towns and villages where the church and town hall are at the center. In rural areas the farmers live in towns and go back and forth to their plots of land outside the town every day. In a French office the leader's office is at the center, and you can tell how important anyone in the organization is by how far his or her office is from the leader's office. It is unthinkable that the city of Paris would suffer from neglect or decay. French leaders follow the tradition of remodeling a section of the city or building a new monument to ensure that the city is as wondrous in the future as it was in the past. The most important buildings, events and organizations are in the center of Paris and the poorer, less important people live in the suburbs.

France is known for its highly centralized government and educational system. It is said that school children all over the country study the same lesson on the same day. Decisions about the curriculum and even specific lessons are made in Paris and communicated through a system of sub-centers until they reach the smallest school in the most remote area. In contrast the American governmental and educational systems are decentralized with local units having much independent authority and responsibility.

In the United States, the capital city, Washington D.C. is the only city built on a French star pattern and it is significant that a Frenchman designed it. In this case all streets are numbered or named in reference to the Capitol building and broad diagonal avenues radiate out from this central point. Every street address indicates how far and in what direction a particular location is in relation to the Capitol. The address of the White House is 1600 Pennsylvania Avenue NW. It is sixteen blocks northwest of the Capitol along one of the radiating avenues. Just a few blocks away you will find a low-income city neighborhood. Presumably a French government would not allow such squalor to exist so close to the center of its nation.

The inside/outside pattern

The Arab culture that dominates the southern and eastern shores of the Mediterranean Sea and extends east through Central Asia is a culture of contrasts and distinctions. Here people distinguish between what is public and what is private, what is male and what is female, and what is inside and what is outside.

Inside	Outside
Female	Male
Private	Public
Home	Market, mosque, coffee house

In the Middle Eastern inside/outside pattern, the inside is female and the outside is male. In the Arabic language, word roots are three consonant groups that carry the main meaning. To form specific words various vowels, prefixes and suffixes are added. The root *hrm* means honor and the word *harem* means the place where the women of the family live. Thus the honor of the family is tied to the women who live away from the public streets and markets. It is the duty of the men to protect the family's honor by protecting the women. The home is private and intimate; the street is where you find the stranger/enemy. Women represent the honor of the family, so if the family is prosperous enough to keep the women at home, they will do so to increase the prestige of the family. The face or head veil and the *abayah* (long black cloak that covers the whole body) are ways of screening women from strangers and are not worn in the

158

intimacy of the family. As we would expect, social life is strictly segregated by sex. Women may be highly educated but often in separate classes from men.

The traditional architecture of this part of the world features high walls and heavy gates. The face the city or a house presents to the outside is plain, not welcoming, even forbidding. The walls are thick to protect what is inside. If you were welcomed into an Arab home you might find a pleasant courtyard full of light and maybe flowers and a fountain. You would see windows, too, but all facing inward toward the courtyard rather than outward toward the street. These days, however, most city residents in Arab countries live in modern apartment buildings, so the rooms of the family's apartment have been arranged to replicate the traditional pattern as much as possible.

The Middle Eastern Home

In most homes the salon is usually the room farthest away from all others, and the closest to the door leading to the outside. Actually, in older buildings, a door leading to the outside opens directly into the salon or guest room on one end and another door opens to the inside of the home. In such a layout the guest knocks at the door and is either led into the salon through the home or asked to please wait until the other door leading immediately to the salon is opened for him. This behavior reflects two of the most important cultural values of the area. The first is the concern with the concept of face, facades, and appearances. The guest is exposed only to the most shining, formal, and stylized part of the home and gets to meet only the members whom the family intends for him to meet. On the other hand, relationships in the Middle East reflect great concern with guest-host relationships. The host is expected to welcome guests and provide hospitality. He should keep the image of an open house. Thus, in receiving the guest in the most distinguished part of the home and in having him meet only the members of the family dressed for the occasion, the guest in honored and the family status is reflected.

As contacts increase and a friendship develops, a guest comes to be accepted by the family and is received in the family room or what is commonly referred to in the Middle East as the sitting room. However, between the time a guest is received in the salon and the time he is accepted as "one of us," certain changes take place in the guest's relationship to the family. When the guest is allowed to meet the members of the opposite sex in the host's family, and how long the guest can stay on a visit depends on the values and lifestyle of the family. For example, it is not unusual in the Middle East for two men to have known each other for a number of years without either of them having met the female members of the other's family, even though they may know a lot about each other's life.

Until a guest is accepted and received informally in the family room his movement is usually restricted to the salon. Unlike the custom in the United States, for example, where a guest wanting to use the toilet just gets up and heads toward the bathroom perhaps mumbling an "excuse me" or perhaps not, in the Middle East, the guest asks for permission to go to the bathroom and for guidance to it. The request allows the host to go out first and check to make sure that the way to the bathroom is clear. That is, he makes sure that there are no family members that the host doesn't want to introduce to the guest, that those around are suitably dressed to meet the guest, and that the place is tidy and in agreement with the image that the host would like to create. Because of all these little inconveniences, it is not common for a salon—only guest to go to the bathroom in a host's house. The situation is of course different in the case of a guest who is invited to a meal.

From John C. Condon and Fathi S. Yousef Out of House and Home 1975

The Hispanic cultures of Spain and Latin American show the influence of Arab culture and their home designs are remarkably similar. Walls usually surround modern homes and more traditional homes include an internal patio that is often a garden with a central fountain. I have traveled to the Middle East and found it difficult as a stranger to move about. The city of Marrakech on the northern edge of the Sahara Desert is an old walled city but even in modern Cairo there are walled neighborhoods. When I wanted to go shopping in Marrakech I had to hire a young boy who led me through the blank walled streets that from time to time opened up into lively markets. I could never have found the markets on my own and once I found them, I could never have found my way back to the central square of the city. The streets seem to be designed to keep strangers out and to lead those who are familiar with the place deeper and deeper inside.

On our scale of low to high context, Arab culture is on the high context end. How people behave depends on the situation they are in. A woman behaves one way in public and in quite another way in the privacy of her home. Even the names people call one another depend on the social context. In the Middle East people generally live according to a widening circle of loyalties. The first loyalty is to the family, then to the clan, then to the ethnic group, and then to those who follow the same religion. Loyalty to the nation state is a new value and can be weak when some more basic group to which one owes loyalty is under attack. Who is an insider in one context may be an outsider in another context. As with Chinese there are many local dialects of the Arabic language, but the culture is unified by the use of a common written language. An Arabic speaker can recognize someone from his own region by the dialect he speaks and this makes them insiders to one another if they are away from home.

Exploring Ideas

1. Which of the basic cultural patterns described above comes closest to describing Chinese culture? Does Chinese culture have some characteristics of the grid, the radiating star and the inside/outside pattern?

2. Once you have identified a basic pattern, or perhaps arranged the patterns in their order of importance in Chinese culture, discuss how each pattern shows up in physical structures, in symbols such as the flag, in language, in social relationships and in other areas of Chinese life.

3. If you think about the inside/outside pattern in relation to Chinese life, you may observe that walls and gates as well as gate men are more common in China than elsewhere. People from other countries are commonly called foreigners (meaning not Chinese) rather than Germans, French, etc. The inside/outside pattern also operates within Chinese society as can be seen in the phenomenon of "localism" in business and social relationships. Also think about the uses of the Chinese words "wai" and "nei" as you discuss this basic pattern. In

what other areas of Chinese life can you see an insider/outsider pattern?

4. Physical structures and social patterns in China also have characteristics of the radiating star. We can see it in the flag and in the central role Beijing plays in national life. It can also be observed in ordinary behavior such as looking to the leader (local, national, work unit) for cues about how to behave. In a traditional family home the largest chair on the right in a reception room is reserved for the oldest male and the left one for the oldest female. Other relatives sit according to their age with the youngest members sitting farthest away from the oldest. In what other areas of Chinese life do you see a radiating star pattern?

5. Read and discuss the following case.

Case 9 Too Much Red Tape?

Too Much Red Tape?

Eric had recently located his first shop in China in Guangzhou. He was optimistic about the prospect of his business, which would be making "American" cookies. He had been successful with several stores in Hong Kong and felt that his operations would prosper in a Chinese market where economic reform was booming and where higher standards of living made it possible for people to buy his product.

He had heard much about the red tape involved in doing business in China but felt he could handle it. Indeed, he had relatively little difficulty in locating his first shop after several weeks of paperwork, and he was open for business sooner than he had thought possible. The local bureaucrats with whom he dealt had seemed favorably impressed when he had indicated his desire to use local workers and even train local

162

managers. His business was quite successful his first few months. People were eager to buy Eric's "unique" product.

A shop owned by local businessmen called "Tianbing Western Cookies" had recently opened providing service similar to Eric's cookie shop and hence, competition. It was time to expand the business. He felt there was enough demand to open another shop in the city and wanted to get a jump on his new competition.

In order to expand the business, Eric would need to apply for additional building permits and so forth. He also needed to arrange for additional suppliers of the various materials used to make his cookies. Eric found, however, that as he began applying for the necessary permits with the local government agencies he was met with responses such as "we've never encountered this request", or "this procedure requires additional information".

After several rounds of trying to understand the official rules, Eric became increasingly frustrated. After all he had been able to acquire the permits to open shop. Moreover, his attempts to secure additional supply channels were as yet unfruitful. It seemed that all suppliers were "already at full capacity", or "unsure of future resources". What really amazed Eric was that Tianbing Cookies was announcing the opening of several shops around town. Eric thought that was particularly odd considering that the owners of Tianbing Cookies had worked through the same government agencies.

Answer these questions:
1. How are the basic patterns of Eric's home culture influencing his behavior and his business strategy?
2. What basic patterns of Chinese culture are influencing the behavior of his competitors and the officials and suppliers he is dealing with?
3. What should Eric do to meet his business goals?

4. What business strategy is the Tianbing Cookie company using? What are the advantages and disadvantages of this strategy? If you had a business would you use this strategy? If not, what would you do to build your business?

Design and behavior

When the members of the House of Commons of the British Parliament were debating how to rebuild the parliament building that had been damaged by bombs during World War II, Winston Churchill argued that the building should be reconstructed exactly as it had been before the war. He said that changing the design of the building would result in a change in the way the government actually works. It was in this context that he made his famous statement, "We shape our buildings and they in turn shape us." He knew that culture is built into physical structures and that these structures do carry messages and influence how we behave.

While there are similarities between the American and British forms of government, there are also significant differences that can be seen in the physical design of the House of Commons as compared to the American House of Representatives. Both countries have two major political parties, but party loyalty is weak in the United States and strong in Britain. The British, who are generally known for being polite and reserved compared to their American cousins, have more heated debates in the Commons than is typical of the US Senate or House of Representatives.

The Commons is a relatively small room in which benches line each side in rows facing the benches on the opposite side of the room. Members of the Conservative Party sit on one side facing their opponents in the Labour party on the other side. Members do not have separate seats or desks but sit shoulder-to-shoulder with members of their own party. From their seats they look across the aisle where they can see the members of the opposition party on the other side of the small room. Senior party

164

members are in the front rows and more junior members are in the back, giving us the British political phrase "back bencher" to refer to a less important member. To vote members get up from their seats and walk out to give their vote to clerks who sit outside each of two doors. Members go through one door to vote no or through the other to vote yes. This system supports party solidarity, because to vote against the party, a member has to move his or her whole body away from party members in full view of everyone in the chamber.

In the US Congress each member has his or her own desk and the desks are arranged in a half circle facing a podium at the center. There is an aisle that separates the desks of members of the Democratic Party from the desks of members of the Republican Party, but each member speaks to the Speaker of the House who sits on the podium. Members are not sitting or speaking as part of a solid group shoulder-to-shoulder with one another and opposing another group, but as individuals. To vote a member merely answers a roll call by saying yes or no or records his or her votes by pushing an electronic button on the desk. As you might expect, members are less likely to vote along party lines than in the British system and party discipline is much weaker. Members are more likely to experience themselves as separate persons making individual choices rather than as representatives of their party.

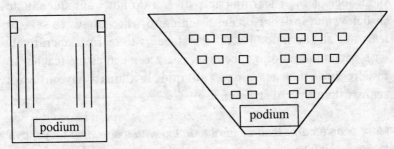

Figure 7 The British House of Commons and the US House of Representatives

165

From this example we see that design and the arrangement of furniture structures communication and influences behavior. We can say that cultural patterns are built into designs and buildings. These physical forms influence our perceptions of situations and play a role in molding our behavior by directing our attention and by positioning us in relation to other participants. Some designs, such as the French café table, draw people together and encourage conversation. Other designs, such as the row seating in train stations and airports, separate people and discourage interaction.

Chinese culture is built into the furniture

As an American teacher at a Chinese university I find the arrangement of classrooms a problem. Most of them have large raised podiums with students sitting in rows below and in front. This design reinforces the authority of the teacher and encourages a teacher-centered style of learning. I prefer classrooms with movable tables and chairs that would make it easier to arrange the students into work groups. I would like to move among the groups monitoring their work and offering advice as needed. As a teacher I prefer the role of facilitator, a person who defines tasks and goals and arranges activities to achieve them. I also see myself as a coach, resource person and motivator. I am not the main source of knowledge for the students but the leader of their learning activities. I do not want students to sit below and in front of me listening to what I have to say, at least not all the time. I want the students to learn cooperatively with each other and to depend on peers as much as the teacher as resources for their learning. To do this in China I have to work against the physical structures.

Most people carry their cultural learning with them when they move to a new situation

My preferences are not mine alone but come from my home

culture, which is also the source of the international business culture. The roles I prefer as a teacher may be similar to the roles expatriate managers from international corporations expect to play in relation to their local professional staff around the world. This is especially the case if the company has a policy of localizing management, that is, of turning over the management of the company's operation to the local people of the country where the facility is located. Students who learn in an exclusively teacher-centered style are also learning to listen to the boss at work and to wait for him or her to tell them what they should or should not do. A manager from a Western company is likely to see such behavior as too passive for someone who aspires to be a manager someday.

Some Chinese report a different experience working for foreign companies. Some find that the management of these companies is more authoritarian than they expected. In this case, it is likely that the foreign executives of the company expect a greater degree of obedience and conformity in their Chinese staff than is usual in a Chinese company. You may conclude that they misunderstand Chinese culture or that they expect Chinese subordinates to remain workers rather than managers for an indefinite period of time. In either case, it is important to be able to "read" the messages in the design of buildings and offices as well as in people's behavior. It is a matter of acquiring the culturally appropriate software for life in the global village.

| **Exploring Ideas** |

1. Look for cultural patterns in the physical structures that are part of your daily life. Think about how the design and arrangement of furniture influences and gently molds your behavior. Are the designs of buildings, homes, classrooms, restaurants, etc. changing? Does this encourage or reflect changes in social patterns? Share your ideas with your class-

167

mates.

2. Read and discuss the following case.

Case 10 How Do Students Learn?

How Do Students Learn?

Karen Randolph had been teaching high school English in the United States before she accepted a teaching job at a teacher's college in China. She found her new environment and her new teaching assignment exciting. Both her students and her colleagues seemed a bit shy of her, but Karen was sure that in time they would all come to be friends.

In the classroom, however, Karen was very frustrated. When she asked a question, the class was silent. Only if she called on a particular student would she get an answer, often a very good one. She could not understand why they wouldn't volunteer when they obviously knew the answers. They were very quiet when she was speaking in front of the class, and never asked questions, let alone interrupt with an opinion, but as soon as the class ended, they would cluster around her desk to ask their questions one-by-one. They would also offer their suggestions about the lesson at this time.

Karen often asked her students to work in small groups during class, especially when they were editing each other's writing. They were slow to move into groups and when they did, they often simply formed a group with the people sitting next to them. Finally she devised her own system of forming groups to get them to interact with students sitting in another section of the classroom.

Most frustrating of all, after she taught her class how to edit essays, she found that the students were likely to write vague and not very helpful remarks on their classmates' papers.

168

They would say nice things about the essays and correct small grammatical errors, but seemed unwilling to criticize them in a way that would help another student revise the essay. They usually accepted her criticism of their writing with good spirits and promises to improve. In fact they frequently asked for more correction of their English from her than she wanted to give. She felt that one hundred per cent grammatical correctness was not as important as learning how to correct what they had written on their own and with the help of others. After all, they would not always have a teacher to tell them what was good and not so good about their English writing.

1. Explain to Karen why students are behaving in the way she experiences as a problem.
2. What do you appreciate about the traditional Chinese way of learning and what do you appreciate about the way of learning some foreign teachers prefer?
3. What do foreign teachers do in class that make Chinese students uncomfortable?
4. What suggestions can you give to foreign teachers about how to teach Chinese students well?
5. What suggestions can you give Chinese teachers about how to teach their students well?

Chapter 10: Thinking Culturally

Language is a code that we use for communication. As we have seen, it is not the only communication code. Etiquette is also a code, a symbolic system of communication, as are painting and architecture. Like the other codes we have considered, language shapes our perceptions and influences our behavior. Among the behaviors it influences is our thinking.

In the last three chapters we have been looking outward to the sensations we take in with our eyes and ears and muscles and to the buildings people create. We quoted Winston Churchill, "We shape our buildings and they in turn shape us." It is the same with language. People create languages and then the languages they create shape the thinking of people who speak them.

Language, culture and thinking

We organize our experience by using language to describe it, and the categories built into our language, its structures, influence our perceptions. Various people have explained this idea about the relationship between language, culture and thinking at different times. Two American linguists who tried to describe the complexities of the relationship of language to culture were Edward Sapir and Benjamin Whorf. Here is one expression of the idea by Edward Sapir:

> No two languages are ever sufficiently similar to be considered as representing the same social reality. The worlds in which different societies live are distinct worlds, not merely the same world with different labels attached.

And one from Benjamin Whorf:

> We dissect nature along lines laid down by our native languages. The categories and types that we isolate from the

world of phenomena we do not find there because they stare every observer in the face; on the contrary, the world is presented in a kaleidoscopic flux of impressions which has to be organized by our minds—and this means largely by the linguistic systems in our minds.

In talking about the categories built into a language, the simplest place to begin is with the names things are given. Many linguists have studied the names of colors in various languages around the world because color is a universal phenomenon and we can describe it scientifically as well as culturally. This makes it easier to compare the way color is named in various languages. In the Navaho language, spoken by a group of Native Americans in the southwest of the United States, there are five basic color terms. One is roughly equivalent to the English white, two correspond to English black, one is similar to English red and one can be translated into English as green or blue. Of course, English speakers can distinguish between the two categories of black used in Navaho, but they do not ordinarily do so. Navaho speakers can tell the difference between green and blue but they usually do not feel the need to do so. What the difference in categories means is that speakers of each language ordinarily analyze color in different ways. They organize their experience into different categories. Usually when we translate from one language to another we do not pay attention to this.

People everywhere name colors but they use different color categories

To test this idea yourself, try to define the English color red by comparing it to the Chinese color *hong*. You can do this by pointing to the clothing or bags of students in your class that could possibly be called red or *hong*. If possible compare your color names with the names given to the same color by a native English speaker. When I have done this with my students, we have found that *hong* describes a wider range of the color spectrum than the English term red does. Some colors that native Chinese speakers usually name *hong* might be called orange, pink, or purple in English. In this case the two languages have roughly the same category but the phenomena that are included in the category are not exactly the same. We rarely consider this when translating from one language to another.

This is a rather simple example, but the same principle applies to other features of specific languages, such as ways of handling time, relationships among people, the actors in any action, and ways of counting and what can be counted. For instance, English has only one counting system. Things and humans are counted using the same words, but in Japanese, there is one set of counting words for things and another for people. In Hopi, another Native American language, people do not count time in the same way that they count things. In English it is possible to say five men and five days. In Hopi people do not count things that cannot be directly observed. They would say five men but not five days. Instead they refer to time as duration. To correctly translate a Hopi statement, we would have to say, "he stayed until the sixth day," rather than "he stayed for five days," but even then, it is still not certain that English speakers really understand how a Hopi speaker experiences time.

Japanese has an elaborate vocabulary for describing shapes and space, so we should not be surprised that Japanese speakers are more sensitive to differences in shape and to characteristics of space than English speakers are. In the Japanese art of flowering arranging each flower is displayed in a clearly defined space and the shape of the flower, stem and vase are highlighted. In Western flower arranging flowers tend to be grouped together according to color. The shapes of individual flowers and stems are lost in the shape of the bouquet.

172

In Chinese there are more words for describing relationships than in English

The Chinese language has many precise terms for describing family and other relationships. Chinese speakers distinguish between relatives on the mother's side of the family from those on the father's side of the family and use different terms to refer to relatives on each side of the family. Chinese speakers use specific terms to address their family members and each name contains the meaning of the precise relationship between the speaker and the person being addressed. Certainly English speakers can distinguish between maternal aunts and uncles and paternal aunts and uncles, but they do not ordinarily do so, and they certainly do not refer to them or address them by different names that include the meaning of that precise relationship. If the situation requires a distinction, then English speakers will find a way to do it. They will say "my maternal grandmother" or "a cousin on my father's side of the family". English speakers find ways to describe relationships that have no precise categories in English, but in learning their language, they learn that these distinctions are not usually necessary.

What are you paying attention to?

These examples show some ways in which the language we speak directs our attention to certain aspects of our environment and encourages us to ignore or pay less attention to other aspects. As a speaker and learner of a second language, there is another issue of attention you should be aware of. In your desire to increase your proficiency in your second language, you probably pay much attention to language when you read or hear English spoken. For you listening to a native speaker, watching an English movie, or reading an English article may be primarily an instance of English. In speech you notice the accents of the speakers, the speed at which they speak, and whether or not you understand the idioms. In reading you may pay attention to words you do not understand. You might try to find useful words and expressions you can add to your vocabulary. Because you are paying attention at that level, you may pay less attention to the content of the message, to the meaning. Native speakers and very proficient English speakers are not focusing on the language. They take the language for granted and use English for communication and self-expression. They are not as interested in English as a language as you are. They are more interested in what they can do with English, whether that is making a new friend, getting or giving information or expressing an idea. To increase your English proficiency you need to put the language in the background and pay attention to meanings.

Exploring Ideas

1. Try the experiment you did with the English term *red* and the Chinese term *hong* with other categories such as family or friend, man and boy and girl and woman. You may find that speakers of Chinese and English include different people in these categories. For instance, Chinese speakers usually refer to male and female university students as boys and girls, while English speakers are more likely to refer to males and females of roughly the same social position as men and women. The categories of boy/man and girl/woman exist in both languages but the boundaries of the categories are not the same. Can you define the boundaries of the categories for each language?

2. From your study of English you have discovered lots of ways in which English is different from Chinese. Make a list of language differences that may indicate differences in how speakers of the two languages organize their experience. For instances, differences in the tenses of verbs may mean that speakers of the two languages organize time in different ways.

174

3. As a second language learner, do you find it difficult to shift your attention from the English language to the meanings carried by the language? What can you do to solve this problem?

What do you really mean?

In an early chapter we said that culture is a system of meaning. We use language to convey many of our cultural meanings. One difficulty in communicating meanings from one language to another is the differences in the ways different languages organize the experience of their native speakers. Another problem is the specific content of categories in one language compared to another. In fact these are relatively small problems compared to the difficulty in translating the meaning of concepts from one language to another. We should not assume that concepts have the same meanings to speakers of different languages. I have learned that when native Chinese speakers use the word god in English that they are thinking of something quite different from what I mean when I use the word god. The concept of god is quite different in Western culture from what it is in Asian culture.

Let's start with a more common concept, family, to see how concepts differ. Every language and culture has the concept of family. There is a great deal of common meaning from one language to another in the concept of family. It usually includes components such as father, mother, brother, sister, son, daughter, etc. In some languages the concept may include ancestors, distant relatives and anticipated births, while in other languages the category is not so broad. When a person speaks or writes the word family, all or some of these meanings come to mind. We could say that the person has an image of family in his or her mind. Even though the word used to describe that image may be a widely accepted translation, the exact mental image will not be the same for the speakers of different languages.

American speakers might have an image of mother as the driving force of the family, while a Korean might have an image of father as the leader of the family. In many Asian languages the image is likely to be of specific persons and relationships, while speakers of some Western languages like English are more likely to think of psychological qualities like love and togetherness. It may be that for speakers of English the concept of family is more abstract, while for speakers of Asian languages it is more concrete.

Even though many concepts are universal , the precise meaning varies by culture

In languages spoken in societies with a Confucian tradition, the concept of family includes the meaning filial duty, the duty children owe to their parents. This concept is meaningless to most English speakers. An English phrase, filial duty or filial piety, has been invented to convey the meaning in English, but this does not solve the problem. For American English speakers particularly, the word duty has a negative meaning. For them performing a duty usually means doing some unpleasant task they do not want to do for someone else. A duty is an obligation and obligations are burdens. I once thanked a young Chinese woman for her thoughtfulness in responding to a need I had. She replied, "It is my duty." At that time I thought she was telling me that she was required to do what she had done and did not do it willingly or joyfully. I would have been more satisfied with "You're welcome." or "My pleasure." Now I can accept "It is my duty." as an appropriate response to my thanks, but I suggest that "I was happy to do it." or "My pleasure." express your meaning more accurately for a native English speaker. If you use the word duty the English speaker is likely to think that what you did was distasteful to you.

I am constantly discovering more concepts that have different meanings in my home culture from their meaning in China.

176

For instance, it was not long ago that I discovered that sometimes in China the concept musician includes the meaning beggar. On one occasion when I was a guest at a wedding in the countryside, a troupe of musicians came to the house and offered to entertain the wedding guests. I was disappointed when the host quickly asked them to leave. I am used to having music at a wedding; it makes the occasion more festive. Later I learned that street musicians are considered beggars in China. In European and American cities they are often seen as serious musicians looking for an audience, a chance to be heard, so that they might get a better job playing music. In some Western cities musicians audition for licenses to perform in the subways and streets, so that the public gets good quality street music. People give them money in appreciation for their performance and not out of pity.

To understand my earlier statement that the concept of god is different in China than it is in areas where Islam, Christianity and Judaism have influenced people's thinking, consider the following chart.

One God			Many gods
All powerful	< West	East >	Limited power
One truth			Many truths

When some Chinese speakers use the word god the image in their minds is likely to include concepts like those on the right of the chart. English speakers are more likely to be thinking in terms of concepts like those on the left. This is an oversimplification and is only meant to caution you that concepts differ from culture to culture and from language to language.

Realizing that concepts differ across languages and cultures may be discouraging for a second language learner. It need not be. As long as we do not make the mistake of taking concepts for granted, we can find out what people mean when they use a

177

particular word.

There are many ways for you to find out more about the meanings of concepts in different cultures. Try some of these:

1. In class take a concept related to your present life such as student, university, research, roommate, friend, holiday, etc. For each concept make a list of images or related ideas that you associate with that concept. Discuss the lists everyone makes to create one list that ranks the components of the concept in the order members of your class think is most important. Then ask a native English speaker what he or she thinks of when using that word. Share your list with the native speaker so you can find out from each other in what ways your concepts are similar and different. This is a more interesting way to approach a native English speaker than saying that you want to practice your English.

2. In a group of people from more than one culture, ask everyone to make a list of the components of a concept. Also ask them to rank each component in terms of its emotional intensity. Give a rating of 10 for a strong feeling and a rating of 1 for a weak feeling. In a work group you can try concepts such as manager, team, competition, cooperation, etc. After everyone has done this individually, have a discussion in which you share your lists with one another.

3. In small groups draw pictures of a concept you are studying. What does a family look like? What does a team look like? Each group can then explain their drawing to the whole class as a way of discovering the important meanings of a concept. If possible, ask people from another culture to make their own drawings. Show your drawings to each other as a way of discovering common and dissimilar meanings in the concept.

4. From the international news we all know that governments

and groups sometimes have disagreements about human rights and intellectual property rights. What does the word rights mean in Chinese? Make a list of the images that come to mind and other terms you associate with rights. What do you think it means in English? Try making a list of images and associations from the point of view of an English speaker. If possible consult a native speaker to discuss the meaning of the concept in English. After doing your research discuss how the differences in the concept of rights is influencing international discussions in this area.

5. Read and discuss the following case.

Case 11 When Is the Film Festival?

When Is the Film Festival?

Zha Xin spent an enjoyable year as a visiting professor at Bradley College in the northeast of the US. He taught Chinese language and culture, which he found a pleasant change from teaching English at his home university in China. His English department had a faculty exchange program with Bradley, so he was able to renew relationships with Bradley professors he first met when they were teaching English at his university. Also, he got to know Frances Howard, a media specialist in Bradley's Communication Department. Zha Xin encouraged Frances to apply to be Bradley's next visiting professor at his university, because he thought her film classes would be as popular with Chinese students as they were with American students. Frances enjoyed getting to know Zha Xin and through him got excited about spending a year teaching in China. With Zha Xin's guidance, she chose a collection of films on videotape and he arranged for her to teach the video classes offered by the department to improve students' English listening comprehension.

Frances found that her students liked movies and had seen many recent American films. At first the students objected when Frances stopped the video machine to make comments about theme or filmmaking techniques, but gradually they began to appreciate her commentary and became more analytical about their film viewing. Sometimes the students said they could not understand all the dialogue, but when she reassured them that they could get a lot of the meaning from the visual images, they relaxed and were able to make intelligent observations about the films.

After several months, Zha Xin asked Frances if she would be his partner for the department's comprehensive activities project. He explained that every spring the English department arranges special student activities to help students to develop their abilities more fully than was possible in regular classes. Frances thought this was a terrific idea and suggested that the students put on a film festival. Zha Xin liked the sound of it. Frances proposed several themes for the festival and Zha Xin said he thought all her ideas were good. He only asked her to select films with female roles as a majority of students were girls and they wanted to dub the films. Frances was glad to get this advice. She had been a theatre major as an undergraduate student and knew how frustrating it was when the best parts went to the boys. Zha Xin would handle the dubbing part of the project, as Frances did not speak Chinese.

Frances selected five films on the theme Good Girls and Bad Girls including two classic westerns "Stagecoach" and "High Noon". She thought the films, recognized classics of Western film art, and the theme would appeal to the whole university community and would give everyone a chance to explore ideas about women's social roles that were especially relevant for young people living in a rapidly modernizing society. She prepared her introductions to the theme and films and showed the films to the student project group. She became confused when students kept asking her questions about the dialogue in various scenes and were unresponsive to her questions about the women characters in general. She noticed that the students talked among themselves about the schedule for using the special dubbing equipment in the audio-visual lab. They did prepare posters for each film but were vague when she asked them about the program and schedule for the film festival.

Finally she talked to Zha Xin about how the students were responding to the project.

"They really like the film festival," he said. "You should not worry about it."

"But they only talk about dubbing," Frances replied. "When are we going to have the film festival?"

"They will present their dubbing at a department meeting next Tuesday," Zha Xin explained.

"But I thought our project was a film festival for the whole campus," said Frances.

"This is a project of our department, Frances. The students show their translation skill by dubbing scenes in Chinese. The teachers then judge which group did the best dubbing. We really like your film festival."

Frances was disappointed and her feelings were hurt. She felt Zha Xin just wanted her collection of films and was politely ignoring everything she said that did not fit his plans. She felt used and thought that Zha Xin had betrayed their friendship by concealing his true purpose.

Answer these questions:

1. What is Zha Xin's concept of a film festival? How is it different from Frances' concept?
2. What is the meaning of films for Zha Xin and what is the meaning for Frances?
3. What are the grid culture versus inside/outside culture issues

in the case?

4. What is Zha Xin paying attention to in the films as compared to what Frances is paying attention to?

5. How can these two colleagues overcome their misunderstanding?

Who are you?

One concept that is so close to us that we rarely pay any attention to is the concept of self. As we have said, the fish notices everything but the water it swims in. It is so taken for granted that it is not thought worth noticing, much less talking about. We are rarely aware that the self is something constructed by our culture, much as buildings are constructed.

One way to explore the concept of self in various cultures is to look at how people are named. We all know that Chinese naming puts the family name in the first position followed by the personal name while English speakers reverse the order. In English speaking countries it is common for women to take their husband's family name when they marry, but they seldom change their personal names. Americans are quicker to suggest that new acquaintances and business associates address them by their personal names than would be the case for people in practically any other culture. Chinese speakers often refer to people by kinship terms – aunt, grandmother, etc. – even when the people addressed in this way are not family members. Chinese speakers also use titles more frequently than English speakers do.

An explanation of names in Bali

The American anthropologist Clifford Geertz doing research on naming on the Indonesian island of Bali found that Balinese babies are given birth order names in cycles of four. The first born child of a couple is given a name that means firstborn. A fifth child is given the same name. If a child is stillborn or the mother has a miscarriage, that unfortunate birth keeps its

182

birth order position and the next child gets the next number. We can see from this that personal names really carry little or no information even about a person's actual birth order. The oldest child could be "number two" if the mother had an earlier pregnancy and the youngest could be "number one" if the mother had four previous pregnancies. Also, everyone has one of only four personal names.

In Bali when people change roles in life, they also change names. An adult might have a name that means "mother of X" or "grandfather of Z". From this and from observing that the Balinese put drama and performance at the center of their social life, Geertz concluded that the Balinese concept of self was entirely different from the concept of self in the West. He says the Balinese experience themselves as performers in a great drama. It is not the person as an individual that counts, but the grand recurring spectacle in which each person plays a part. What is important is the stage on which people perform and the parts they play at different times in life. The individual will die but the play will go on. Geertz notes that people try to stylize all aspects of expression, behaviors, emotions and language. They try to make their behavior fit their part in the play, the great human drama that continues generation after generation. In that context it is not surprising that the Balinese name the roles people play rather than the people who play them.

The significance of personal names in American culture

Because you are not familiar with the details of Western practices in giving people names, you might assume that English personal names are an expression of Western individualism. This is not necessarily the case. In most American subcultures, there is a limited supply of personal names and you may meet several people with the same personal name. Often American parents give a baby a particular personal name because they think it sounds right with the family name. Other considerations are the associations with the name, the nicknames the name suggests, and the possibility of the child being teased by childhood friends because of the name. If a name sounds old-fashioned it may be rejected for that reason. If a name has a positive association because it is the name of a popular figure, it may be chosen. Possibly many girl babies born in the last year have been named Diana or Diane because of the association with Princess Diana. People rarely change their personal names, but they do change the nicknames based on their personal names. Katherine may want to be called Kate, Kathy, Katie, Kath, or Katherine at different times in her life. From this we can see that personal names are used to project a personal image to the society. People do attach a lot of importance to their personal names, in part because they consider the name an important message about who they are.

Exploring Ideas

1. Make a list of the characteristics of Chinese naming behavior and a list of the characteristics of naming in various Western societies. Compare the two lists and from the differences make some guesses about differences in the concept of self in the two cultures.

2. Use the form below or write the phrase "I am..." on a piece of paper. Quickly finish the sentence in various ways. Do not spend much time on each sentence. Simply write whatever comes into your mind. Continue until you have 20 "I am" sentences.

Who am I?
1. I am
2. I am
3. I am
4. I am
5. I am
6. I am
7. I am
8. I am
9. I am
10. I am
11. I am
12. I am
13. I am
14. I am
15. I am
16. I am
17. I am
18. I am
19. I am
20. I am

After you have finished writing, put your sentences into categories.

1. Physical characteristics (tall, short, dark-haired, etc.)
2. National or ethnic identity (Chinese, American, etc.)
3. Regional subculture (hometown, province, northerner, speaker of dialect, etc.)
4. Gender (girl, boy, man, woman)
5. Social status (student, department, university, occupation, top student, monitor, etc.)
6. Character (hard working, kind, sympathetic, lazy, good friend, etc.)
7. Age or generation (young, old)
8. Family relationships (son, daughter, older sister, etc.)
9. Activities (music lover, sports fan, basketball player, etc.)
10. Identity (your name, "I am who I am," etc.)

Count your responses in each category. Which categories did you use first? Which ones did you use later? If you have a sentence such as "I am a boy from Guangzhou," count it as two categories: gender (boy) and regional subculture (Guangzhou).

Ask everyone in the class to report what category they used for the first sentence, second sentence, etc. If your first sentence is "I am my parents' daughter," that is category 8, family relationships. Make a list of the categories that were used most frequently by the students in the class.

Put the categories in order from the most important to the least important. For instance, you may find that ethnic identity, family relationships, social status and character were the most frequently used categories. Be sure to give greater weight to the categories at the top of each list as these are the categories that came into each person's mind first. When I did this with my class, I found that gender was a category for girls but not for boys, so pay attention to such differences within your class.

When you have finished collecting and analyzing the results from your class, discuss what is most central to your sense of who you are. You might call it "The Chinese Concept of Self."

Another way to do this activity is to compare your responses to those of another group of people who come from a different culture. If possible ask another group, perhaps a group of foreign students on your campus, to do the same activity. After each group does its own analysis, the two groups can get together to discuss similarities and differences in the concept of self.

Chapter 11: Comparing Cultural Values

The objective of our work in this chapter is to increase your awareness of the basic values of your own and other cultures. To do this we will use a scheme developed by the American anthropologist, Florence Kluckhohn. She identified five orientations, five categories of beliefs and behaviors that are universal. This means that all cultures have to work out solutions to these issues. Every human group needs to adapt to the natural world and every human group has to order relationships among members of the group. Each culture has done this and continues to do it in its own way, but we can identify some similar values in the practices of various cultures. These are the three basic values that appear on Kluckhohn's chart for each orientation. Theoretically we can analyze a culture and figure out which of the three values it most often uses to resolve the issues for each of the orientations. Once this is done, it becomes possible to compare the basic values of the various cultures of the world.

The ways in which basic values are expressed in behavior are very complex. We cannot necessarily predict how someone will behave in a specific situation just because we know the basic values of that person's home culture. One reason for this is that values differ somewhat according to age, gender, social position, occupation and region. Another reason is that people combine and establish priorities among conflicting values in order to solve real problems. Also, each culture has developed as the result of influences from a number of different philosophies and religions, so each society has inherited different, sometimes conflicting values. We usually do not recognize these contradictions when making decisions about how to behave. We usually just follow our common sense, which means we do what we take for granted is the right or reasonable thing to do. Basic values are often part of the cultural iceberg that lies hidden from our view.

Orientation	Basic values		
Human Nature	Basically Evil	Mixture of Good and Evil	Basically Good
Relationship to Nature	Nature controls Humans	Harmony with Nature	Humans control Nature
Sense of Time	Past	Present	Future
Activity	Being—who you are	Growing—becoming	Doing—what you are doing
Social Relationships	Hierarchy	Group	Individual

Figure 8 Categories for comparing values across cultures

People usually state their values more concretely than the chart shows. In fact, we offer the chart so you can see the basic values that are the source of the more specific values you use to guide your decisions. The more specific values are expressed as social attitudes, the principles we hear when people give us advice and the principles we rely on when we give advice to others. These attitudes rather than the basic values are what we hear in proverbs, slogans, wise sayings and advice from parents, teachers and friends.

	Social attitudes as expressions of basic values		
Human Nature	**Basically Evil**	**Mixture of Good and Evil**	**Basically Good**
	Expect to find evil and fight against it	Separate good from evil	Protect people's virtue
	Punish bad behavior	Identify strengths and weaknesses	Reward good behavior
	Save people from their evil nature	Reward the good in people and punish the bad	Find the most virtuous people
Relationship to Nature	**Nature over humans**	**Harmony with Nature**	**Humans over Nature**
	Accept your fate	Live according to the rhythms of nature	Make life comfortable and convenient
	Life is outside the individual's control	Everything has its own character	Problems can be solved once we know the facts
	Be humble	Be balanced	Be objective

188

Sense of Time	Past	Present	Future
	Tradition is the best teacher	Pay attention to what is going on here and now	Control the future by planning for it
	What happened in the past is important today	Everything will happen in its time	What is past is past and not important
	The old are wise	Events occur in cycles	The young know what is happening
	Break with the past to change society	Look for causes in the present situation	Study history to shape the future
Activity	**Being**	**Growing**	**Doing**
	Protect your dignity and the dignity of others	Develop your potential as a whole person	Achieve specific goals
	Fulfill your role	Follow values and lifestyles appropriate to your stage in life	Develop procedures and measure results
	Show the world who you are	People change and won't be the same tomorrow as they are today	Show the world what you can do
	Pay attention to people	Pay attention to possibilities	Pay attention to actions
Social Relationships	**Hierarchy**	**Group**	**Individual**
	Obey authority; know your place	Respond to what others think and feel	Express your own feelings and ideas
	Treat others according to their position	Depend on others and let them depend on you; be loyal	Be as independent and self-reliant as possible.
	Look to leading figures to know what to think and do	Look to others in your group to know what to think and do	Make your own decisions and choices

Figure 9 Social attitudes as expressions of basic values

Even at the level of social attitudes, we may not be fully aware of what values we are acting on. For instance, everyone living in a cold climate wants to stay warm in winter, but people in different cultures will go about this in different ways depend-

189

ing on their basic values. Americans use central heating built into their homes, offices and factories. Japanese, with the same level of technology and standard of living, are more likely to use space heaters and wear warmer clothing. Americans will not explain their choice in terms of humans being the masters of nature, but they may say they value material comfort. Japanese may say they do not like central heating because then they have to keep the house closed all day; they want to be closer to nature in their daily lives than Americans do. Their basic value is harmony with nature.

Before I lived in China, I did not realize how strong a value material comfort is for Americans. When my family got together recently at my brother's desert home, everyone suffered from the heat. They all stayed in air-conditioned cars and buildings as much as possible. I also thought it was hot, but from living in China, I knew that if I changed my behavior I would be comfortable, stay out of the sun, wear a hat and cool clothing, drink lots of water, don't do too much physical exercise, enjoy the cooler evening hours, etc. In short, adjust to conditions. My relatives were so accustomed to the material comforts of the American lifestyle that they looked for a comfortable environment rather than adjusting to the environment they were in.

Florence Kluckhohn's original idea was to compare the basic values of various cultures. Often it is only by looking at our own values in contrast with other values that we really understand them. While we do this, we need to recognize the limitations of this approach.

1. Not everyone in a culture has the same basic values. Keep the various layers of cultures in mind when using this chart. Expect to find differences within cultures as well as across cultures.
2. Cultures change over time. Values and beliefs also change as societies respond to changing conditions. People know what is going on elsewhere and import technologies and ideas from

190

other cultures. People frequently reinterpret traditional values to meet new needs and solve new problems.

3. The concept of basic values is itself a generalization. People combine and give different importance to various values as they create institutions and social practices. As a result of historical circumstances each culture has an inheritance of values, combinations of values and ways of acting on values that is quite unique.

With these cautions in mind, consider another chart. This one shows the generalizations people most frequently make about the differences between basic Chinese values and basic Western values. It expresses broad generalizations. Almost anyone can give examples of behaviors and social attitudes that show that sometimes Chinese are more individualistic than Americans and more intent on dominating nature than many Westerners. For that reason, we will discuss the values in detail to see how they work in practice.

Orientation	Chinese values	Western values
Human Nature	Basically Good	Mixture of Good and Evil
Relationship to Nature	Harmony with Nature	Humans control Nature
Sense of Time	Past orientation	Future orientation
Activity	Being—who you are	Doing—what you are doing
Social Relationships	Hierarchy	Individual

Figure 10   Comparison of Chinese values and Western values

Human nature

The traditional Western belief about human nature is that humans are basically evil. We see this in the Bible story of Adam and Eve. God throws them out of the Garden of Eden because they ate the fruit from the Tree of Knowledge. From that time on, according to Christian teaching, all humans have been born with original sin. That means they do evil as part of their nature and can only be saved from evil by God. As a result of the rise of humanism in the West, this basic belief has changed to one of

191

seeing humans as a mixture of good and evil. The original belief continues to flourish alongside the more modern belief. For instance, Westerners who are called fundamentalist Christians, those who follow the Bible as a guide to daily life, still believe that humans are basically evil and must be saved, that is, must accept God to become good. The traditional view has also been incorporated into Western institutions in various ways. The distrust of human nature can be seen in American political institutions with their checks and balances. The legislative branch of government and media journalists should keep an eye on the president, state governors and other government officials to make sure they do not do anything evil. If some wrongdoing is discovered, the person should be punished, usually by being removed from office.

The traditional Western view of human nature shows up in modern theories that seem to have nothing to do with religious beliefs. The psychological theories of Sigmund Freud include the idea that infants are controlled by primitive desires (evil) and learn to control them (become good) as the personality develops. This contrasts sharply with the Chinese view that children are pure and good and learn to do bad things as a result of contact with bad influences in the society. Typically Westerners stress the ability of people to change for the better. Now, however, they are more likely to think that education and other good influences, rather than God, will save them.

To Westerners good and bad exist side by side but should be separated. The good should be encouraged and the bad eliminated to the extent possible. The categories of good and bad appear everywhere. Students and employees have strengths (good) and weaknesses (bad). Policies have costs (bad) and benefits (good). Individuals and organizations should act to increase the good (build strengths, increase benefits) and reduce the bad (overcome weaknesses, reduce costs). In this way, human nature can be improved, even perfected in time. In the Western

192

moral universe it is necessary to confess the bad you do. You should admit to your mistakes and shortcomings. This is the first step in becoming good. Even a US president can be forgiven for his mistakes, if he publicly admits his wrongdoing and promises not to do it again.

Advice from an American teacher in China

I think it is important for anyone coming to China to watch, listen, and learn with an open mind. There is no right or wrong culture, no sides to pick, as there is no utopia on earth. There is good and bad in every society because they are all made up of good and bad people. I just try to remember that along with the freedoms I hold dear comes the freedom for people to make bad choices as well as good; comes the freedom for evil as well as good.

In China, as in other Asian societies that have accepted the teachings of Confucius, people are believed to be basically good. As we said, children are believed to be pure and innocent but may become corrupt as they grow older and have more contact with society. The direction of moral change is more likely to be from good to bad, rather than from bad to good as it is in the West. Because of this danger, it is the responsibility of those in authority, such as parents, teachers and political leaders, to protect the morality of those under their care and to be models of virtue themselves. I find that when my students write about their mothers, fathers, grandfathers, teachers and honored historical figures, they tend to idealize them. They invariably possess all virtues and have no defects. Now I understand that my students are presenting these people as models of virtue, which is how they have been taught to see them. In the West even the noblest figures usually have flaws. The story of President Nixon's fall from power conforms to the Western expectation that great men can be ruined by something bad within their character. This is a typical theme of Western tragedy.

In Confucian cultures people are encouraged to be good by the people around them and are likely to feel ashamed if they fail to live up to others' expectations that they be virtuous. If China has what some experts call a **shame culture**, then the West is dominated by **guilt cultures**. In guilt cultures the person is expected to know the difference between right and wrong and to feel guilty if he or she does or even thinks something wrong, whether or not anyone knows about it. In shame cultures, the good is an ideal everyone hopes to realize but may not be possible to achieve in every situation. What is important is that you meet your obligation to be a model of virtue for a particular group of people to whom you have such a responsibility.

Chinese people share with Westerners a belief that education should be a good moral influence on people. In fact Chinese expect schools and universities to be places of virtue. My students often regret leaving the relatively pure world of the university for the less pure world of business. Westerners do not expect particular institutions to be more virtuous than other institutions. They think it is as possible to be a virtuous businessman as it is to be a virtuous college professor. Good and bad are found everywhere, within each person, and therefore within

194

each organization.

Exploring Ideas

This discussion of human nature has been very general. I should tell you that what I have said is most characteristic of countries in the West where the Protestant form of Christianity has been most influential. This includes the countries of northern Europe and North America. Beliefs and social attitudes about human nature are somewhat different in the Roman Catholic countries of the Mediterranean region.

Look at the levels of culture within the larger Chinese national culture to identify differences in basic values depending upon

- Regional and/or ethnic and/or religious and/or linguistic differences;
- Gender differences;
- Generation differences that separate grandparents from parents from children;
- Social class differences associated with educational opportunities and with a person's occupation or profession.

Answer the following questions:

1. Are different virtues expected of different kinds of people? Are women expected to be more virtuous than men are? Are women expected to have different virtues than men are expected to have? Are educated people more virtuous than uneducated people are?
2. When you compare your values to those of your parents or grandparents do you see evidence that Chinese values are changing?
3. Do people from various regions have the reputation of having certain virtues that people in other regions are less likely to possess? What are the virtues you associate with specific re-

195

gional or ethnic subcultures?

4. Do you expect to increase in goodness as you go through life or do you expect to become less virtuous? What are the moral dangers you face? How will you overcome them?

Relationship of humans to nature

In our previous discussion of Chinese gardens we saw that the designs reflect Chinese cultural ways of using the senses. Taking another look we see that the gardens also reveal Chinese social attitudes about the relationship between humans and nature. Pavilions, paved pathways, and other structures are integrated with the natural features of water, trees and rocks. There is no sharp distinction between being inside a building and being outside in nature. In the West buildings tend to dominate their surroundings and interiors and exteriors are distinct spaces. In the history of the West, nature was usually seen as either a wilderness or a paradise. The wilderness should be tamed and the paradise should be kept pure. In both cases, nature is outside of human society.

The Western experience of human life being separate from nature can be found in the Bible story of creation. When God creates Adam, he is given dominance over all of God's creation. Adam and his human descendents stand apart from and above nature and are told to use the natural world to meet human needs. As masters of nature, humans are encouraged to control it and exploit it in any way they choose. To master the natural world, people need to study and explore it to figure out how it works, much as you might figure out how a machine works before you use it. This attitude of looking at the natural world as an object contributed to the development of Western science.

Chinese traditional medicine shows the cultural value of harmony with nature

Like many foreigners, I caught a cold soon after I first

came to China. I did what Westerners usually do when they have a minor illness. I taught my classes as usual. If I were Chinese I would probably have stayed home to give my body a chance to recover. It just happened that an auditor in my class was a pharmacist and he asked if he could visit me to bring me some medicine. That evening he introduced me to Chinese medicine and told me that it would take longer to work than Western medicine, but that it would be gentler on my body. In Western medicine the human body is an object that can be studied and then controlled. This has led to the invention of powerful medicines, but the medicines may have unpleasant or even dangerous side effects. In Chinese medicine the human body is part of nature and needs to be brought back into balance. Medicine should work with the body's own resources. It should be integrated with the body.

Western values are changing because people now realize that the Western mastery over nature philosophy causes problems as well as providing benefits. In the last twenty years scientists have identified an astounding number of problems caused by Western technology and thinking, everything from over-fishing the oceans to global climate change to air and water pollution. At first technical experts tried to solve these problems by using more technology to clean up the pollution technology had created. Now more people are saying it is not enough to develop technologies for recycling trash or cleaning dirty water. What we need are alternatives to the polluting technologies.

In an effort to find a way out of this dilemma, some people in the West are looking to other cultures to find alternatives. Americans, for instance, have a growing appreciation for Native American beliefs about the sacredness of nature. In this view, the first one on Kluckhohn's chart, nature is powerful and humans are weak. Nature is alive in the sense that plants, animals, the wind and the ground itself have spirits. A Native American might say, "The earth is our mother." Native Ameri-

197

cans traditionally offered prayers of thanks to animal spirits that gave their lives so that people could eat. They believed that nature would treat them well if they treated nature well, so the relationship was one of love, respect, wonder and fear. In an age of environmental crisis, we need those feelings as we work out a new relationship with nature.

The Western value of mastery over nature extends to human engineering

The values that people hold toward nature usually extend to other areas of life. If your culture teaches integration with nature, harmony and balance, you are likely to seek harmony and balance in social relationships as well. If you are in awe of nature and feel helpless in face of its power, then you might also feel powerless in other areas of your life. If you think you are separate from nature and can control it, then you probably think you are separate from others and can use scientific methods to control people and events. This is true in the West where technology extends to the human world in the form of human engineering. The scientific study of human motivation and the invention of technologies to control it are the basis of professional practice in fields such as advertising, psychology, education, sociology, public relations and management.

Exploring Ideas

1. As China modernizes there is an emphasis on using Western technology to achieve national goals. Do you think China must adopt the Western attitude toward the natural world to achieve its goals? What examples can you give to show that China is keeping its values concerning the integration of humans with nature as it modernizes?

2. How can the Chinese value of integration with nature contribute to the global culture? For instance, what does Chinese medicine have to contribute to Western medicine?

198

Sense of time

Florence Kluckhohn and her assoatciates developed their chart for comparing basic cultural values before Asian countries entered a period of rapid economic growth. At that time Asian societies, including China, appeared to many Westerners to be firmly traditional, even though China had already undergone a revolution which proved that Asian societies could change quickly. Does this mean that rapidly developing Asian societies have become future oriented rather than past oriented? Not exactly. Past-oriented societies are those in which tradition is very important. People usually know their history and may talk about an event of a hundred or a thousand years ago as if it happened yesterday. They can do this because the past is kept alive in history, storytelling, language, music and dance, religious practices and customs. In past-oriented societies, the cultural memory is rich and deep. People in these cultures often look back to a period when their culture was at the height of its power and glory and may quote respected philosophers and leaders from the past as a guide for action in the present.

Present-oriented cultures find it easier to combine tradition and modern ideas

The past may have such a hold on people that extraordinary means must be used to create change. Leaders advocating something new may feel it is necessary to erase parts of the cultural memory in order to create change. In future-oriented societies leaders feel less need to rewrite or reinterpret history because people do not know their history in much detail or do not see it as a barrier to change. In those societies overcoming the limitations of the past or surpassing the accomplishments of the past are good reasons for doing something new. In present-oriented societies the past and present often exist side by side and people do not see any contradiction in that fact. Traveling in Thailand and Indonesia I saw modern office buildings and department

199

stores full of the latest technology with shrines to nature gods in front. After work in modern offices, people put on traditional clothing and participate in activities similar to those of their ancestors.

Whatever their attitude about the past, people from past-oriented cultures may feel more secure when something new is defined as similar to something that occurred in the past. For instance, if a new policy is introduced, it may be given the authority of the past by comparing it to a historical event or by supporting it with a quotation from a respected leader of the past.

Future-oriented societies often have a strong belief in progress but this is not necessarily so. People may have negative expectations for the future and their efforts may be directed at preparing for or preventing bad times ahead. We can see this in predictions about future consequences if environmental problems are not solved or the spread of illnesses is not prevented. Whether the future is seen as probably good or probably bad, time is seen as a straight line that leads from the past and is swiftly moving into the future. In these societies the past is studied scientifically to find trends and patterns. The causes of present and future conditions can be found in the past, so it is useful to investigate it in order to create a better future.

In future-oriented societies people ask "What if . . . ?"

Westerners are good at projecting themselves into the future. Sometimes they do this by thinking in terms of "what if . . . ?" George Orwell in his novel 1984 and Aldous Huxley in his novel Brave New World took trends they saw in their society and wrote novels predicting what society in the future would be like if those trends continued. Today managers and financial analysts do the same thing when they analyze trends and assess future markets using sophisticated statistical measurements. Even people who do not know how to use these technologies treat the future as concrete and knowable. People set goals, target dates for meeting them, and outline specific steps for getting to the goal. Working people plan their careers, their summer vacations and their retirement. Western managers want to know the personal goals of their workers. It is hard for them to believe that workers without goals for the future will be motivated to do their work well. Their attitude is that people act today because that action is a step toward the future they are preparing for. For them the future is not something to dream about or fear but something made real through concrete actions and thinking. Their attitude is that the future can be controlled if you act today.

In future-oriented societies time is linear, which means that it moves in only one direction, from the past to the future. In present and past-oriented societies people are more likely to experience time as cyclical, as repeating itself according to some pattern. They may pay more attention to daily, seasonal, and historical cycles than people in future-oriented societies do. People in present-oriented cultures are more likely to look to factors in the present situation to find the cause of a phenomenon than they are to see causes as originating in the past.

Exploring Ideas

1. A friend from the US sent me "Time is Money" by email to inspire me to make the most of each minute of the day. Using the descriptions of the three time orientations, decide whether you think the passage reflects a future or a present time orientation.

> **Time is Money**
> Imagine there is a bank that credits your account each morning with $86,400. It carries over no balance from day to day. Every evening it deletes whatever part of the balance you failed to use during the day. What would you do? Draw out every cent, of course!

Each of us has such a bank. Its name is TIME. Every morning, it credits you with 86,400 seconds. Every night it writes off, as lost, whatever of this you have failed to invest to good purpose. It carries over no balance. It allows no overdraft. Each day it opens a new account for you. Each night it burns the remains of the day. If you fail to use the day's deposits, the loss is yours. There is no going back. There is no drawing against the "tomorrow".

You must live in the present on today's deposits. Invest it so as to get from it the utmost in health, happiness, and success! The clock is running. Make the most of today. And remember that time waits for no one.

From my perspective in China I replied by sending my friend "Time is Rhythm."

2. What would you add or change to more accurately express the Chinese orientation to time? Is the orientation to time changing? What is your evidence?

Time is Rhythm

In Asia time is more like the rhythm of the waves, the ebb and flow of hourly, daily, annual and historical cycles. Pay attention to these rhythms and stay in tune with them. Each activity has its time. It is a pleasure to enjoy the strawberries when they come into season. They will only be available for a few weeks, so enjoy them and do not think about them when the time is not right.

It is the same with the day. There is a time to work, a time to rest, a time to eat, a time to enjoy friends. Don't try to impose an unnatural rhythm on the day by skipping meals or working when you should be with your family and friends. If you miss a dear friend today, don't worry. The cycle will come around again, and there will be another right time to meet.

Pay attention to the past. It is a cushion that softens the pressures of life. It is a reservoir of the wisdom of your ancestors. It is the precious life experience accumulated by your parents and grandparents who lovingly pass it on to you. It is where all our rich humanity, including virtue, can be found in the endless stories of heroes, leaders, scoundrels, enemies, lovers, and sages. Be thankful for them, as they never fail to guide and help you.

The future is where you are going and where you hope to prove yourself worthy of your inheritance from the past. It is where you live out the virtues you have learned and where you pass on your inheritance to those who will come after you, to your children, students, friends, and countrymen. It is where you join your ancestors in the drama of history.

3. Chinese people often think of themselves as hardworking. You will see in our next case study that Westerners do not al-

ways agree.

Case 12 How Much Is Hard Work?

How Much Is Hard Work?

A team of four Chinese from a large prestigious organization were in Honolulu for ten days to meet with six American colleagues from several different US universities. The ten scholars were getting together to finish up a project that they had been working on together for more than three years. The data had been collected, with great effort and many bureaucratic tangles, in several villages in central China. The Chinese team had been tireless and super-humanly patient in working out every problem so that the data collection had been extremely successful.

The researchers had been working separately for nearly a year on analysis, reports and papers based on their data. The Americans felt very lucky to have obtained the financial and institutional support to give the group an opportunity to get together one last time—this time in the US—to read each other's papers, work out problems with the analysis of data, fill in missing bits of information that "the other side" had, and to make sure that everything had been handled in a politically sensitive way. They were to meet for ten days in Honolulu.

The Chinese delegation arrived on Friday morning and were installed in a comfortable, inexpensive hotel in Waikiki. When the Americans arrived last in the afternoon everyone was eager to talk about what they had been doing and to begin work. They met for dinner and got right down to business at the home of one of the researchers, who had recently taken a job at the University of Hawaii. Since everyone was tired from traveling, they quit at ten o'clock, but on Saturday morning they were back at work at nine. At one o'clock, the Chinese were becoming very distracted. The interpreter, Yuan Bing, a Chinese who had been in the US about six years and was married to an American, suggested that everyone break for lunch, but he was ignored. The Americans called out for pizza at two and kept arguing, writing, calculating, and discussing straight through the late meal. At seven, the Chinese were sent back to their hotel at their request; the Americans didn't get back to the hotel until ten.

Sunday was, as planned, another work day. The Chinese participated actively in the discussion in the morning, and after lunch, which at Yuan Bing's urging was served by one o'clock. By six, however, the Chinese were anxious to return to their hotel, though the Americans were equally anxious to keep working. On Monday morning, the Chinese announced that they were taking the afternoon off. The Americans were rather annoyed, since they felt pressured to get as much as possible accomplished in the short time they had together, but they agreed to arrange a car for the Chinese.

The next two days the Chinese worked hard and cheerfully all morning and into the evening, though they insisted on taking off a full hour for lunch right at noon, and another for dinner promptly at six, even when they were in the middle of something. The Americans lunched on doughnuts and fruit provided at the conference center and kept on working. The interpreter could sense tension and resentment building between the two groups. Finally, on Wednesday morning, the Chinese told the interpreter to announce that after Friday at noon they were not working any more, that they were going to spend the last 48 hours sightseeing. The Americans were clearly dismayed, and protested. Yuan Bing decided it was time to step outside his role of interpreter and intervene.

As you work on the case, consider:

1. How can Yuan Bing explain the behavior of the Chinese team to the Americans?
. 2. How can Yuan Bing explain the behavior of the American team to the Chinese?
3. Why Yuan Bing didn't do something sooner to prevent this problem?
4. What can he and others do now to improve the situation?

Activity

When a middle aged American couple showed up to help a young Chinese couple move into their new apartment, they were surprised that the Chinese couple would not allow them to do any work. Instead they found a place for them to sit and gave them tea. The Chinese couple didn't think it was appropriate for an older distinguished professor to move furniture and carry boxes for them. It would not be dignified. In the United States when someone moves into a new house, it is a custom for friends to help clean and carry, so the Americans were eager to help and were upset that their presence only created more work for their young friends. The housing staff where I live once got upset when I climbed a ladder to get something off the roof. They felt they had lost face because I thought it necessary to do something they saw as their job and as a violation of my dignity. They would have preferred that I ask someone on the staff to do it. In the US climbing ladders is acceptable for people of any age or social position and necessary for anyone who owns a house.

What we are concerned about as we discuss activity is the purpose and character of human activity in different cultures. In cultures of the first category, being, people's actions express who they are. For that reason people behave in ways appropriate to their position in life. People's actions should be suitable to their status, social roles, and character. It is these roles and statuses that determine what is socially acceptable or dignified, because the person should act to enhance their roles and statuses. Important roles or statuses that determine behavior include gender roles such as woman, wife, and mother. Other important statuses include student, intellectual, government official, grandparent, manager and leader. (See Case 4 Can We Talk About It?)

In being cultures people often behave in ways considered suitable to their social roles

In being cultures, social status and position may be more significant than what the person does. This is often a problem for Westerners who are doing-oriented. Westerners sometimes experience the talk and behavior of Chinese people as performance, as dramatization of the self and as not very relevant to what is important, which in the Westerners' minds is to get something done. The Chinese in these situations are likely to be showing that they are friendly, virtuous, or sufficiently important to be worthy of the Westerner's attention and relationship. Westerners may not understand this because they are looking for concrete information and action. They often find Chinese conversation to be lacking in information. They do not understand that Chinese speakers are often showing who they are with their talk. The Chinese say things that a person of their status and character should say to show that they are educated, polite, humble, high-ranking or hospitable.

I once taught a group of professionals that had been sent by their company to the university for intensive English training. Because it was a work group, I started the oral class by asking everyone what they did in the company. They were all able to give me job titles but few could describe what they actually did in their jobs. Their company was soon to become a joint venture with a Western company, and I knew the Western managers and technicians would not be satisfied with their "I am" statements. They would be listening for "I do" statements, so I taught them how to describe what they do.

In doing cultures much talk indicates an intention to act

A person from a doing culture doesn't necessarily do any more than someone from a being culture. People are active everywhere. Doing culture people often talk a lot and may not be especially physically active. If you ask such a person what they are doing with their talk, they might say that they are planning, problem-solving, gathering information or making decisions. These are important concepts for people from doing cultures because these are the mental activities that lead to action or are the equivalent of action. They consider these activities as well as their achievements to be important, usually more important than their social status or position. When two people meet for the first time, one of the first questions asked is, "What do you do?" The answer is usually a statement of activity – I design software – rather than a job or position title.

Because the stress is on action in doing cultures, the goals toward which action is directed are also emphasized. As we have already said, personal goals are important for the person, as these are what motivate action. Similarly groups and organizations should have goals. It is also important to be able to identify and measure the outcomes of actions. Were the goals met? To what extent were they met? The concern with visible and measurable outcomes has stimulated the development of a wide variety of measurements. It is much more difficult for Westerners, and particularly for Americans, to value qualitative outcomes that are not measured quantitatively. It is frequently noted that Westerners serving as technical advisors in developing countries often do not feel they have accomplished anything as a result of their stay abroad. When local people reassure them that cooperative relationships have been built, that they now have a better idea about what needs to be done, or that they feel more confident about solving a particular problem, the Western technical

207

advisors do not feel any better. They cannot measure the outcome of their work so the results do not seem real.

In doing cultures there is often a sense of urgency about getting things done. Deadlines are important, as is the schedule. To have a full schedule, to be busy, indicates that you are accomplishing things. Take another look at **Case 3 Finding an Interested Buyer**. Mr. Li was indirectly saying he did not want to meet with George Hall when he said, "This week is very busy." George replied, "It sure is. How about 10 o'clock?" George thinks that all effective people are busy and have tight schedules. He heard Mr. Li saying that he was an active businessman, which only encouraged him to press for an appointment.

In being-in-becoming cultures people are experienced as changing

The middle position on the chart is called being-in-becoming or growing. Here the stress is on development of the self, whatever the self is understood to be in a particular culture. The idea is that we are all on our way somewhere and have not yet arrived. This form of activity emphasizes change, the idea that no one will be the same tomorrow as today. Hindus and Buddhists, for example, use the concept of karma to express the idea that how we live today influences how we will fare in life in the future, even in future lives. In India the social attitude that there are different ways of life and different virtues for people at various stages of life is widely accepted. A student should possess certain virtues. Later when someone goes to work, marries and raises a family, new attitudes, ways of behaving, and new virtues are expected. At this stage a person usually seeks worldly success, takes on worldly obligations, and pursues worldly pleasures. After fulfilling the family obligations of middle life, a person may become detached from worldly life and become more spiritual. Some may even leave their families and give up the material things they worked hard for in order to live a religious life. Once the leader of a training workshop I participated in asked all of us to discuss our personal goals. My partner for the training activity was a middle aged Indian general manager who told me that his personal goal was to become a good human being. In cultures that stress being-in-becoming, people may be more tolerant of how things are than is true in being or doing cultures. If each person is different at different stages in the journey through life, then it is to be expected that there will be significant differences among people in the present. The possible journeys and the paths that people follow may be endless, and the material conditions of people's lives may not reflect their true nature or show what they will become. For these reasons, people in being cultures may be more accepting of differences in beliefs, lifestyles, standards of living, and behavior. What is important is to respond to the possibilities and potentialities in situations and in people. The growing form of activity can be seen in many of the cultures of South Asia, but even there it is not the exclusive or even dominant form of activity. It exists side by side with doing and being in South Asia, and to a lesser extent in other cultures of the world.

Social relationships

In the original version of the chart we are using, the first category under social relationships was called authoritarian. This term emphasized the power or authority of the person at the top, but the essential characteristic of social systems in this category is that each person has a position in a hierarchy. It is the person's position within a hierarchy that dictates how the person should behave toward others in that hierarchy. The society as a whole consists of a series of hierarchies. A person who is at the top of one hierarchy may be at the bottom of another hierarchy that is above it. The chairman of an academic department is at the top of the department's hierarchy, but is low on the hierarchy of university administrators. The university may be at the top of the hierarchy of universities in a local area, but low on the hierarchy of universities in the country as a whole.

In cultures with hierarchical values people are aware of their position in relation to others

In a hierarchy people have clearly defined privileges and obligations according to their position. For instance, an older brother is expected to protect and advise a younger brother, while the younger one is expected to listen to and serve the older one. I always ask my students if each of them can identify their oldest roommate. They are always able to tell me the exact birth order of all their roommates. Even in relationships, which to people from other cultures appear to be non-hierarchical, Chinese people are aware of a hierarchy. It may be based on age, family social position, academic achievement, or some other criterion. In both obvious and subtle ways people's relationships with one another are influenced by where they perceive each other to be in a number of different hierarchies. When I first started teaching in China I noticed that the same few students always responded to the questions I addressed to the whole class. In time I figured out that these students were at the top of the class hierarchy. It was their right and duty to speak for the whole class.

Hierarchical societies differ from one another depending on the criteria used to assign a person a place in the hierarchy. If the criteria all depend on the circumstances of birth such as race, ethnic group, or inheritance from one's parents, then the hierarchy may be rigid and unchanging with certain groups permanently on the bottom and others permanently on the top. Recently Chinese young people could be heard discussing the red, gold, and black paths to success. They were recognizing that Chinese hierarchies are based partly on achievement, so there are ways to move up through them by acquiring education, wealth or political credentials. They also know, however, that

210

the criterion of age slows a person's advancement through most Chinese hierarchies.

In cultures with group values people often make decisions by consensus

As an American teaching in China I noticed that students in my class act according to hierarchical principles, but I also notice that their behavior reflects the group pattern of social relationships. In societies where relationships are based on groups, each person's social identity comes from their group memberships. People feel dependent on the group, safe within it, proud, and competitive with other groups. I discovered that I could get the students to be active in class by asking them to act as members of small groups. Students were willing to speak as a representative of their group when they were unwilling to speak for themselves. I found that I could get the students to be even more active by asking the groups to compete against one another. If I had a contest among groups, students usually were highly motivated to help their group win.

Unlike decision-making in individualist societies, which is usually based on majority rule, in the group pattern decisions should satisfy everyone and people will compromise to reach agreement. No one should be completely defeated. Sometimes standing in front of the class waiting for groups to make a decision, I have become impatient. I have given them a deadline and the decision is not such a critical one. Why is it taking them so long to decide? What I have not fully appreciated is that it is important that members of the group understand one another and sense one another's feelings and desires. The groups need time to find out what each member is thinking and feeling. Once the group has made the decision, the whole group rather than one person is responsible for it. The students are much faster and more efficient in acting on their group decisions than they are in making them. Everyone wants to act in the way the group decides because no one wants to let the group down. Each person puts aside their own feelings and interests to contribute their energies to the group project.

Loyalty is important in cultures with group values

In the group pattern of social relationships members of groups may be relatively equal or they may be arranged in a hierarchy. What distinguishes this pattern is that the group act out of concern for all its members, make decisions by consensus, and that members are loyal to the group. Individuals are not simply members of groups but belong to groups. In teaching I learned that I could increase the motivation of my students by praising or even criticizing the work of the whole group. Everyone was proud when the whole group had accomplished something and everyone worked hard when I challenged them to do better. Gradually I adapted to a new pattern of social relationships in which hierarchy and group membership are more important than they are in the individualist culture from which I come.

In cultures with individualist values each person is seen as autonomous and separate

In the United States and other individualistic societies, social relations are based on the autonomy of each person. That means that each person should be treated as an individual first and only secondarily as a member of a group or the occupant of a position in a hierarchy. In practice Americans often fail to act on their strong belief in equality. Class and race continue to be important factors in American society, even though most Americans will say they do not like hierarchies or that hierarchies are not so important. There are many hierarchies in American society as there are in other individualist cultures, but people in the US are uncomfortable with them and try to communicate with one another in a way that denies they exist or reduces their im-

212

pact. The frequent use of first names is one way they do this. People often address one another as individuals rather than as roles or positions. Those in high positions often send messages that say they are just like everyone else. The president while addressing the whole country may even say he consulted his wife when making a decision. It makes him sound like an ordinary citizen.

In individualist cultures people tend to be less aware of others' feelings and may talk more than people from group-oriented cultures. In individualistic cultures people must establish their own relationships. In less individualistic cultures, relationships come to the person from their membership in a group or a position in a hierarchy. Frequent talk is a way of expressing the self, giving information, and expressing opinions, all of which is necessary to find out if there is common ground on which to build a relationship.

Members of individualist cultures value self-reliance

In individualist cultures, self-reliance and independence are important, and it is considered weak to be dependent on others. In the group social pattern people accept dependence on the group and do not think their dependence is a sign of weakness. Sometimes Chinese people will say they think Americans do not take care of their elderly parents as well as Chinese do. I answer that Americans do care for the elderly but they have to do it in a way that does not interfere with the autonomy and independence of the older person. Children often work hard to preserve the independence of their parents because they know that the parents will experience a terrible loss if they must become totally dependent on their children.

In individualist cultures, people are more likely to express pride in themselves and their accomplishment rather than to express pride in their group, company, family, or hometown. Because an individual's position in life is seen to be the result of his own efforts and ability, it is difficult for him to feel good when things are not going well. Unemployed workers may blame themselves for their unemployment, because the social attitude is that if you really want to work, you can find a job. Personal initiative is highly valued, and failure to solve your own problems is your fault. Americans cope with this tough code by using consultants and professionals of all kinds when they need help. If you can't do something yourself you hire a lawyer, consult a counselor, or take a course that will teach you how to do it.

People learn the social patterns of their culture early in life. In individualist cultures where each person acts independently and is responsible for his actions, children learn to express their individual desires and make individual choices when they are very young. The mother of a two-year-old child might ask her son what he wants for breakfast. She gives him a choice between two different breakfast cereals and two kinds of fruit juice. The child is learning to make choices and decisions and to experience his needs and desires as more important than other considerations. In a group or hierarchical society the mother is more likely to decide what the child will eat. In that case the child is learning to accept what is given and to experience himself as part of a group in which others know best what he needs and therefore make decisions for him.

Exploring Ideas

Now that you have read the descriptions of the basic values from Kluckhohn's scheme, you are ready to decide to what extent you agree with the chart in **Figure 10 Comparison of Chinese values and Western values**.

1. Assign 100 points for each orientation on the chart. Then assign some portion of the 100 points to each of the three basic values for that orientation to indicate your opinion about the relative importance of each value in Chinese culture as a

214

whole.

Do this individually first and then meet in small groups to compare and discuss your rankings of the values. As you discuss your rankings try to reach a group consensus on how the 100 points should be distributed among the three values for each orientation.

Ranking Chinese values				
Orientation	Basic Values		Scores for each value	
Human Nature	Basically Evil	Mixture of Good and Evil	Basically Good	100
Relationship to Nature	Nature controls Humans	Harmony with Nature	Humans control Nature	100
Sense of Time	Past	Present	Future	100
Activity	Being	Growing	Doing	100
Social Relationships	Hierarchy	Group	Individual	100

2. After the groups have finished their work, compare the rankings from all the groups. Give each group an opportunity to explain why they rated the values as they did and to persuade others with examples. If possible, reach a consensus that everyone in the class can accept.

3. Do the activity again, this time making distinctions for levels of culture. For instance, rank each value according to how important it is for people of different generations.

4. Continue in this way using other levels of culture such as gender, occupation, rural and urban residence, region, and ethnic group. When you have considered the levels that you think are significant, write an essay or hold a class discussion on "Changing Values in Chinese Culture" or "Value Differences In Chinese Culture".

5. Discuss the chart with a group or individuals from another culture. Explain the values for each orientation and ask them to rank the values for their culture. Ask them for examples of behaviors, feelings, and attitudes that support their rankings.

215

Differences in Chinese Values by Age					
Orientation	Basic Values			Scores for each value	
Human Nature	Basically Evil	Mixture of Good and Evil		Basically Good	100
Under 25					
25-55					
Over 55					
Relationship to Nature	Nature controls Humans	Harmony with Nature		Humans control Nature	100
Under 25					
25-55					
Over 55					
Sense of Time	Past	Present		Future	100
Under 25					
25-55					
Over 55					
Activity	Being	Growing		Doing	100
Under 25					
25-55					
Over 55					
Social Relationships	Hierarchy	Group		Individual	100
Under 25					
25-55					
Over 55					

6. Recognizing differences in basic values in Chinese culture can be disturbing because an important part of cultural identity is sharing values and attitudes with other members of your culture. In practice cultural identity has two meanings:

   1) The idea of a national character that describes what the members of the culture have in common above and beyond their individual differences. This is the meaning when we say, "Chinese culture is..." or "Chinese people are..."

   2) The identity of the person in relation to the culture he is a member of. In this meaning cultural identity is part of each person's personality. This is the meaning when

someone says, "As a Chinese I..."
In class discuss the ways and the extent to which Chinese national culture is changing. What is the impact of those changes on your cultural identity as a Chinese?

Chapter 12: Taking Cultural Values to Work

In the last chapter you learned that becoming aware of cultural values increases your self-knowledge and helps you more fully appreciate your cultural heritage. Now it is time to take that increased awareness with you when you go to work.

Young Chinese professionals in all fields recognize that the conditions of work are changing. The students I teach accumulate certificates for various skills, write and rewrite résumés, and rehearse job interviews. They know that work is becoming more competitive and that they have to prepare for it while they are still university students. As I watch them, I admire their energy and determination. Still, I know that they lack information and ideas that could help them to prepare better. When they practice job interviews they assume that the interviewer has the same cultural values they have, even though the interview is in English, and the company they are role-playing has its roots in a European culture. As so often happens, when we are in a situation that we know demands more of us, we respond by doing more of what we did in the past. What my students need is new cultural software.

Recognizing how basic values and the social attitudes associated with them vary from culture to culture is only a first step in becoming effective in a cross-cultural work situation. Because more and more people are working in organizations that employ people from several different cultures, it is important to understand how basic values and attitudes get translated into work attitudes and behaviors. Fortunately a lot of research has been done in the last twenty years on just this topic. By learning about and applying knowledge from the research findings on work related values, you can add new software to your operating system. You can learn how to adapt your behavior to the cultural requirements of your job.

In 1980 Geert Hofstede from the Netherlands published a book, Culture's Consequences: International Differences in Work Related Values, that takes a different approach to analyzing cultural differences in values from Kluckhohn's. Rather than categorizing values, he began by conducting opinion surveys of workers in companies around the world. He then used statistical methods to analyze the responses to the surveys. From the analysis he identified four pairs of contrasting values that he used to compare values across cultures. He found a way to assign each country a score for each pair of contrasting values. The advantage of this method is that it makes it possible to identify differences in cultural values more precisely. One limitation of this method is that differences within nations and cultures are not identified. Because each country or region is assigned a score for each value, it is not possible to know how much variation exists within a country or region. In other words, Hofstede's work emphasizes national cultures rather than the layers of culture within nations.

The four pairs of contrasting values Hofstede identified are:
- Large and small Power Distances
- Individualism versus Collectivism
- Masculinity versus Femininity
- Strong and weak Uncertainty Avoidance

His original study did not include China but did include Taiwan, Singapore, and Hong Kong. Because these regions and countries are culturally Chinese, it is reasonable to expect that values in the People's Republic of China are similar in some respects. China was included in later studies, so more data is becoming available for China.

In the Kluckhohn scheme there is only one category for social relationships, which she divides into three basic values: hierarchy, group, and individual. In Hofstede's research there are two pairs of contrasting values to describe social relationships. The first, power distance, is roughly similar to the value Kluckhohn calls hierarchy. The second, individualism versus collectivism, is roughly the same as individual values and group values. This chapter deals with these first two pairs of contrasting values. The second two pairs of contrasting values are covered in **Chapter 14: Managing in Organizations.** Even though these values were discussed in the previous chapter, Hofstede adds more details and describes how these values are reflected in the attitudes and behaviors of people working in organizations.

Power distance

The first value contrast, power distance, is an attempt to measure cultural attitudes about inequality in social relationships. In all cultures some people have more power or higher status than other people. There is no society in the world in which everyone is precisely equal to everyone else. Hofstede is not trying to measure how unequal people actually are in a particular country. He is trying to measure how equal or unequal the people in a particular culture think people should be. In some cultures position in a hierarchy is considered to be natural and important. People are unequal by nature. These cultures are high power distance cultures. In other countries, people believe that everyone is by nature equal to everyone else. There are differences in power and status in these countries, but people think they should be eliminated or minimized. These are low power distance cultures.

The title power distance emphasizes the emotional and social distance between people who occupy different places in a hierarchy. In a large power distance country there is likely to be a greater emotional distance between bosses and subordinates. Employees will show great respect for the boss and be reluctant to criticize him. They will probably think that it is natural for the boss to enjoy special privileges that his employees do not have. Children are likely to be taught to respect and obey parents, teachers, and others in authority. In small power distance countries, an employee is more likely to approach and criticize a boss. The boss may occupy a higher position in the hierarchy, but that does not mean he deserves any special treatment.

A brochure advertising a Chinese company may feature a photograph of the headquarters building with a big expensive foreign automobile in front. This is meant to show the status of the company and perhaps of the manager. A reader from a small power distance country will probably find the brochure distasteful. To that person the display of status symbols indicates that the company is not spending its money in a businesslike way. In small power distance cultures, it is not acceptable for a company to spend money on useless status symbols. Employees in low power distance countries may criticize the boss for claiming special privileges or enjoying a significantly higher standard of living than they have. It is better for the boss to drive a more modest car. The brochure for a Western company will show that it spends its money on business necessities rather than on status symbols.

In low power distance countries if a teacher reports to parents that their child has misbehaved, the parents will try to find out if the teacher used his authority over the student in the proper way. If they think the teacher did not treat the child fairly, they might take the child's side. In every society children have less power than adults, but in a low power distance society children are encouraged to become adults as soon as possible. They are encouraged to claim the privileges of adults whenever possible. Their parents believe that the differences in power between teachers and students, between parents and children, and between bosses and workers should be reduced and not emphasized.

The following chart summarizes Hofstede's contrast in attitudes and behavior between cultures with large power distances and those with small power distances.

221

Attitudes and behaviors	Large power distance	Small power distance
Hierarchy	Hierarchies reflect the basic inequality of people	Hierarchies are only convenient ways of organizing activities.
Relationships	Comfortable with hierarchical relationships	Prefer equal relationships
Power	Accept differences in power	Dislike or distrust authority
Use of power	Whoever holds power is right and good.	Whoever uses their power will be judged as to whether they use it in the right way.
Dependency	The less powerful are dependent on the powerful.	Interdependence between less and more powerful persons
Decision making authority	Decision-making tends to be centralized; the leader decides.	Decision-making is dispersed throughout organization. People at all levels make decisions.
Leadership	Leaders direct the activities of subordinates by giving specific instructions.	Leaders motivate their subordinates to work toward goals. They do not give as much specific direction.
Initiative	Only the leader initiates.	Everyone is expected to initiate.
Communication flow	From top of organization to the bottom	From the top down and from the lower levels to higher levels
Status	High status people enjoy privileges.	People disapprove of special privileges and symbols of status.
How to change the organization	Replace people at the top.	Reform the organization.

Rules about behaving according to one's position in a hierarchy are first learned in the family, but they are carried over into work. In large power distance countries a good boss is like a good father, protective and caring, but at the same time requiring obedience. A good boss may be loved like a father, and a poor boss may be despised. In either case he is the boss, and whether you happen to have a good one or a poor one is not something you can control. In countries that put less stress on hierarchical relationships, people generally do not have such strong emotional feelings about their bosses. They are more likely to see differences between themselves and their superiors as nothing more than differences in organizational roles.

In an organization in a large power distance country, more information flows from the top to the bottom of the hierarchy than from the bottom to the top. Often the leader of one hierarchy is passing down instructions he has received from a higher authority. Decisions are made by the leader and then passed down to the staff in the form of instructions. Those in lower positions usually wait for the leader to tell them what to do. They hesitate to act on their own, because they do not want to do anything that would seem disrespectful. The result is that the staff is able to perform jobs that are known and familiar, but they are less likely to initiate action on their own when they encounter new or unique situations. Without specific instructions, they wait for the leader to tell them what to do.

In organizations in countries with smaller power distances, the leader is likely to give the staff guidance in the form of general principles and then expect the staff to apply those principles in their work. For instance, a small power distance leader might tell his staff to provide good service to customers by doing whatever can be done that is permissible according to company policy. The employee then has to decide what he should do when customers make unusual requests. If what is requested is allowable within company policy, then the employee will do it without checking with his leader. If the employee is not sure, he will ask someone for advice, but not necessarily the leader. He may think another colleague with more experience can help him decide what to do. If he makes a good decision the leader will praise him for his initiative. If the leader does not like the decision, he will instruct the employee on how to make a better decision in the future.

Countries and regions that are culturally Chinese score high on Hofstede's Power Distance Index. Some Southeast Asian, Latin American and Arab counties have even higher Power Distance scores. The United States has a lower score than France and Italy, but a higher score than Northern European countries.

Country or Region	PDI	Country or Region	PDI
Malaysia	104	Iran	58
Philippines	94	Japan	54
Mexico	81	Italy	50
Arab countries	80	USA	40
India	77	Netherlands	38
Singapore	74	Australia	36
Brazil	69	Germany	35
France	68	Great Britain	35
Hong Kong	68	Switzerland	34
South Korea	60	Sweden	31
Taiwan	58	Israel	13

Figure 11 Power Distance Index for selected countries and regions

Hofstede also found social class differences within each country in terms of the Power Distance Index. Employees of organizations who had higher levels of education had lower Power Distance Index scores than for the country or region as a whole. He concludes that in all countries, the most highly educated segment of the population prefers work situations with smaller power distances than exist in the country as a whole.

Exploring Ideas

Use what you have learned about large and small power distance relationships to analyze the work experiences of the four Chinese secretaries described in the following case. Finland like other Northern European countries has a low Power Distance Index score (33).

Four Secretaries and Their Jobs

Four classmates from a top Chinese university all took jobs as secretaries after graduation. Five years later the four former classmates had a reunion and discussed their jobs.

Chen Qi and Dai Yun both work as bilingual secretaries for a Finnish company in Beijing. Chen Qi is secretary to the Finn general manager, and Dai Yun is secretary to the Chinese local manager, a position only slightly lower than that of the Finn manager.

Zhang Ying is from a politically prominent family and was hired as the secretary to the leader of a small government bureau in the capital city of her home province. Lu Yan works for a state run enterprise in the same city where she was hired as the secretary to the new manager for international marketing. The company has never marketed its products abroad before so this office and Lu Yan's position are new to the company.

Five years later Chen Qi is satisfied with her job with the Finnish company but Dai Yun is not. The Finn manager receives orders from the company's home office in Finland, and he gives orders to those below him in China, including his secretary Chen Qi. He tells her how he wants his time scheduled and she then makes appointments for him according to his instructions. She translates memos and other documents and interprets from Chinese to English and English to Chinese. If the manager does not think Chen Qi has done her work well, he tells her right away. He is very demanding, but Chen Qi feels that she knows what her duties are and knows what her manager expects. She is confident that she is doing a good job.

Dai Yun often does not have as much work to do as Chen Qi does, because her boss schedules his own appointments and does a lot of the office paperwork himself. When he is out of town she has time to study for the graduate entrance exam. However, she is not sure whether or not she is doing a good job. Her manager tells her what she is expected to do, but he does this day by day. When people call or come to the office to see her boss, she greets them in English or Chinese as necessary. She receives their memos and other messages as well as their questions and requests and passes them on to her manager. Dai Yun thinks of her job as doing what her manager wants her to do. She pays close attention to his moods and behavior, and sometimes she is able to anticipate what he would like without him telling her.

Zhang Ying looks and sounds confident when the four former classmates get together. She reports that she and her boss have a close working relationship. Like Dai Yun she thinks of her job as pleasing her boss, but she has more responsibility than her former classmate does. Zhang Ying's boss often has to write reports for other government bureaus and usually he simply tells her what the report is to be about and she writes it for him. After all, she keeps up-to-date with public affairs and is more familiar with the details of the day-to-day operation of the office than he is, because he is away much of the time attending meetings. It is also part of her job to decide who among the many people who want to see her boss will be given an appointment, to handle some personal business for her boss, and to inform him of people and events that it is important that he know about.

Zhang Ying is proud of the fact that her boss depends on her so much. She feels that his trust is deserved because she quickly learned how things are done in political circles in her province. She is now able to handle all the complexities of relationships in exactly the way her boss would handle them. Zhang Ying is excited that her boss may soon be given a new and better position and she expects to move to the new office with him.

Lu Yan is the picture of the busy career woman. In the last five years she has put in long hours and has acquired many new professional skills. She says the first years with her company were difficult, because no one had a clear idea how to handle international marketing. She was able to help her boss with several projects by making use of what she had learned about marketing in her university studies. Because she could speak English she accompanied company leaders on several trips abroad to visit companies with which her company was doing business. She feels she and her boss have been colleagues as much as boss and secretary. Her hard work is starting to pay off, as she was recently assigned responsibility for the marketing of a product the company has developed in conjunction with a foreign company. Now, she says, I have to hire a secretary for myself, because I have become a businesswoman.

Answer the following questions:
1. Using a scale of zero to one hundred, rate each of these work situations on power distance. You might want to give a different power distance score for each (1) boss-secretary pair and to each (2) organization. In a class discussion defend the scores you give. Consider all the factors on the chart comparing large and small power distance relationships.
2. Since all but one of the secretaries have a Chinese boss, factors other than national culture seem to be influencing power distance relationships at work. How do you explain the differences in the work experience of the four secretaries?

People from relatively small power distance countries often have different expectations about how decisions should be made than do people from countries with larger power distances. Consider the next case.

Case 14 A Question of Safety

A Question of Safety

At 1:00 p.m. on a pleasant spring afternoon Dick Jones returned to his fourth floor room in the Foreign Experts Building on the campus of a Chinese university where he had been teaching for eight months. As Dick approached his room he thought he smelled smoke. He didn't see anything suspicious but went back downstairs to report this to the front desk.

Jiang Qing was on duty that noon. She had been working in the building for five years and, like others on the staff, was proud of the improvements in service and facilities that had been made in the foreigners' residence in recent years. She listened to Dick's report but did nothing about it. Dick's requests always sounded like demands. She and other staff members were annoyed by his frequent complaints and by his failure to notice their efforts to make his life comfortable. He could wait; after all it was the staff's rest period.

About twenty minutes later Dick angrily returned to the reception desk, this time insisting that Jiang Qing investigate the fourth floor for a possible fire. As the two went door to door through the vacant rooms, the smell of smoke became stronger. When they opened the last door on the hall they were faced with a wall of thick black smoke. They quickly closed the door. Jiang Qing ran back to the first floor to alert her co-workers, and Dick knocked on doors on the third and second floors to tell people to get out of the building.

Soon workers had run a water hose from the adjacent

hotel and stood on the top of a covered walkway trying to extinguish the fire. Despite their efforts they could not get the water high enough to put out the fire, which by this time was flaming out of the window. Residents were calmly but quickly leaving the building, but Dick was upset because he could not persuade Jiang Qing to call the fire department. She and the cleaning women were also visibly upset and doing what they could to respond to the crisis. Jiang Qing called the assistant manager of the Reception Unit at her office and at home. When Jiang Qing located her, she came immediately and, seeing the situation, instructed Jiang Qing to call the fire department.

The firefighters arrived and soon put the fire out. They poured additional water on the area to make sure the fire would not start up again. No one was hurt and the damage was confined to the empty fourth floor rooms. Several third floor rooms had water damage.

Chinese and foreigners alike crowded into the building to survey the damage. At this time the assistant manager was heard to say that she was the first one to see the fire. When this was translated for the foreign teachers, they were indignant. "It was Dick who discovered the fire and he had a hard time getting anyone to listen to him," several exclaimed. "Who is she? We've never seen her in the building before." Thus began a discussion among the foreign residents of the poor way the staff had responded to the fire.

"We always thought the building was unsafe, but now we are sure of it. If this had happened at night, we might have been killed." Others commented that it was not the staff that told them to evacuate the building, but Dick. And why did it take so long to call the fire company? By evening the foreign teachers had a long list of complaints about the staff's disregard for their safety to present to the Foreign Affairs Office.

Answer these questions:

1. What are the differences between how the housing staff and how the foreign residents think decisions should be made?
2. How would you explain the behavior of the housing staff and the assistant manager to the foreign teachers?
3. What would you advise the foreign teachers to do now that the immediate danger is past? What will happen if they go to the Foreign Affairs Office with their list of complaints about how this crisis was handled?
4. What can the Reception Unit that manages the building do to improve its ability to respond to emergency situations in the future?

Individualism versus collectivism

The second of Hofstede's contrasting pairs of values is also concerned with social relationships. The Individualism Index measures the extent to which the interests of the individual are considered to be more important than the interests of the group. Countries that score high on the Power Distance Index tend to have low scores on individualism. There are enough exceptions, however, to convince Hofstede that these are separate values. France, for instance, is highly individualistic but also high on power distance.

What Hofstede adds to our earlier understanding of individualism and collectivism is the concept of ingroups and outgroups. This in an important feature of Chinese social life that we first met in Chapter Nine: Building Culture into the Landscape in the discussion of the inside/outside cultural pattern. Another concept used to describe this pattern is **localism**. This means that when decisions are made, the interests of the local group are given priority over the interests of a more distant group.

One semester when my workload was particularly heavy, I asked the department to find me two teaching assistants to help me read student essays. The leaders of my department were very cooperative and promptly assigned me a capable MA student from the applied linguistics program. They would get me a second one soon, they said. Several weeks passed but no teaching assistant appeared. Later I discovered that the department couldn't find a second graduate student because they were only willing to give this assignment to graduate students who had already agreed to work for the department after they finished their studies. Learning to teach writing was a resource the department wanted to keep within the group.

This practice of favoring members of the ingroup contrasts sharply with academic practices in individualist countries. In the US, for instance, university departments rarely hire their own graduates. Even the most promising graduate student is expected to find a position in another university. This policy favors the professional group as a whole rather than the immediate interests of the local department. The reasoning is that in order to compete with academic departments across the country or the world, the local department has to be faithful to impersonal academic standards rather than to its own graduate students. When other respected universities hire graduates, the high academic standards of the department are affirmed.

Western sociologists have long been aware of the contrast between a universal orientation and a local or particular orientation, and describe this contrast within cultures as well as across cultures. Coming from individualist cultures, they associate universal values with urbanization and modernization. They say that when people move to cities and become more educated, they adopt more universal values. Their reasoning is that urban life requires more impersonal patterns of relationships, while rural life rests on a sense of solidarity with others. If their theory applies to Asian cultures as well as Western cultures, you would expect to find differences within Chinese culture based on urban or rural residence and level of education. Keep in mind, however, that both Singapore and Hong Kong are highly urbanized and have well-educated populations and yet have low scores on individualism.

People from individualist cultures are more likely to act on principles that apply to everyone, principles that are universal and apply to associates and strangers alike. Individualists are more likely to treat people they do not know as if they can be trusted, as if they, too, will behave according to the same universal principles. Individualists are generally concerned about the processes of decision-making such as the process of selecting an employee for a job or a promotion. For them rules that define processes are important because they are necessary to assure that impersonal or universal standards are used in making decisions. Any behavior that attempts to seek an advantage for one person over another based on a personal relationship is seen as unfair or even as corrupt. Often individualists strongly disapprove of attempts to gain preference, and the person who does this may be seen as dishonest or unprincipled.

Collectivists are not unprincipled, but when making decisions they tend to give a higher priority to relationships than individualists do. They expect people who are involved in a group relationship to have duties and obligations to one another. Duties include being loyal and furthering the interests of the group, so it is their obligation to give preference to ingroup members. This is considered more important than following impersonal rules that do not distinguish between strangers and associates.

Attitudes and behaviors	Individualists	Collectivists
Self	Each person is separate from others; children learn to think in terms of "I"	Each person is part of a group; children learn to think in terms of "we"
Identity	Identity is based in the individual	Identity is based in the social network
Communication	Low context	High context
	Speak your mind and tell the truth	Maintain harmony and avoid confrontations

Social values	Personal freedom is more important than equality	Equality is more important than personal freedom
Decision-making	Follow universal rules; the decision-making process is important	Fulfill obligations to ingroup; relationships are important
Group Membership	The individual belongs to many groups but his attachment to them is relatively weak	The individual belongs to few groups but feels strongly attached to them
Conformity	Group has relatively little influence on the behavior of group members	Group greatly influences the behavior of members
Behavior toward ingroup and outgroup members	Relatively little difference in behavior toward ingroup and outgroup members	Big difference between ingroup and outgroup behaviors
Relationships with group members	Less intimate with ingroups and less hostile to outgroups	More intimate with ingroups and more hostile to outgroups
Competition	Occurs within groups as well as between groups	Occurs between groups but not often within groups
Cooperation	Cooperate with people who are not members of one's group plus group members	Cooperate with members of ingroups but not with members of outgroups
Strangers	Value meeting new people; meet them easily	Formal and distant with strangers
Self-reliance	It is a pleasure to do as much by yourself as possible	People depend on each other but should not burden ingroup members unnecessarily
Typical relationship pattern	Short-term, voluntary less intensive relationships	Long-term, involuntary more intensive relationships

Figure 12   Contrasts between individualism and collectivism

Countries and regions that are culturally Chinese have the lowest individualism scores. Among the world's cultures, individualism is the exception rather than the norm. Over fifty countries were included in Hofstede's original study and most were low on individualism.

Country or Region	IDV	Country or Region	IDV
USA	91	India	48
Great Britain	89	Japan	46
Netherlands	80	Iran	41
New Zealand	80	Brazil	38
Sweden	71	Arab countries	38
France	71	Philippines	32
Switzerland	68	Mexico	30
Germany	67	Malaysia	26
Austria	55	Hong Kong	25
Israel	54	Singapore	20
Spain	51	Taiwan	17

Figure 13 Individualism index scores for selected countries and regions

Exploring Ideas

1. If you have not already worked on **Case 7 Who Are You Trying to Fool?** read it now. Even if you have already discussed it, it is worthwhile to review it for your discussion of individualism and collectivism.

2. Read the following case and answer the questions.

Case 15 Sharing the Wealth

Sharing the Wealth

Anna Bilow had been working for a Chinese-owned and operated company in Nanjing for about six months. The division she was working in had a small collection of Chinese-English dictionaries, English language reference books, and some videos in English including a couple of training films and several feature films that Anna had brought at her new employer's request when she came from Europe. Anna knew that some of the other sections had similar collections. She had sometimes used her friendship with one of the women in another department, Gu Ming, to borrow English novels and reference books and in turn had let Gu Ming borrow books from her section's collection. On other occasions, she had seen friendly, noisy exchanges, where one of the other workers in her division had lent a book or video to a colleague from another section.

Anna thought it was a great idea when a memo was circulated saying that the company's leaders had decided to collect all the English language materials together into a single collection. The plan was to put them in a small room that was currently being used for storage so that all employees could have equal access to them. Now she would no longer have to go from department to department trying to find the materials she needed.

Anna was surprised to hear her co-workers complaining about the new policy. When the young man in charge came to the department to collect their English language materials, she was astounded to see them hiding most of the books and all but one of the videos in their desks. When she checked out the new so-called collection, she found that the few items were all outdated or somehow damaged. She also noticed that none of the materials she had borrowed from Gu Ming were in the collection. She asked her friend why the Chinese were unwilling to share their English language materials with all their co-workers, when they seemed willing to share them within their departments.

1. What explanation do you think Gu Ming gave Anna?
2. What problems do you expect to encounter if you are asked to share resources with people who are not part of your ingroup?
3. Discuss the advantages and disadvantages of the ways people in both individualist and collectivist cultures share resources.
4. Read the next case and answer the questions that follow.

The Entrepreneur

Charles was excited about his new promotion and transfer to China. He had done well in the marketing department of his company and had been promoted to assist the director of marketing at the company's recently established operations in Shanghai. He had studied a bit about Chinese, but so far had worked only in the United States and had little experience with Chinese individuals or culture. In the two months before relocating, Charles often went to the local university library to try to absorb all he could about China, its culture, and the ways of doing business. In addition, his company provided a week-long cultural seminar just prior to his departure.

After arriving in Shanghai, Charles found that his work was exciting and that marketing to the Chinese was a new challenge. During his cultural seminar he had learned several concepts that were important in the Chinese business environment such as the concept of *guanxi*. He had also learned about individualism and collectivism and that China tended to be collectivist, while his own American culture ranked high on individualism. He felt he understood these concepts and was sure he would learn more.

Because the marketing director had two assistants, Charles worked closely with Dashan, his Chinese counterpart. Charles learned that Dashan came from a fairly influential family in the area. Dashan was quite motivated and worked very hard. To Charles it seemed that Dashan was quite "individualistic" as he worked hard for bonuses, was always going the extra mile, and had set a number of work-related goals for himself.

After a few months, Dashan left the company to start a venture of his own. Charles kept in touch with him and noticed that Dashan's business was doing very well. One weekend, Dashan invited Charles for dinner. Many of Dashan's relatives were present as well as some friends whom Charles had not met. Charles found that Dashan's house was quite nice and equipped with many big-ticket consumer items, such as a personal computer, air-conditioning, and modern kitchen appliances. Charles also learned that Dashan had recently bought a new car for his parents. It was clear that Dashan's business was very profitable and successful. Dashan was managing it himself and already had 40 or 50 employees. It seemed to Charles that Dashan was doing quite a good job of being "individualistic."

1. Is Charles correct to interpret Dashan's behavior as individualistic?

2. In what ways is Dashan's behavior consistent with his culture's values?

3. What can you tell Charles to help him correct his understanding of Chinese cultural values?

4. Read the following comments about doing business in China made by an American attorney. Answer the questions that follow.

Problems of doing business in China

Stanley Lubman, an American attorney who has represented companies doing business in China for 25 years, lists the problems that international companies experience when setting up a business in China. (From PBS Newshour interview 10/31/97)

- Chinese government policy is changeable.
- The law is general rather than specific. It is interpreted and applied by officials locally with a great deal of discretion.
- China is politically decentralized. There is not really one China. There are many and each of them interprets national policies and laws quite differently, sometimes contrary to Beijing's intent.
- It is difficult to find out what an agency's practice actually is because they do not make their interpretations public.
- Contracts are difficult to negotiate. Both sides may have very different expectations.

1. Do you think Stanley Lubman's conclusions about doing business in China are accurate?
2. To what extent do his comments reflect the frustrations that a businessman from an individualist culture might experience when trying to work in a collectivist culture?
3. What advice would you give to someone from an individualist culture who was starting a business in China?

Chapter 13: Working in Groups

Contemporary Western management theory stresses working in teams. The first thing to notice about this is the terminology. Teams are groups, but the almost universal use of a sports metaphor to describe them is significant. Westerners, though individualists, are fond of team sports. Athletes from the individualist cultures of Europe and North America excel in team sports such as soccer, basketball, cricket and hockey. Athletes from collectivist cultures such as China excel at individual sports such as track and field and swimming. Understanding this apparent contradiction is essential for both individualists and collectivists if they want to be successful in cross-cultural work environments.

To encourage my students to think more deeply about the contrast between individualism and collectivism, I asked them to solve the riddle of Chinese success in individual sports and Western success in team sports. In response they told me a Chinese saying that expresses the same idea: "One Chinese is a dragon; three are a worm." Hearing this reassured me that my observations of Chinese group behavior have some basis in fact. On the other hand I wanted to object. Chinese groups also have advantages. Fans may gloomily discuss the failure of the Chinese national team in World Cup football competition, but this does not tell the whole story of group life in collectivist cultures. I have to agree, however, that Chinese groups are not typically organized in a way that resembles a modern sports team.

It is not easy to generalize about groups in one culture as compared to groups in another culture, because every culture has many different types of groups. Even so, the contrast between individualism and collectivism as dominant cultural patterns does provide a way to understand the typical group patterns in a particular culture. Both Chinese (collectivist culture) groups and Western style (individualist culture) groups can be effective. Problems usually arise when members of different cultures are the members of the same group. When a Western manager says to his Chinese staff that he wants them to be a team, the Chinese staff may be confident that they know what he means. Probably they do not, because their expectations for how they should behave as members of teams may be quite different from the way the Western manager expects them to behave.

The lifecycle of a group

In the following discussion, the lifecycle of a group is divided into four stages with a comparison of the typical behavior of individualists and collectivists at each stage. The stages show that the focus of attention and the issues of group life change over time. The diagrams at the beginning of each section are an attempt to show in abstract form what a group feels like to members at each stage. During the first stage, for instance, the new group is unknown and members are relating to the groups from which they come. At the second stage, members are aware of the complex and sometimes conflicting relationships within the group. At the third stage members are aware that their group is distinct from other groups, while at the fourth stage members are busy with the work of the group.

Groups change gradually, so the stages are not as separate as they at first appear. For instance, when new members join the group, the group reconsiders issues from the first stage. Each group will have its own particular structure and patterns of relationships at each stage, but some structures are more typical of collectivist culture groups and others are more typical of individualist culture groups. Individualists who are trying to be effective in a collectivist culture group should pay attention to the challenges at the end of each chart. The same advice applies to collectivists who belong to a group with members or a leader from an individualist culture.

Stage One: Forming

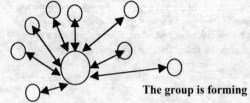

When a group is forming, members expect the new group to be like their previous group experiences.

The group is forming

Members discover what the new group will be like

To individualists all groups are temporary. They form and reform. A professional footballer plays for the term of his contract. A soldier is subject to military authority only for the term of his enlistment. Workers change jobs to find more desirable conditions, increase their skills, and advance their careers. The manager of a company appoints a task force to research an issue and make recommendations. Even families are relatively short term in that children are expected to become independent from their parents and create families of their own when they are adults. Marriage is voluntary, not just in selecting a mate but in terms of how long the couple will stay together.

People join professional organizations, neighborhood groups, and personal interest groups of all kinds. Individualists think groups can accomplish things a person cannot do alone, so forming or joining a group is a way to achieve personal goals. For these reasons individualists have more experience joining and leaving groups and belong to many groups at the same time. They can do this because their personal identity is quite separate from their group memberships.

241

An individualist anticipates a new group

When an individualist joins a group usually he is doing so as a separate person. He doesn't give much thought to how his family would expect him to behave in the group. If the group is a work group, he may be thinking about what his boss expects of him, but the boss has probably instructed him about achieving certain goals and has left decisions about how to do it to him. Also the individualist has personal goals and sees each new group as a chance to achieve them. Maybe the individualist wants to be a manager some day. If the boss assigns him to work on a task force, the individualist is likely to see his boss's assignment as a chance to develop his leadership skills. Even if he is not much interested in the work of the task force, being a member could benefit him. The benefit might be the opportunity to learn new skills that a leader should have. A collectivist is less likely to think in this way. When his boss assigns him to participate in the work of a task force, he is more likely to be thinking about what the boss expects him to do as a member.

Because the individualist has participated in many different groups, he expects each one to be different. Whether it is a task force at work, a community orchestra, a neighborhood football club, a parents' organization at his child's school, a group of employees supervised by the same boss, or a workshop at a professional conference, each group has its own requirements and benefits. The potential member wants to find out what each new

242

group will be like. How will the group function? How much time and effort will be required? What will members of this group actually do? Is the group likely to succeed in achieving its goals? Is the leader effective? Are the other members capable and easy to work with? When considering joining, the person evaluates these issues of group life and then decides whether or not to participate and decides how much energy he will devote to the group.

A collectivist anticipates a new group

When a collectivist enters a new group, he carries his other group identities along to a greater extent than the individualist does. He is likely to see himself as a representative of his important ingroups. In the work of the task force he participates on behalf of his boss. In another group, he may be participating on behalf of his work unit or even his family. The collectivist usually decides to join or form a group in response to instructions or recommendations from an important ingroup. Participating is not a personal choice but a response to the wishes of others. A Westerner is likely to see group membership as voluntary, so he decides whether or not to join. This is true even if the group is not actually voluntary, as in a work assignment or a required course at university. If the individualist decides participation is not a benefit, he may comply with the requirement to attend, but give little more than his physical presence. Collectivists also use this strategy occasionally, because most of their groups are not voluntary.

The usual attitude of a collectivist is to expect the new group to be similar to other groups he has participated in. He knows it takes time to form relationships and he knows that the leader plays a critical role. He should be aware of the status of group members and behave according to his position in the hierarchy. The collectivist is less conscious of making a personal choice to participate or of having a choice about how to participate. He

243

receives the group as it is presented and tries to fit into the program of the group. He is not usually thinking of the group as an opportunity to pursue his personal goals.

Challenges for individualists and collectivists

The challenge for individualists working with groups in a collectivist culture is to recognize the relationships, or lack of them, that already exist in the new group. He shouldn't expect members to participate as independent individuals. If the individualist is the group leader, he can make use of relationships that already exist by asking subgroups rather than individuals to offer suggestions. He should give members a chance to form relationships, and he should be sensitive to hierarchies in the group.

At this stage the challenge for collectivists is to recognize that all groups are not alike. If the new group is one in which individualist expectations apply, the collectivist should pay less attention to status and hierarchy than in other groups. Western groups usually prefer smaller power distances between leaders and members, so deferring to the leader too much will make a poor impression. The leader's words should be heard as a call to action and not simply as an expression of his leadership status. A Western leader is likely to expect the group to be a way of achieving his personal and organizational goals. He will probably give many direct orders at first, but this does not mean you should remain silent. He also wants any relevant information you have and expects independent opinions from you.

Forming: Members discover what the new group will be like		
Group Issue	**Individualists**	**Collectivists**
Initial attitude	A new group is a good way to achieve a specific purpose	A new group requires time to form new relationships
Other members	Assess attitudes and abilities of group members. It is not necessary to know much more about them	If members are strangers it will take time to form relationships; if they are from outgroups, adopt the attitude of the ingroup toward them
Personal choice	Assess advantages and disadvantages of belonging to group	Accept membership if it is assigned
What to look for	How group goals match personal goals	What the leader expects
	Probability of group achieving its goals	What ingroups expect
Challenges	Focusing on group rather than on self	Recognizing choices
	Sensitivity to relationships	Responding to group purpose

Exploring Ideas

1. Make a list of all the groups you belong to. Include family, dormitory, university department or program, group of present classmates, friendship group from middle school, school committees or project groups, work groups of supervisors and workers, and any other groups you can think of. How involved are you in each group? In what ways are the groups similar to one another and in what ways are they different?

2. For each group draw a diagram using circles, lines, and arrows, or any other symbols to show feelings, relationships, and communication patterns. In small group discussions, explain some of your group diagrams to others. Ask one another questions to learn as much as possible about the life of each

group.

3. How important are your ingroup relationships (family, university department, etc.) in influencing your behavior in any new groups you enter? Do you think you participate in new groups as an individual or as a representative of your important ingroups?

Stage Two: Storming

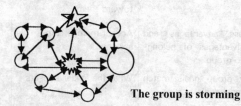

The group is storming

When a group is storming, members compete and cooperate as they negotiate important issues of group life.

Members find their places in the group

The second stage is called storming because the relationships among members at this stage are often unsettled or in turmoil; relationships are stormy. The main theme is conflict as members negotiate relationships trying to gain an advantageous position in the group. This stage is a challenge to both individualists and collectivists working in mixed culture groups, because the typical ways of competing in the two types of cultures are very different.

Individualists prefer to compete and negotiate openly. In an individualist group, members will say things like, "I don't agree with you"; "I don't see it that way"; "It won't work"; "What we need to do is. . ." or "Your analysis doesn't go far enough." Such comments are said politely most of the time, but the words carry messages of disagreement or even conflict. There is likely to be debate about what the group should do and the decisions made have implications for who wins and who loses in terms of

246

status and prestige in the group. Because status in hierarchies carries relatively less weight than in collectivist groups, the contests are supposed to be about ideas and issues rather than about power. Nevertheless, they are debates about who will be a more powerful influence in the life of the group.

The American Argument Culture

Deborah Tannen, Author of The Argument Culture

We have a tendency to approach every problem as if it were a fight between two sides. We see it in headlines that are always using metaphors for war. We see it in our public conversations, which are always debates, and we see it in an attack culture where journalists, intellectuals of all sorts think unless you're attacking and criticizing, you're not really thinking. This goes back to Aristotle, the idea that opposition is the best way to think about anything. The seeds of it can be found in our classrooms. A teacher will introduce an article or an idea and rather than asking students to explore the idea to find what's good and useful in it will only ask how can we attack it. This sets up debates where people learn not to listen to each other because they're so busy trying to win the debate.

There is a tendency to frame everything as an either/or. Sometimes this can be great, as when journalists want to be balanced and show both sides. But sometimes there aren't two sides. Sometimes there are more; sometimes there are less. Often we give a platform to discredited views in our eagerness to show the other side. Only in the United States have we given a platform to a few discredited scientists, who say global warming isn't a problem, just so that we can show the other side.

We need to develop other metaphors and not talk about two sides, but talk about all sides. The most dangerous effect of this is to the human spirit. It has a corrosive effect on us, to be constantly surrounded by this unrelenting contention. And people do respond when you give them a fuller view. Let's ask people who have opposing views to find common ground. Ask them how they have influenced each other. There is drama in seeing people actually listening to each other and changing their view. It's the drama of a new solution.

Groups in collectivist cultures have an advantage at this stage, because the hierarchy provides an automatic structure and a stable position for each member. The collectivist value of maintaining harmony is also helpful in controlling conflict. I have participated in many groups with both Chinese and Western members. When the Westerners start debating issues, the Chinese members usually agree with both sides. Maybe someone will make a comment on the way out the door to one of the de-

247

baters that subtly conveys agreement or disagreement. Maybe no one will. In my experience Chinese group members instinctively avoid open competition in a group unless there is a high level of trust among group members, but that does not mean there is no competition. I have seen Chinese group members vie for power by talking about their children, by praising someone's virtue, and by making jokes. To see the competition, one has to be able to see the context in which these seemingly harmless statements are made. That is not easy for low context, individualist culture communicators to do. The disadvantage for collectivist culture groups in the storming stage is that conflict is usually disguised and often occurs behind the scenes. This can make it more difficult to resolve.

Collectivists, including Chinese, sometimes compete with others by creating problems for rivals rather than by trying to outperform them. This strategy maintains a harmonious surface for group life but often inhibits the initiative of group members. Over time it can drain off the energy of the group.

Jealousy

Xu Meiyan, Student

It is said that one Chinese person is a dragon while two are worms. That means one Chinese person can achieve a lot when he does something alone, because he can be wholly devoted to the work. Two Chinese will achieve nothing when they are competing with each other because what they think about is not how to do better than the other but how to make things harder on the other.

Most people struggle with one another for power, money, fame or love. They think that these things are limited and cannot be divided equally among everyone. One's winning must mean another's losing. If you want more, you must beat your competitors. Everybody wants more than others have, so the struggle is fierce.

Then how to win the competition? There must be some people who are more talented, learned, diligent, stronger in body and luckier than others. They are more likely to be winners, but most others are unwilling to be losers. The losers may blame their failure on unfair treatment during the competition, the winners' dishonest methods or their own momentary carelessness. They do not admit that winners are really better than they are. They are tortured by the winners' triumph and their own failure.

The jealous losers will try to recapture what they have lost. Because they are not able to beat the winners face to face, they will use dishonest methods, such as finding fault with the winners, defaming them or threatening them. A few jealous losers even destroy the things they have lost because they are determined that no one else can have those things, if they can't have them.

Jealousy is not always a defect and does not always bring harm. Some people may lose at first but refuse to take the defeat lying down. They put the blame on their own shortcomings and learn from their failure. They turn failure into motivation and strive harder. They believe they can win fairly and justly.

Individualists compete for leadership roles

In individualist culture groups members openly compete for leadership roles because the formal leader is seen as only one of the leaders of the group. Members are expected to play important roles such as identifying problems, providing information, clarifying issues, and initiating action based on the leader's general statements of purpose and goals. The Western or individualist view is that an individual needs to show that he knows how to lead, because that is how others recognize his qualifications for formal leadership positions. It is not unusual for someone other than the highest-ranking member to be the formal leader of an individualist culture group, although his status should not be much lower than any higher-ranking members of the group. The lower ranking person might be appointed leader because the task of the group is in his area of special expertise. Whatever the official rankings of members, they will tend to treat one another as equals, while at the same time they might compete with one another by trying to outperform each other or even by challenging the leader. The status and prestige a member enjoys in a group is only partly determined by the member's position in formal hierarchies. How a member handles relationships with other members and how he contributes to leadership and communication are also important. Since harmony is not a strong value, issues can be debated openly and disagreeing with the leader and other members is acceptable. The result is often a complex pat-

249

tern of cooperation and competition that looks disorderly to a Chinese observer.

Collectivists expect one strong leader

Many Chinese have told me that they think it is foolish to behave like a leader if you are not a leader. I think what they mean is that relatively large power distances and the obligation to show respect to those in higher positions usually determines their behavior in a group. Because leadership is hierarchical and also personalized in many collectivist culture groups, members sometimes compete for the good opinion of the leader. Several times when I have asked students to form project groups, the members were so focused on me as the leader-teacher that they paid no attention to the other members of the group. Instead of presenting their project as a group, they each presented their own piece of the project to me. My classroom group experiences are not necessarily typical of groups in collectivist cultures, but probably the usual teacher-centered teaching methods encourage Chinese students to expect groups to have strong leaders and relatively weak working relationships among members.

Competition for approval from the leader often prevents other subgroups from forming. Relationships among members may be neglected as members focus most of their attention on the leader. The usual exception is when members are co-members of other important ingroups. In that case they may stick close to their ingroup members and not reach out to form relationships with other group members who are strangers or members of outgroups. I have sometimes been surprised to discover that two students who have been in the same English department section for several years never had a substantial conversation with one another until I put them in a work group together in class. Even though they spent several hours a day in the larger group, they interacted mostly with their own ingroup members within the class.

Non-hierarchical Chinese groups

Most of my group experiences with my collectivist culture Chinese students have been very positive. Usually students have already formed close-knit cooperative groups in the department, class and section by the time I meet them in their second year of university study. These groups have small power distances between formal leaders (class monitors) and members. Even if members are similar and the leader's rank is not much higher than that of the members, it takes time for members to know one another well enough to establish an intimate relationship in which everyone participates. These groups develop structures that more closely resemble group culture social relationships on Kluckhohn's chart. In this case the storming stage is not focused on the leader as much as on the group members. Informal hierarchies develop in these low power distance, collectivist culture groups based on regard for particular classmates' academic standing, cooperative attitude, or attractiveness. Even within these mostly harmonious and cooperative groups, some members have higher status and prestige than others. Sometimes the students do form subgroups that are relatively distant from one another. Occasionally one or more students will have a bad reputation if some behavior or characteristic puts them outside the range of acceptable group behavior. Once these group roles and positions have been negotiated among the members, they tend to remain stable over the life of the group.

Storming: Members find their places in the group		
Group Issue	**Individualists**	**Collectivists**
Position and status	Achieve status and influence by forming alliances with leader and group members	Status depends on status in the organization or status in important ingroups
Relationships with other members	Friendly and informal with everyone	Polite and determined by status; stay close to ingroup members
Group structure	Negotiated among members	Defined by hierarchy or leader
	Complex division of roles	Less division of roles
	Sub-groups may form to complete tasks or to gain a competitive advantage within the group	Sub-groups are used only if the leader requires them
Leadership	Leadership is shared among members	Only the leader should behave like a leader
	Formal leader role is only one leadership role, so rank of leader is not so important	Formal leader must be highest ranking member
	Leader gives guidelines; members decide the specifics	Leader defines specific tasks
	Challenge the formal leader if necessary	Defer to the formal leader; offer ideas and give advice indirectly
Competition among members	Open and focused on group issues	Hidden and focused on the person
	Members may compete for status and influence with any other member	Members may compete for a favored relationship with leader
	Compete by out-performing competitors	Compete by creating problems for competitors
Challenges	Stabilizing relationships	Competing openly
	Maintaining harmony	Thinking and behaving independently

252

The challenge for an individualist participating in a group with collectivists is to respect the need for harmony and find less confrontational ways of competing. The individualist also needs to learn to work within a more stable pattern of hierarchical relationships. Collectivists in individualist culture groups need to build relationships with other members, including strangers and outgroup members, and not devote too much energy to pleasing the formal leader. They should also experiment with open debate on group issues and compete with other members by performing well on group tasks.

A danger for both individualist and collectivist groups is that conflict and vying for position will go on and on, so that the group is not able to develop further by moving to the next stage.

Exploring Ideas

1. What characteristics of individualist groups and collectivist groups are evident in the groups you participate in? To answer this question, consider the characteristics listed on the charts.

2. How does the group you are describing handle its relationships with other groups? Do the relationships between groups follow a hierarchical pattern? What groups are above and below the group in the hierarchy?

3. How is competition among members handled in the groups you participate in? Is it open or hidden? What strategies do people use to compete? To what extent is jealousy a problem in your groups?

Stage Three: Norming

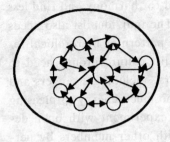

When a group is norming, the focus of group life shifts from "I" to "we."

The group is norming

The group establishes its identity and values

The title of the third stage refers to norms or values the members of the group agree upon as basic to group life. At this stage members of the group are aware of themselves as a group. The focus shifts from specific relationships and conflicts within the group to the group as a whole. Notice that the diagram shows the group boundary at this stage. It is dark and thick to show that members are focused on activities and relationships inside the group and are aware of the boundary that separates the group from other groups.

When members are competing or vying for favored positions during the storming stage, among the issues they work out is what behavior and attitudes will be valued in the group. Are members expected to defer to the leader at all times, or is it permitted to propose an alternative course of action? Are members who compete by trying to perform well on group tasks valued members, or do others consider them too ambitious? How much variation in personality and ways of participating in the group is acceptable? Is it permissible to be a little different, or should all group members try to be as much alike as possible? Is this a good group to belong to, or is it a burden to be a member of this group? Once most of the members agree on some basic issues like these, the group becomes more cohesive. They have reached agreement on norms, and by doing so have achieved an identity as a group.

Individualists commit themselves to goals

This is much easier to achieve if all the members are from the same culture and have similar expectations for the group. In general individualist culture groups will form around agreement on goals and tasks. Western teambuilding training often emphasizes this aspect of group life and refers to it as team spirit. Members have team spirit when they are committed to reaching the goals of the group, when they believe their team will prevail over competing groups, or when the team members are committed to working together to achieve a high standard of excellence in their work. Team spirit can be strong, but in individualist culture groups it may falter if members start to doubt whether the goals of the group can be reached. Sometimes collectivists observing individualist groups are surprised by how readily individualists will compromise on issues that are important to collectivists. For example, an individualist culture negotiating team may change its position on an issue in the middle of a negotiating session. The explanation is that individualists are so committed to achieving goals that compromising on other issues seems like the right thing to do. This cultural difference has often been noted when Chinese business groups negotiate with Western business groups.

Collectivists commit themselves to people

As a general rule collectivist culture groups form around commitment to the members of the group. Goals may be important but feelings of closeness among group members are often more important. Some collectivist culture groups may reach this stage more quickly and easily than is typical for individualist culture groups. The exceptions are when members participate primarily as representatives of other groups, or when conflicts are

255

so hidden that they never get resolved. The relative ease with which collectivist culture groups coalesce may be because members can influence one another with appeals to collectivist values such as loyalty, duty and harmony. The problem for collectivist culture groups at this stage may be that the values around which the group forms stress relationships rather than goals. The norms may help the group to form, but in the long run, they may become barriers to further group development.

Individualists emphasize procedures for decision-making

An important norm in any group concerns how decisions will be made. Because individualists prefer smaller power distances and consider processes important, members of individualist culture groups usually think that everyone in the group should participate in planning and decision-making. The formal leader has an important role in defining issues and goals and then may ask the group to make some choices about how to work toward those goals. In discussing issues, group members may expect everyone to give an opinion or state a preference. Typically various options are discussed in a meeting. If members disagree and the issue is not one the leader feels he has to control, then the group may decide by voting. For instance, if a work group is deciding in which restaurant to have a holiday party, voting works well. The decision is not critical to the life of the group and neither the group as a whole nor individual members have much to lose if a poor decision is made. It is a way to show group members that they have a role in making decisions and that the group makes decisions by following processes that are fair and impersonal. More important decisions are not usually made by voting, but often involve discussion among members about the advantages and disadvantages of each option available to the group. If the group members can't reach agreement through discussion, the decision may go back to the leader or may be delegated to a particular member who will have primary responsibility for acting on the decision.

Collectivists emphasize the leader's role in decision-making

In collectivist cultures the authority of the leader is likely to be more central in decision-making. If the group is one with a large power distance between leader and members, the leader may make all decisions, large and small, and simply tell members what to do. In groups with smaller power distances, the leader may still be central to decision-making, but will consult with members privately, so that most important decisions are a synthesis of everyone's thinking. I have seen this consultative style of decision-making and it is often very effective. The leader may begin by announcing a new project for the group. The discussion in the group meeting is mostly a matter of the leader giving information and inspiring group members to get involved with the project. After the meeting the leader informally talks to group members to hear their ideas and suggestions. The leader considers all the ideas, analyzes and synthesizes, and then announces the decision at a formal meeting. The advantage of this decision-making method is that the group is not asked to choose between options presented by various members. Because there is no public debate, group members do not have the feeling that some members won and others lost. Because the leader is responsible for synthesizing, often decisions incorporate all or many of the suggestions made by group members. When this happens, many members are affirmed, because they recognize their ideas in the final decision. The whole process encourages a strong commitment to decisions once they are made. If the collectivist group leader does this well, the group will probably function well.

If any leader, either collectivist or individualist is only passing on instructions from a higher level in the hierarchy, then decisions may not be as good. Members will not be very committed to these decisions, but collectivists may be more willingly to comply based on their cultural value that those in authority should be obeyed. Compliance, however, is a weak form of commitment and may result in members devoting only minimal energy to group tasks. They may comply in a superficial way while they pursue their own interests and goals, even when those interests are inconsistent with the intentions of the higher authority.

Members become more aware of boundaries

At the norming stage of group life, members are especially aware of the boundary between their group and other groups. Sometimes a group will achieve its sense of togetherness or identity of this stage in a way that leaves some members outside. These members are still technically a part of the group, but they feel like outsiders and may behave like outsiders. Another possibility is that the group will develop a series of groups within the group. At the center is the leader. Next is a small group of people who are closest to the leader and who are most frequently consulted when decisions are made. Further from the center are other members who have less influence and less critical roles to play in the life of the group. Membership in the various rings within the group may be determined by a member's position in the formal hierarchy, or may be the result of personal selection by the leader.

In individualist culture groups, boundaries both within the group and between the group and other groups are usually easier to cross than is typical of collectivist culture groups. To understand the issue of boundaries, review the contrast in Chapter Nine: Building Culture into the Landscape between the grid pattern and the inside/outside pattern. Because Chinese culture follows an inside/outside pattern, thick, difficult-to-cross boundaries are especially typical of Chinese groups. The danger for collectivist groups at this stage is that members become overly dependent on the group and feel so secure within the group that members fail to look beyond the boundary for relationships and resources that it needs to do its work well. At this stage members cooperate with one another, so they are able to do the work of the group, but if norms discourage cooperation with other groups, the group may have to rely too much on the expertise and other resources held by members of the group.

Individualists are more likely to specialize group roles

Individualist culture groups usually have an easier time developing a system of specialized roles within a group than collectivist culture groups do. Individualist culture norms stress doing, that is, achieving results on tasks. Tasks are often seen as technical problems so that technical solutions are required. This attention to technique supports the efforts of individual members to develop special skills, and this in turn leads to the development of specialized roles within the group. This is what we see in Western sports teams. One team member may be a specialist in defense while another specializes in offensive play. The specialization of roles enables the group to develop a high level of expertise, but the weakness is that the group may suffer if it loses one of its experts. Another problem for individualists is that group norms are often so focused on tasks and goals that the emotional needs of members are neglected.

Norming : The group establishes its identity and values		
Group Issue	Individualists	Collectivists
Commitment	Commit to goals of group	Commit to people in group
Loyalty	Be loyal to personal goals and team goals	Be loyal to people, in-groups, and leader
Negotiation	Compromise to accomplish goals	Honor important principles; maintain dignity
Motivation	Work hard to get the job done efficiently	Work hard to avoid burdening group members
Group boundary	Relatively open	Relatively closed

259

Decision-making	Include everyone in planning and decision-making	Planning and decision-making are the leader's responsibility
	Follow proper procedures	Sense opinions and desires of members
	Make decisions by discussing issues openly	Leader decides after consulting members privately
	Speed up by voting	Speed up by having leader decide
Group roles	Specialized roles	Members have similar roles
Communication norms	Express opinions and persuade others	Maintain harmony
Challenges	Maintaining a warm group feeling	Crossing boundaries; differentiating roles
	Building consensus	Using procedures for decision-making

In collectivist culture groups the pressure for conformity to group norms may be very high. If the norm is that everyone in the group should be the same and essentially do the same things, then the group may not be able to create a system of specialized roles. This is a weakness when the job of the group requires new and sophisticated methods to achieve its goals, but it can be an advantage because all members are able to do the various jobs the group needs to accomplish. Another problem that collectivist culture groups sometimes have is that norms stress relationships over tasks. Issues tend to be more personalized than in individualist culture groups. A collectivist culture group can benefit by taking advantage of strong group feeling and high levels of cooperation to look more objectively at how the group is functioning. Perhaps members need more technical skills or could improve their communication skills. There may be advantages to adopting some Western attitudes toward planning, assessment and measurement as a way of improving the group's functioning in the future. This may be difficult to accomplish if group norms support stability over change. Some members may be afraid that

260

introducing changes will upset the familiar and comfortable patterns of group life.

Challenges for individualists and collectivists

At this stage individualists are challenged to consider the advantages of the consultative style of decision-making used by effective Chinese leaders. This is a way of overcoming the disadvantage of having to choose between a limited number of alternatives advocated by various members. Individualists also often need to devote more energy to maintaining and supporting a warm group feeling and to valuing members who contribute more to group feeling than to achieving group goals. Collectivists are challenged to use procedures for decision-making to reduce dependence on the leader as the focal point for all decisions and to develop a system of specialized roles. Collectivist culture groups often need to open their boundaries and look outside the group for additional resources.

Exploring Ideas

1. Based on your own group experience, make a list of the characteristics of a good leader. Consider what you appreciate about the leadership of your parents or grandparents in the family, your class monitor and your university department or program leaders. Share your list with others in a small group discussion. In the group compile a list of important leadership characteristics to present to the class.
2. Analyze the flow of communication for each of the groups you participate in. Do messages move more easily from the top of the hierarchy down? How easy is it to move information from the bottom up? Is it best to wait for the leader to ask for information or do members offer information even when no one asks for it? What kinds of information move from the top down and what kinds of information move from

the bottom up? Who receives the most information and who sends the most? Does the sending and receiving of information depend on the person's position in the group hierarchy?

3. Analyze member-to-member communication for the groups you participate in. Does the communication between members stress feelings or tasks? Is one member more important than others in setting the values the groups will follow? Such a person is often called the normative leader whether or not he has a formal leadership position. Do group members look to one member more than others for guidance on how to complete a task well? This person is called the task leader whether or not he has a formal leadership position. Is one member more influential than others in creating the feelings that other members tend to adopt? This person is the emotional leader. If you continue this kind of analysis you may find that group leadership is shared even though the group thinks that only the formal leader is leading.

4. Analyze the boundaries in your important groups. Is there a smaller group of group members who seem more central to the life of the group than other members are? Do some members seem detached from the life of the group, only participating when they are required to and not sharing the group feeling? Try to diagram your group using a series of circles around the center of the group showing where each member is in relation to the center. If identifying with the group, sharing group values and feelings is the true measure of group membership, then where is the actual boundary of the group?

5. How much pressure is there in your important groups to conform to group values and standards of behavior? To what extent can you be different from other members and still be considered a good group member? Is it easier to be an individual in the group at one stage in the life of the group than at some other stage? Do group members become more or less accepting of individual differences over time? To what extent

do the values of the group change over time to accommodate individual differences?

Stage Four: Performing

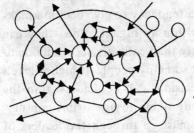

When a group is performing, it is doing its work.

The group is performing

The group acts to achieve results

In the fourth stage of group life, the members have found their places in the group, and the group has decided on its basic values and patterns, so more energy becomes available to accomplish the work for which the group was formed. Members do not need to devote so much energy to working out relationships and deciding how decisions will be made, as these features of group life have stabilized. Unfortunately not all groups successfully resolve the issues of the earlier stages. In that case, the group will be able to accomplish some work, but the weaknesses in the group's structure may prevent it from being as productive as it could be. Some groups keep on storming forever. Other groups form with a negative identity that discourages members from devoting themselves to the goals of the group. Other groups are hampered by poor decision-making methods or inadequate communication patterns.

Often, however, this is an especially pleasant period of group life and it can continue indefinitely. The challenge for groups that reach this stage successfully is to continue to change and adjust with changes in its environment. The group needs to be both stable and adaptable. Individualist culture groups and collectivist culture groups typically have to deal with different problems as they try to do that.

Individualists may require more time to implement decisions

Because individualists have a tendency to give decision-making authority to various levels within an organization, they can often make decisions more quickly than collectivists. Individualist groups do not have to consult so many people at higher levels in the organization, so many decisions can be made within the local group. Collectivists are more likely to use a time-consuming process of consultation that must go through the leaders of several levels of the hierarchy. Individualist culture groups, however, are often slower to act on decisions. Individualists continue to think of themselves as separate persons even when they are members of groups. Just as they think it is necessary to negotiate during decision-making, they also think it is necessary to negotiate how the group will act on its decisions. This slows down implementation. Once a collectivist group has made a decision, no further negotiation is necessary, so acting on the decision does not take much time.

Individualists can cross group boundaries more easily

Individualist groups do have some advantages at the performing stage. They are not limited by group boundaries. The relatively more open boundaries of individualist culture groups enable them to cooperate with other groups and share resources more readily than is typical of collectivist culture groups. Individualists often have broad horizons and search widely for resources. The individualist culture practice of delegating decision-making authority makes it easier for subgroups to work independently and form their own relationships with other groups. It is not necessary for all these matters to go through the leader.

Collectivists may have difficulty sharing leadership roles

In collectivist culture groups the leader is the main communication center, so members have fewer ways to coordinate their work with one another. Everything has to go through the leader. It can be a difficult burden for one person no matter how conscientious or capable.

Strong personal leadership has definite advantages in the early stages of group life. When the group is forming the leader defines the goals and objectives and lets the members know how things will be done in this particular group. Strong leadership in a hierarchical pattern helps members orient themselves to the group quickly. This pattern causes problems in later stages as it prevents members from developing their own leadership capacities. Once members are familiar with goals and purposes and commit themselves to them, they can benefit from a more flexible leadership pattern and more open patterns of communication.

The challenge for collectivists is to share leadership with members when they are ready. This enables the group to take full advantage of the expertise of all group members. A Chinese manager educated in the West once told me that he gave a worker on his project team a raise in pay because the worker had disagreed with him in public. He wanted the other team members to know they were not expected to defer to him all the time.

Sharing leadership and working out a system of stable but flexible roles enable the group to take on more complex tasks. This is what happens on a modern sports team. Winning a match usually requires a complex strategy in which each player can be depended on to play his specialized role and coordinate his actions with those of other team members. If each player is relating to the coach as an individual and competing with other team members for the most favored position on the team, the team is unlikely to win. This may help explain Chinese success in individual sports in which the athlete's close working relationship with the coach helps to improve performance. A different pattern is needed for a successful team.

Individualist culture groups also excel at evaluating outcomes and using information from their evaluations to change the way the group operates. This objective attitude toward their own functioning enables them to see their group as a piece of technology to accomplish tasks. If the technology is not working well, figure out what the problem is and make the necessary changes. They reorganize the group and reassign roles more readily and more often than collectivist culture groups.

Performing: The group acts to achieve results		
Group Issue	Individualists	Collectivists
Acting on decisions	Negotiate how decisions will be carried out	Once decision is made everyone does whatever is necessary to carry it out
Specialization	Assign specialized tasks according to abilities of members	All members do essentially the same tasks or tasks are assigned by rank
	Integration of specialized tasks is an important job	Assembling individual contributions is usually enough
Relationships with other groups	Share resources across groups if everyone benefits	Keep resources and information within the group
	Cooperate with other groups if helpful in achieving goals	Use personal relationships to link to other groups
Evaluation	Outcomes should be measurable	State outcomes positively and in general terms
Group learning	Use outcomes to improve performance	Learn by following models
Rewards	Publicly acknowledge individual effort and achievement	Publicly acknowledge group effort and achievement
	Some members may contribute more so will receive greater rewards	All members contribute so all should receive the same reward

Personal Outcomes	Build skills and accumulate accomplishments to achieve long term goals	Build social network to use in the future; pursue goals of important in-groups
Challenges	Strengthening group relationships	Strengthening task and evaluation functions
	Caring for members	Sharing resources across group boundaries

Collectivists are proud of their group

When evaluating outcomes collectivist groups tend to celebrate the accomplishments of the group rather than reporting its strengths and weaknesses and making concrete plans for improving performance in the future. Collectivist culture group members identify with their groups more strongly and are genuinely proud of their accomplishments. They want to uphold the dignity and honor of their group in relation to other groups. These expressions of group pride are more acceptable in a collectivist culture than expressing pride in your own personal accomplishments. Collectivists also tend to view the group more subjectively and are not accustomed to analyzing its functioning as if it were a piece of technology. Another factor that discourages objective analysis of outcomes is that the structure of roles within the group may be more fixed than in individualist culture groups. If members are assigned their group roles according to their positions in formal hierarchies, the group has fewer options for reassigning roles.

Individualists are less loyal to their groups

Individualist culture groups are not usually as good at meeting the emotional needs of group members as collectivists are. They may excel at specializing tasks and then integrating all those specialized tasks, but they are not as attentive to the relationship needs of group members. With a stronger commitment to tasks than to people, they break their ties with the group

267

more easily than collectivists usually do. The individualist moves on to pursue long term goals. This makes individualist culture groups less stable.

Because individualists tend to be members of a particular group for a shorter time, they have less opportunity to learn from more experienced group members. Individualist culture groups are more likely to use formal training as a way to provide group members with the skills they need. In collectivist culture groups, the preferred way of learning is for newer member to follow the models provided by the senior and more experienced members of the group. A Chinese working for a joint venture company complained to me that when the joint venture replaced foreign managers with Chinese managers, the opportunities for special training decreased. Her Chinese manager saw training as a reward for loyalty rather than as a way to increase the expertise of the staff.

The issue of loyalty also helps explain the difficulty collectivists have in sharing resources and information across group boundaries. Emotionally collectivists are looking inside the group and experience other groups as "not us". Exchanges of information and other resources occur in the context of personal relationships, and the relationships with members of other groups are not close. The only way to solve this problem is to communicate through the formal hierarchy or to establish personal relationships with members of other groups. Often collectivist culture groups have to identify a member who has a relationship with someone from a specific group in order to gain access to a resource the other group controls. This tendency to personalize all relationships severely limits the resources each group has access to. I once expressed my frustration at not being able to get a resource I needed from another university department by indignantly asking, "Are we a university or a collection of walled cities?" I was told that in order to get what I needed the head of my department would have to talk to the head of the

268

other department.

Individualists expect to be rewarded as individuals

Because individualist culture groups assign different roles to various members, and because members do not identify as strongly with the group, members expect to receive different rewards. After all, each member made a different and measurable contribution to the work of the group. In collectivist culture groups it is typical for all members to be rewarded equally. When a foreign coach was offered the job of coach for a Chinese national sports team, he said, "I can't take the job unless I'll be allowed to control salaries." Until then the team had been following the collectivist culture practice of paying all team members the same salary. In individualist culture team sports some positions are considered more crucial to the success of the team, so players in these positions receive higher pay.

Exploring Ideas

The purpose of this activity is to give you experience evaluating the functioning of a work group. It takes approximately four hours to complete.

1. Divide the class into four groups, one for each stage of the lifecycle of a group. Each group will prepare a presentation for the whole class for its assigned stage of group life (one hour).

2. Each group gives its presentation (approximately 10 minutes per group).

3. After all the presentations have been given, evaluate the work of your group (one hour):

   Group feelings: Describe your feelings as a group member by rating the statements below from 1 (never) to 10 (most of the time).

   When everyone has completed the form, meet as a group to

discuss the feelings in your group.

Feeling	Rating
Not involved with work of group	
Energetic	
Worried about doing the job well	
Confident the group will succeed	
Confident I will perform well	
Eager to follow the lead of others	
Irritated by behavior of some members	
Comfortable with group members	
Enjoying myself	
Bored and uninterested	
Competitive with other groups	
Proud of the group's accomplishments	

Group roles: Rate each group member from 1 (little or none) to 10 (does frequently) for each of the following group roles. Complete the form individually. Then meet as a group to discuss the roles each member in the group played. Also describe the leadership, the communication patterns, and the task roles for your group.

Group role	Member	Member	Member	Member	Member
Speaks as representative of whole group					
Speaks for self only					
Resolves conflicts and reduces disorder					
Remains calm					
Defines own role					
Encourages initiative and decision-making in others					
Offers suggestions					
Makes decisions					
Directs activities of group					
Asks for information from the teacher					
Asks for information from other groups					

270

Supports other members					
Stays focused on the task					
Integrates work of members					
Evaluates what group is doing					

Group effectiveness: Rate each of the following outcomes from 1 (not achieved) to 10 (achieved very well). In your group, discuss the extent to which goals were achieved.

Outcomes	Ratings for:		
	Self	Group	Class
Strengthened relationships with group members			
Performed well in group presentation			
Increased ability to observe group process			
Improved communication skills			
Improved decision-making skills			
Improved leadership skills			
Improved ability to evaluate strengths and weaknesses			
Improved ability to set goals			
Improved ability to work toward goals			

4. Meet as a whole class to share results of the small group evaluations and to evaluate the work of the whole class on this activity (one hour). What needs to be done to improve learning from this kind of activity in the future?

271

Chapter 14: Managing in Organizations

When taking cultural values to work, the first step is to recognize cultural differences in the extent to which people think relationships between people should be equal, that is, look at power distance. At the same time, notice the other important contrast in social relationships, the one between individualism and collectivism.

The remaining two pairs of contrasting values we learn from Hofstede's research,
- masculinity versus femininity, and
- uncertainty avoidance,

are useful for making more precise distinctions between cultures that seem to be similar when using only the first two pairs of contrasting values.

For instance, we know that Northern European and North American cultures tend to be low in power distance and high in individualism while Chinese culture is high in power distance and low in individualism. The next step is to understand the ways in which Swedes are different from Americans and the ways in which the British are different from Germans. Similarly, Westerners can use Hofstede's Masculinity Index and Uncertainty Avoidance Index to recognize differences between Japanese, Malays, Koreans and Chinese.

Toughness and tenderness

Hofstede named his third pair of contrasting values masculinity versus femininity, but this is misleading. What he is measuring with this scale is the extent to which everyone in a society embraces values that have traditionally been associated with men, that is assertiveness, competitiveness and toughness. On the feminine side of the scale we find societies in which people generally embrace values that have traditionally been labeled as feminine, that is modesty, cooperation and tenderness.

According to Hofstede, in the most masculine countries, both men and women are relatively tough, but in these countries there is a significant difference in expectations for men and women. Men are expected to be strong; they should fight to protect their interests. Women are expected to be nurturing and sensitive to feelings. In more "feminine" countries there are fewer differences in expectations for men and women. In these countries no one should fight and no one should be too ambitious. Everyone should be concerned with maintaining good relationships with others. Because the more tender values are characteristic of both men and women in more feminine countries, these values are more influential in the society as a whole. The fact that Hofstede is from one of the world's most feminine cultures, Netherlands, may account for his identifying this previously ignored cultural difference.

In the United States, a relatively masculine country on Hofstede's scale, the women's movement emphasizes encouraging women to become more like men. Women are encouraged to seek jobs traditionally held by men and to take training courses in assertiveness and self-defense. Advocates for women's rights have worked to get laws changed so women now earn the same salary as men for the same work, and work rules have been changed to eliminate special privileges for women. Women are encouraged to be just as career-oriented and ambitious as men.

In the Scandinavian countries, which are more feminine on Hofstede's scale, the women's movement has stressed sharing family responsibilities between men and women. Both men and women have a legal right to take time off from their jobs to take care of children. These countries also have strict rules against using physical punishment to discipline children.

In Japan, by far the most masculine country included in Hofstede's survey, men are expected to devote themselves to

273

their careers, while women stay at home with the children. While at home, however, women spend their time supervising their children's study so they can compete successfully on examinations. Women and children also have to be tough because failing in one of the many examinations has serious consequences. Young women go to work when they finish school, but at work they often perform roles such as greeting, entertaining, and serving others. In more feminine countries, school failure is not as serious, and women's work roles are similar to those of men.

Attitudes and behaviors	Toughness (Masculinity)	Tenderness (Femininity)
Social values	Ambition, achievement, and material success	Caring for people and cooperation
Social goals	Economic development; progress	Protecting the environment; preserving what already exists
Gender role differences	Different expectations for men and women; men are tough and women are less tough	Few differences in expectations for men and women; both should be tender
Assertiveness	Men should be assertive and ambitious; women should not be ambitious but should teach children to be tough	No one should be too assertive or ambitious; everybody should be modest
Family roles	Fathers deal with facts and mothers deal with feelings	Both fathers and mothers deal with facts and feelings
Expectations for children	Girls cry; boys don't; boys should fight back when attacked; girls shouldn't fight	Both boys and girls are allowed to cry but neither should fight
Resolving Conflicts	Resolve conflicts by showing strength and fighting them out if necessary	Resolve conflicts by compromise and negotiation
Management style	Managers should be resourceful, decisive and assertive; they are visible	Managers should be resourceful but not visible; they use intuition and strive for consensus

Decision-making	At meetings individuals show how good they are; decisions are made elsewhere	At meetings common problems are discussed and solutions sought
Social attitudes	Reward the strong; big and fast are beautiful	Sympathy for the weak; small and slow are beautiful
Opinion leaders	The top student in class; the most successful businessman	The average student; the ordinary person

In his research Hofstede found many differences within national cultures on the values of tenderness and toughness. He found that young people, regardless of gender, tend to have more masculine (tough) values than older people do. He also found differences by occupation. Sales people regardless of gender have tougher values than managers do, and managers have tougher values than unskilled industrial and office workers do. He explains this by pointing to the competitive nature of sales work. Managers have to be good at both achieving goals and relationships. Unskilled workers are not able to compete as well as highly educated workers, so they are more likely to value cooperation among colleagues and the security of their jobs.

Because the values of toughness and tenderness combine with other values and vary within cultures as well as across cultures, it is a good idea to consider them as modifiers of other values. For instance, in China with its large power distances and strong focus on collectivism, the value of harmony restrains competitiveness within groups, while tough values support competition between groups. The implementation of market reforms supports competitiveness and tough values in general, while those working in more traditional industries may have more tender values regarding work. Those with higher positions in work organizations may be expected to be tough, while those occupying lower positions may be expected to be more modest.

For several years I noticed that the boys in my classes tended to sit in the back rows of the classroom and did not answer my questions unless I called on them. In general the girls were more cooperative and tried hard to win my approval. As is true in most foreign languages departments, the girls outnumber the boys. As English majors the boys were already seen as being less tough than boys studying science or business. They did not want to make matters worse by openly competing with the girls. In the last few years, this has changed. Now the boys are more active and cooperative. In recent years the department has stressed the business uses of English, has installed computers, and has sponsored many contests and debates. I think the boys see the departmental culture as more masculine now, and that accounts for the change in their attitudes.

Country or Region	MAS	Country or Region	MAS
Japan	95	Arab countries	53
Austria	79	Malaysia	50
Switzerland	70	Brazil	49
Mexico	69	Singapore	48
Great Britain	66	Israel	47
Germany	66	Taiwan	45
Philippines	64	Iran	43
USA	62	France	43
New Zealand	58	Spain	42
Hong Kong	57	Netherlands	14
India	56	Sweden	5

Figure 14 Masculinity Index for selected countries and regions

The scores for countries and regions on Hofstede's Masculinity Index cover a wide range. The Scandinavian countries and the Netherlands are the most feminine, while Japan is significantly more masculine than Austria, the next most masculine country. For countries in the middle of the scale, it is necessary to pay attention to the particular ways that tough and tender values are expressed in each culture. The countries and regions that are culturally Chinese all fall in the middle of the scale, although Hong Kong seems to have significantly tougher values than Singapore and Taiwan. Among Asian countries Thailand (34) and South Korea (39) are the closest to the tender side of

276

the scale.

Exploring Ideas

1. How do you explain the significantly higher score for Hong Kong as compared to Taiwan and Singapore on Hofstede's measurement of tough and tender values?

2. Do you think that your country's social welfare system should protect the weaker members of society such as the elderly, children, and people who are poor or disabled? Or do you think that it is more important that laws and policies reward members of society who are capable and hardworking? Where do you think the balance should be between the values of toughness and tenderness?

3. Hofstede found that people working at different jobs have different values. In thinking about your present or future work, do you think your chosen field requires relatively tough or relatively tender values? Does this match well with your personal values?

4. Europeans do not like it when Chinese think that all Westerners are like Americans. A Swedish friend gave me her views on the differences between Swedes and Americans that reflect differences in cultural values of tenderness and toughness. After you read it, try to predict additional differences between Swedes and Americans.

Swedes and Americans are not alike

Swedes tend to think Americans are superficial and overly proud of themselves because they talk a lot. Swedes generally don't mind silence. If you pause for a while before answering a question or saying something about the topic being discussed, to a Swede that means you find the question or topic important and you're thinking before you talk. It also tells a Swede that you're intelligent.

Also, Swedes don't like it when people talk about how good they are at something. You may be very good at something, but you're supposed to deny it and say you need to learn more or something like that. And don't interrupt!

If someone offers you a gift, it would be suitable to seem a bit embarrassed or moved, and always offer to pay for your meal if you go out together.

Americans are always surprised when I say I think American women are not very liberated. In Sweden, men on the average do forty per cent of the housework. Younger men do more, and older men do less. In the US men can't stay home with their babies. In Sweden they can receive several months of paid leave to take care of their babies. In the US you find more women in top executive positions but it seems they had to give up a lot to get there.

Uncertainty avoidance

How do you prefer to organize your life? In a structured way, making decisions and knowing where you stand, or in a flexible way, discovering life as you go along? If you prefer structure and want to know what to expect in most situations, then you are trying to avoid uncertainty. A person who is relaxed and at ease, even when he does not know what will happen next, is showing low or weak uncertainty avoidance.

I once met a group of Chinese teachers traveling on a train from Lanzhou to Nanjing. It was almost midnight when we arrived. I had a home to go to, but they had to find a hotel for 15 people in an unfamiliar city. I was surprised that they all seemed so at ease. If I had been in their situation I would have been anxious about where I would sleep that night.

The Uncertainty Avoidance Index seeks to measure the extent to which people in a particular society are able to tolerate the unknowns of life. Are the unknown and unfamiliar seen as threatening or is the unknown merely curious and perhaps even stimulating and interesting? If a country scores high on uncertainty avoidance it indicates that for most citizens the unknown is assumed to be undesirable. It is also a measure of tolerance for ambiguity. People from low uncertainly avoidance countries do not have a strong need to control things, people, and events by clearly defining and categorizing them.

Germany and Great Britain have similar scores on the first three of Hofstede's pairs of contrasting values, but Germany is higher than Great Britain in uncertainty avoidance. In Germany there is more emphasis on following rules precisely, on having the trains run on time, and on formal structure in organizations, all ways to reduce the unpredictability of life. In high uncertainty avoidance countries people experience more stress and a sense of urgency as they go through their daily routines.

Attitudes and behaviors	Strong Uncertainty Avoidance	Weak Uncertainty Avoidance
Sense of well-being	High stress; anxiety	Low stress
Emotional Expression	Aggression and other emotions can be expressed	Aggression and other emotions should not be expressed
Diversity	What is different, is dangerous	What is different, is curious
Motivation	Security, esteem or belonging	Achievement, esteem or belonging
Innovation	New or unusual ideas are resisted	New or unusual ideas are tolerated
Time	Time is money	Time is only a framework

Country or Region	UAI	Country or Region	UAI
Japan	92	Switzerland	58
France	86	Netherlands	53
Spain	86	New Zealand	49
Mexico	82	USA	46
Israel	81	Philippines	44
Brazil	76	India	40
Austria	70	Malaysia	36
Taiwan	69	Great Britain	35
Arab countries	68	Hong Kong	29
Germany	65	Sweden	29
Iran	59	Singapore	8

Figure 15 Uncertainty Avoidance Index for selected countries and regions

Management styles

The value differences of tenderness and toughness and weak and strong uncertainty avoidance are frequently overlooked. If you are working for a manager from another culture or serving a customer from another culture, it helps to know the person's home culture score on these pairs of contrasting values. With that information and an understanding of the values the indices measure, you can better anticipate what the manager or customer is likely to expect from you.

Even these finer distinctions among cultural values are still generalizations. Not everyone in a culture is the same, and every culture includes people of various personality types. The purpose here is to encourage you to notice value differences so that you can adapt to them. You will have to do your own observations to improve on the generalizations presented here. With this caution in mind, we can identify four different management styles, each with variations, by combining what we have learned from studying these two pairs of contrasting values.

Weak Uncertainty Avoidance

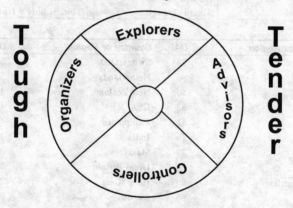

Strong Uncertainty Avoidance

Figure 16 Management styles

Explorers are risk takers who value their own and other people's ideas

Managers who can be characterized as explorers are risk takers so they like new ideas and like the people they work with to have ideas also. If the explorer type manager has the tender values typical of countries with low scores on the Masculinity Index, he is likely to be good at promoting other people's ideas as well as his own. He will notice your new or unusual ideas even if you have not fully developed them and will help and encourage you to communicate them to others. With tougher values this manager is likely to stress the development of new methods, technologies and ways of working. He wants to find out if the new approaches will work. The explorer manager values creativity.

Controllers value accuracy, dependability and efficiency in their workers

Controllers value predictability, so they emphasize inspecting the work that has been done and controlling the procedures for producing quality work. They want things to be done correctly so they value accuracy and precision in the people they work with. With more tender values this manager is likely to emphasize maintaining and safeguarding standards in all aspects of work. With tougher values he is likely to focus on production. He wants to see things moving on toward completion. Is the output satisfactory? Are the contracts ready to be signed? This manager values accuracy, dependability and efficiency.

Organizers value efficiency and effectiveness in themselves and others

Organizers with their masculine cultural values are good at making things work. They are active as they implement procedures and methods to make everything go. If they are risk takers they will use their organizing skills to develop new products, methods and ideas. They will figure out how to test and assess to find out if the new idea is practical. This type of manager emphasizes outcomes and wants to keep things moving. If the manager is more inclined toward security he will focus on making what already exists more productive. This manager values efficiency and effectiveness.

Advisors value resourcefulness and appreciate sensitivity to relationships

The managers who are described as advisors tend to have tender values and are, therefore, apt to be modest about themselves but attentive to other people. They are good at getting information, perhaps because others find them trustworthy and non-threatening. As good listeners and observers they often know more about what is going on than others do. Other managers and staff like to discuss problems with them, because they are attentive and resourceful. They are more effective managers of people than technical processes as they pay more attention to people than to things. If they are risk takers they reach out beyond the organization to find new information and resources. If they value security they stress maintaining a good work environment and relationships. They are good at resolving conflicts because they try to find a way to reconcile opposing viewpoints. This manager values resourcefulness and sensitivity to relationships.

Exploring Ideas

1. Try to predict what managers and customers from various cultures are likely to expect from the people they work with by analyzing the scores on all four of the indexes. For instance, if a Human Resources Manager from a Singaporean company were coming to your campus to recruit university graduates for positions in his company, what do you think he might be looking for in a potential employee? What should you emphasize in an interview with this manager? Try the same exercise with other countries and regions for which you have scores.

2. Imagine that you are applying for a job. Prepare a résumé describing your education, work experience and qualifications. Then write four different letters of introduction, each one suitable to be sent to one of the four types of managers described above. Do not change any facts about yourself to

282

meet each manager's expectations, but decide what to emphasize about yourself and how best to interpret or present the facts to each of the four managers.

The culture of organizations

Recently experts in management have been discussing organizational cultures. By this term they mean that every company or organization has a unique culture. Each company has its own values, history, customs, attitudes, relationship patterns, and preferred ways of working. We can also describe the special language, symbols and emotional atmosphere of a particular company. Organizations, however, are not like national cultures in some important respects. People usually have a choice about joining them; they join them later in life, and they only participate in them during the hours of work. Despite the limitations of using the concept of culture to describe organizations, it does encourage us to see organizations as a whole. Using the concept of culture directs our attention to the out-of-awareness or less obvious characteristics of organizational life.

If you are applying for a job with a foreign company or working for one, it is helpful to understand the characteristics of its organizational culture. As with national cultures, interviewers and managers often have difficulty describing their organizational culture because they take it for granted.

In a later book Cultures and Organizations: Software of the Mind (1991) Hofstede extends his analysis of work related values by using his pairs of contrasting values to describe the cultures of organizations. He begins his analysis by telling a story.

In the 1970s Owen James Stevens, an American professor, was teaching at a business school in France. He adopted the customary practice in business schools and gave his students a case study for the final exam in his organizational behavior course.

The case described a textile company in which two managers were in conflict. The marketing manager wanted to accept small orders for fabrics from fashion companies. Often these orders had to be filled on short notice, but the manager felt that if the company filled these small rush orders, then they would get larger orders from the fashion companies later. The production manager disagreed. He had the job of changing the dyes in the machines, and he felt that these small orders were costing the company too much money. He had to shut down machines and clean them before processing each order. From his perspective, too much time was spent cleaning machines and not enough time was spent dying fabrics. He wanted the company to refuse the small orders.

The students were asked to diagnose the organizational problem and make recommendations for solving it. Over the years Professor Stevens noticed that students gave different answers depending on what country they came from.

The French students said they thought the problem was that the general manager had not resolved the conflict. The two managers should take the problem to the general manager who would tell them what to do. He would give orders that would settle how this conflict was to be handled in the future. Stevens felt that the French students saw organizations as pyramids of people with the manager on top.

The German students said they thought the organization lacked the proper structure. The areas of responsibility of the two conflicting managers had not been clearly defined and there were no procedures for making this type of decision. The German students described methods that could be used to develop the necessary structure and procedures for making these decisions. Stevens felt that the German students saw organizations as well-oiled machines.

The British students said the problem was the result of the poor negotiation skills of the two managers. They recommended that both managers be sent to a management course to improve their relationship skills. Stevens felt that the British students saw organizations as village markets in which people have to negotiate each new situation.

Stevens's observations of his students' preferences for how to solve organizational problems can be explained by combining the country scores on the Power Distance Index and the Uncertainty Avoidance Index.

When Stevens made his observations he did not have any students from Asia. And when Hofstede first described organizational cultures using the values of power distance and uncertainty avoidance, he did not identify a type for cultures with large power distance and low uncertainty avoidance scores. Later when he discussed these models with colleagues from India and Indonesia, they suggested that in their cultures organizations resemble extended families. The owner manager is like the father or grandfather. He resolves the problems that occur, and he assigns tasks to the workers. Typically workers do not have very specific job descriptions and activities are not highly structured.

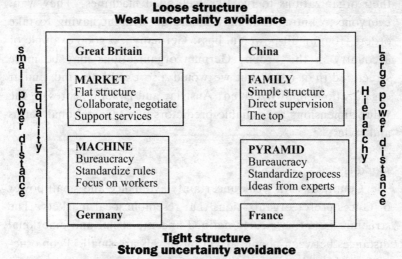

Figure 17   The culture of organizations

Pyramids

In countries with large power distance and strong uncertainty avoidance, people like power and authority to be concentrated in one person and they like activities to be structured. A country with this combination of values is France, but this organization type might also be found in countries with a similar combination of power distance and uncertainty avoidance scores. This group of countries includes Guatemala, Mexico, Korea, Japan, and Greece. In Japan it is not formal rules, but informal rules in the form of customs and accepted ways of do-

285

ing things that define the structure. These informal rules are quite fixed and have the same effect as formal rules.

Machines

In countries with small power distance and strong uncertainty avoidance, people prefer to structure activities without concentrating authority at the top of the organization. They want their organizations to run like well-oiled machines. They want everyone to know what they should do without having to take orders from an all-powerful boss. Germany is a good example of a country in this group. German organizations may be more structured than most, but we would also expect to find similar organizations in Switzerland, Austria, and Israel if scores on the value dimensions are reliable predictors of organizational forms and styles.

Markets

Countries with weak uncertainty avoidance and small power distances prefer organizations that resemble local markets. The structure is not as clearly defined and the social and emotional distances between people at various levels are small. People negotiate, bargain and generally work out problems as they arise. Good relationship skills are essential for managers in this type of organization. Hofstede cites Great Britain as an example, but Ireland, Denmark, Sweden and, to a lesser extent, the United States, Canada, Australia and Norway also fit into this group of countries.

Families

Countries and regions rooted in Chinese culture tend to combine large power distance and weak uncertainty avoidance. People in other Asian countries such as India and Malaysia show similar patterns. In these places the preferred organizational form is a strong leader and a rather loose structure. The very powerful owner-manager operates like the father or grandfather of an extended family. The boss makes decisions and his policy takes precedence over formal procedures. Employees at lower levels in the organization may have high level professional skills and good ideas about how something could be improved, but they will not contradict the boss. The issue is not what the employee achieves but whether or not the leader favors him.

Exploring Ideas

1. Organizational cultures also vary within national cultures. Study job postings, advertisements, public statements, brochures and personal reports about a particular organization. From these sources of information, describe the culture of the organization. Give specific examples to support your conclusions about the basic values of the organization that you are studying.

2. As a class project form small groups to investigate several foreign-owned, joint venture and Chinese organizations in your area. Use several different sources of information to get as objective a view as possible of each organization. For instance, interview people who work for the organization, study brochures and advertisements, read news reports of the organization's activities, and listen to public statements leaders make. Report your findings about the culture of your group's organization to the class. Compare the cultures of the organizations your class has studied.

Chapter 15: Persuading across Cultures

As China increases its contact with people around the world, Chinese organizations and individuals are busy preparing messages they hope will persuade audiences in other countries. Often the people involved realize they need expert help in crafting their messages. As a native speaker of English I am sometimes asked to give that help. The local television station has asked me to edit texts and read the English narration for television programs they plan to send abroad. Students ask me to read the personal statements they plan to send to universities in the US or Europe. Usually the people who ask for help think that what they need is a native speaker to read a text translated from Chinese, or someone with a good feel for English grammar to make sure the sentences they first composed in Chinese and then translated are correct.

The Chinese people who ask me to help them prepare messages for readers, listeners or viewers abroad nearly always underestimate the requirements of these communication situations. They mistakenly assume that the problem is only a matter of using the basic language code properly and correctly. With few exceptions, they are totally unaware of cultural differences in how people use language to communicate. They do not realize that a message that carries a particular meaning in the sending culture will be interpreted as having a different meaning in the receiving culture, even when the words are perfectly grammatical. Achieving a perfect translation does not solve the problems of communicating across cultures.

How to improve a Chinese student's essay

A student writes a short essay that is poorly expressed and grammatically incorrect. Perhaps she is translating from a Chinese essay:

> Many people would like to feed a pet when they were a child, it is because they are lovely, cute and they would not cause any unfortune to people. People can speak out their unhappiness and secret to these little creature and make sure those secret would not be heard by themselves from others mouth. For this reason, animal become a good friend of human being. If you like to start feeding a pet, there are a number of questions you should first consider, for example: Choose a suitable animal as a pet for yourself, make sure you can prepare a reasonable place for them and can spend time on them etc.

Correcting the language does not make it a good essay by Western standards:

> Many people like to keep pets when they are children. That is because pets are lovely and cute and do no harm to people. People can express their sadness and reveal their secrets to these creatures and know that they won't hear these secrets coming out of someone else's mouth. For this reason, animals become good friends of humans. If you want to keep a pet, there are several issues you should consider. First, choose a suitable pet. Then, make sure you are able to provide a suitable place for the pet to live. Finally, think about whether or not you have enough time to spend with your pet.

A Westerner who reads the corrected version of the Chinese student's essay will not be satisfied, and will undoubtedly consider the essay boring and meaningless. The essay is not persuasive, because it does not include enough information to convince the reader that the writer knows what she is talking about. It does not sound authentic or sincere. It carries no authority, even though the writer is bold enough to give the reader advice.

An American teacher gives the following advice for improving the writing:

> I suggest helping the student to find something meaningful to write about. Does she have a pet? Does she want a pet? Does she know someone who

has a pet? She should write about something she knows. Even with assigned topics, students can learn how to make the topic personally relevant and to write from observation.

I discourage (sometimes prohibit) the use of words like lovely and cute. What did the student observe about the dog, cat, or child that made her think it was lovely or cute? Ask the student to describe the appearance or behavior that led to that evaluation.

Maybe the student can write about choosing a pet. Does she have experience in choosing a pet? Does she know of people who made good or poor choices? Encourage her to write from observation and experience. The important thing for her is to discover what she personally has to say about the topic. After she writes something meaningful, then you can help her correct the grammar. That is the last step in the writing process, polishing.

The problem is that the Chinese student is following the rules of writing from her home culture. This includes a tendency to use words in ways that are characteristic of high-context cultures. (See "How people use words" page 61.) In the student's mind, it is important to write a proper essay. Writing an essay is a social situation with its own rules and social expectations. The Western reader also has some concerns about the form of the essay, but to him words are primarily meant to convey information. If the essay only follows a form and does not include information that is useful or interesting, then the essay has no meaning. That is why the American teacher stresses the content and makes correcting the form of the language code the final consideration in helping the student to improve her writing.

A writer or filmmaker from one culture who thinks he has prepared a message that will persuade his international audience as surely as it would persuade his home culture audience, is probably mistaken. In Chapter Seven: Perceiving Culturally you saw that it is often difficult to find meaning in a painting from another culture, because the way that people represent or depict the world varies from culture to culture. It is the same when the world is represented in language. In translating messages created in one language for listeners or readers or in another culture, we

290

cannot be certain that our meaning will be understood. Further-more, we cannot be sure that even if the meaning is understood, that the receiver will find the message convincing or even appro-priate for the situation.

Painting pictures with English

When I teach English composition, what I read in student essays often reminds me of a Chinese painting. For instance, a student might use the phrase "naughty boy" without further de-scription. Over the years I have come to understand that "naughty boy" is an image, a fixed phrase, that represents a perceptual object in the mind that carries with it details that it is not necessary to describe further. When a Chinese writer uses the phrase "naughty boy" or "lovely girl" he expects the reader to have many associations with that phrase and to use those asso-ciations to fill in the details. The problem is that a Western reader does not make the same associations with these phrases that the Chinese writer does. The Western reader does not have the same perceptual object in his or her mind. Western readers are accustomed to having details described concretely and fully, so they will not make those associations or even use their own as-sociations to fill in the details. To them these phrases sound vague and empty.

Native English speakers teaching writing in China often comment that their students' writing is rich in visual and other sensory images, but at the same time they also say that it is too sentimental. What they mean is that Chinese students tend to idealize what they are writing about. The writer is presenting a person, memory, or situation as he or she thinks it should be rather than how it is observed to be. The writer may not intend to portray a realistic picture of the world. Foreign teachers cau-tion one another, "Don't ask them to write an essay about their mothers or grandmothers. All you will get is stereotypes about devotion and sacrifice. They will all sound alike."

Another problem is the way essays are organized. We saw that in Chinese painting the eye of the viewer is assumed to move across the surface of the painting, while in the Western painting there was one focal point, one spot from which the viewer looks at the painting. Again this cultural feature from art shows up in written language. Chinese essays frequently begin with very general statements. The paragraphs often contain information that seems to be unrelated to information in other parts of the essay. The writer's opinion or recommendation is often not expressed directly or is stated in a weak form. A Western essay has a fixed focal point and all the details in the essay are arranged in relation to that focal point. The opinion of the writer is expressed strongly near the beginning of the essay.

Below are the contrasts I have noticed between Chinese and Western writing in English.

	Chinese writing	Western writing
Style	Poetic	Objective
	Present an ideal picture	Present a real picture
Purpose	General; make a good impression	Specific; persuade the intended audience
Main Idea	Reader infers the writer's intention	Main idea is stated at the beginning
Introduction	Broad perspective	Opens close to the specific topic
Language	Create an impression	Convey concrete information
	Sensory images	Observable facts
	General statements	Specific statements
	Reader fills in detail	All relevant details included
Structure	Loosely structured	Tightly structured
	Points need not be related to one another	Points are related to the main theme
Argument	Present all sides and let reader decide	Convince the reader
Statistics	Included in text	Given in separate chart
Conclusion	Present an optimistic view of the future	Restate and expand main idea
	Urge reader to behave well	Urge the reader to take a specific action

Chinese colleagues and friends inform me that precise, accurately observed writing is also highly valued by Chinese. This is undoubtedly true. Why then, does so much of the English writing I read have the characteristics I have described?

Part of the problem might be the way English is taught. Often teachers and students are focusing on mastering the forms of the language and are not emphasizing its communicative function. The result is that students display their mastery of English rather than learning to use English to convey meaning. They are writing beautiful English essays rather than writing informative essays for particular readers. This is not the only problem, however, as the serious miscommunications also occur when the original text is written in Chinese.

One problem is that writers are following principles that we saw in Chinese landscape painting. They are following their home culture rules about how to represent the world in the literary form of the essay.

Other cultural characteristics also contribute to the problem. I often read texts that seem to be oriented to the writer or to groups that are important to the writer rather than to the intended audience. For instance, the text may refer to important people, events or political positions that are not meaningful to an international audience. The writer's purpose in these cases appears to be to demonstrate that he is a loyal member of his significant groups. Writers often show their regard for hierarchies by using terms like "top", "leading", and "famous". Writers should keep in mind that readers from cultures with lower power distances do not find these statements convincing unless they are supported by specific facts.

This is my advice for translating Chinese verbal pictures into English verbal pictures.

Translating concepts from Western art into English writing	
Paint a clear realistic picture.	Avoid giving a general impression and do not expect the audience to use their imagination to fill in the details. Do not idealize your topic, your audience or the facts.
The eye of the viewer is held constant.	The speech or report should have a clear constant theme or organizing idea that is stated at the beginning. This is what is meant by a clear focus. Remember that the Western painting has a known light source. Your "light source" is your main idea. Everything in your speech or essay should be related to it.
The eye does not move around from one thing to another.	The facts or observations should be organized in relation to the central idea. Other material is considered irrelevant. Your reader or listener is staying in one place, that is, focusing on your main idea. Don't expect them to move away from it.
Facts are solid, objective, unchanging, and separate from the observer.	Support recommendations with objectively observable facts. Facts should be related to each other in a logical way.

Exploring Ideas

Read the following case and answer the questions that follow. The criticisms Wu Weimin received from his boss indicate that he may have been painting Chinese pictures with his English words.

Case 17 Work Performance Review

Work Performance Review

Wu Weimin had just started working for a Swedish company that had extensive business commitments in China. A large part of his work concerned advising his expatriate colleagues on Chinese business practices. This involved both writing reports and recommendations and addressing meetings.

As he was very anxious to succeed, Wu Weimin always researched his topics thoroughly and tried to make his presentations as clear as possible. However, he gradually became aware that something was wrong. It often seemed that nobody listened to him and his advice was ignored. When he spoke at meetings, he felt that people were impatient and uninterested in what he had to say. He got more and more unhappy and began to feel that his colleagues were not interested in his opinions because he was Chinese. This, he thought, was racism.

The company had a policy of annual review, which meant that every staff member met with the managing director once a year to discuss his or her progress. When the time came for Wu Weimin's review, the managing director gave him a copy of the company's assessment of his performance. The assessment praised his hard work, but made the following, very serious criticisms:

1. When speaking at meetings, arguments are often unfocused and speeches lack clear direction.
2. Written reports contain too much irrelevant material.
3. In both speaking and writing, material is poorly organized, with important recommendations often appearing only at the end of the report.
4. Often appears uncertain about the points he wants to make.

Wu Weimin was shocked by these criticisms. He could not understand why they had been made and he was not sure what to do about them.

1. Why do you think the company criticized Wu Weimin in this way? Do you think he is correct to conclude that the problem is racism?
2. What cultural expectations about presenting information oral-

ly and in writing may account for the negative evaluation of
Wu Weimin's work?
3. Give advice to Wu Weimin to deal with each of the specific
criticisms the managing director made.

Moving beyond translation

What follows are a few segments from the narration for a
videotape prepared by a local commercial district. The visual
images matched the text, so you can probably imagine what they
looked like. Some were entirely appropriate, but the pictures
were "sentimental" in the beginning when the text is poetic.
Graphics and maps should have been included to convey information that is hard to remember when it is presented in sentences. In later sections the visuals showed new buildings without any people. Obviously the local people are proud of the
buildings, but they would be more successful if they minimized
expressions of local pride and considered what would be attractive to the audience that was watching the video. Another problem was the sound track. It featured American music that was
slow and traditional. Choosing a particular piece of music simply
because of the country it came from was a mistake in this case
because the music did not convey the energy this type of video
should have.

When I went to their TV studio to record the English narration, they gave me the script that had originally been written in
Chinese and told me that they intended to take the video to the
US to seek investors for the commercial district. That was their
purpose, but they stated it only weakly and at the end.

Welcome to JN Commercial District	
The English translation reflects the poetic quality of the opening of the Chinese version	Nanjing is a city of ancient capitals with the Purple Mountain soaring in the east and the everflowing Yangtze River running through.

296

A Western audience needs precise geographic orientation. Rewrite: "Southern Jiangsu Province is located at the intersection of two of the most prosperous and rapidly developing areas of China: the East Coast and the Yangtze River Valley"

The purpose of the video should be stated at the beginning.

Numerical data is not presented effectively. Give data that demonstrates economic strength to support the claim that it is a top county. Give population of Nanjing and NJ county. Give all data in graphic form.

Remarks about Dr. Sun Yatsen are not responsive to the audience. To Americans he is not an authority on economic development. The statement is idealized and too general.

The local fame of Qinghuai River is not relevant. Potential investors want to know if it is scenic (tourist development) or navigable (transportation).

Show a map that locates nearby economic enterprises. A potential investor wants detailed information about neighboring facilities to assess the market potential of the area.

Businessmen also want to know about telephone and postal service.
General statements are giving an ideal rather than a realistic picture of transportation.
Insert a transportation map showing markets that are accessible from the District.

This part of China is known as Southern Jiangsu. It is a land of treasures, of cultural relics, of numerous legends and a land of marvels. And Nanjing, capital of the province, is the central metropolis on the mid and lower reaches of the Yangtze River.

To the southeast of this modern city lies its close neighbor, JN County of Jiangsu Province, one of the top hundred counties in China in terms of overall economic strength. With an area of 1600 square kilometers, JN County surrounds Nanjing on three sides, and is closely integrated into the city. The county enjoys a long history, a well-developed economy, beautiful environment and rich natural and human resources.

Dr. Sun Yatsen, leader of modern Chinese democratic revolution, once stayed in Nanjing and he remarked, "This is a piece of land rarely to be found among the world's metropolises. It will surely enjoy a bright and boundless future.

Covering an area of 38 hectares, JN Commercial District has at its back Dongshan Hill which is of historical interest, and is surrounded on its three sides by the famous Qinghuai River. To its east we can find China's largest high-tech agricultural development zone and the largest gold foil producer; bordering on its west is the National JN Economic Development Zone. To its south is the province's first private-run High Tech Industrial Park.

The Commercial District is a hub for air, water and land transportation, with a number of national highways running through it, which provides easy access to the neighboring cities including Shanghai and Hangzhou. The city is only 8 kilometers away from Nanjing and is 18 kilometers from Nanjing's Lukou Airport.

Numerous tourist attractions are within easy reach of JN Commercial District. If you head east, a dozen kilometers drive will bring you to the world renowned Dr. Sun Yat-sen Mausoleum and the eastern suburbs of Nanjing, a beautiful place to visit at any time of the year...

Greatly encouraged by Deng Xiaoping's South China tour in 1992, the people of JN were determined to complete the Commercial District in five years time. In fact, the District is a totally new area in Dongshan Town. Its layout is well-planned, with business facilities, office and hotel buildings, residential quarters, restaurants and entertainment centers.

It is really a hard job to accomplish to complete a totally new district within five years without outside investment. People of JN realized that to attract investors, they had to provide the basic facilities.

The forward looking developers didn't hesitate to pour money into the facilities. Over 15 million US dollars has been invested in the infrastructure and other projects . . .

Investors keep coming. The first was Yiming Real Estate from Guangdong Province that spent 1.2 million dollars in the purchase of a piece of land here. Within two years time, two phases of apartment buildings were completed and most of the apartments were sold out. The next to come was a Hong Kong real estate group whose first phase construction of apartment buildings has also been completed.

In 1995 The Commercial District cooperated with the local government's department of supply and established the largest auto market in the county. The business there has been prosperous.

Statement of purpose is weak and comes at the end. Avoid a vague and inflated ending. "We welcome forward looking investors who want to position themselves well in the Chinese market."	We, the developers of JN and its Commercial District, are expecting all forward looking investors who see the potentials here and will give serious considerations to JN when they are trying to well position themselves in a highly competitive world of business. Let us share the opportunity, the potentials and the benefits. Welcome to JN and JN Commercial District!

Displays of status symbols, text that communicates local pride rather than giving information, and numerical information that is irrelevant or lacks the context to make it meaningful are not effective. Large photos showing an enterprise's product and people at work, and text with a clear purpose that is responsive to the information needs of a foreign reader are effective.

Understanding the role of the translator

In this case a translation of the Chinese text, however well done, will not be persuasive. When I am asked to edit similar texts, I tell the translators who bring them to me that they need to rewrite the text rather than translate it. Any corrections I make in the English sentences will not solve the problem. They usually tell me that they realize the text is not suitable for an English speaking audience, but say they have no choice, because they have been told to translate. The manager involved mistakenly believes that it is the job of the English translator on the staff of the business enterprise or government agency to translate from one basic language code to another. Money is wasted, time is lost, and opportunities are missed because managers of enterprises have such a limited understanding of the true value of having an English translator with the appropriate cultural skills on staff.

When this happens, the translator first has to convince the manager that communicating to an international audience re-

299

quires putting the facts and information in a form that is attractive, meaningful and persuasive to the Western audience for which they are intended. It also means that someone on the staff needs to be sensitive to cultural issues in visual presentation as presentation of language. In fact, all the cultural knowledge you have acquired is relevant to the design of a publication for an international audience.

Exploring Ideas

1. Rewrite the text of a Chinese brochure, pamphlet, magazine or advertisement with a Western audience in mind. Describe what pictures, graphics, charts and other visual elements should and should not be included. Design a new layout that is sensitive to the cultural expectations of a Western reader.

2. Design a bilingual pamphlet for a self-directed bicycle tour of a section of your city. Keep the needs of both domestic and international visitors in mind. What sites will be attractive to each group. What are the information needs of each group? The user of the pamphlet should be able to follow the route you lay out without a guide. Show placement and layout of pictures, maps, etc.

3. Design a web page to introduce your department, program or organization to a specific international audience. Define your audience as concretely as possible. Consider the cultural background, possible motivations and expectations of the specific visitors you hope to attract to your Internet site. View Internet sites developed in Western countries to identify their characteristics. What can you offer visitors that will make your site appealing? How can you get the attention of people who visit your site? How can you keep them looking at and reading what you have to offer?

Negotiating

As we have seen, publications and videos that are intended to persuade are not necessarily persuasive to readers or viewers from a different culture. This also occurs when people try to persuade one another face-to-face, that is, when they negotiate. How do you persuade a company to offer you a job? How do you persuade the members of a negotiating team to accept your company's terms for a contract? How do you resolve a disagreement that occurs between two people from two different cultures? Strategies of persuasion in these and other situations vary from culture to culture.

You need to use all that you have discovered about the hidden aspects of culture from your experience and from reading this book when choosing strategies for negotiation. For instance, Westerners tend to stress process when making decisions. Their emphasis on process encourages them to develop what are known as "fair play rules", rules about procedures that assure that decisions will be made fairly. They also expect others to be as concerned about following the rules as they are. Sometimes Westerners are described as legalistic, meaning that they expect people to follow precise rules contained in laws, contracts, and agreements. People from high context, collectivist cultures are more likely to be concerned about relationships, ingroups and outgroups, and status than about particular rules. These differences influence the negotiation strategies used by each side.

Westerners think negotiations progress when the parties get down to work on specific details. A good relationship comes from reaching agreement on many specific items. A Western negotiating team may begin by enthusiastically promoting their ideal position as to how the details can be worked out, then gradually pull back through a series of compromises to whatever positions the Chinese negotiators are willing to accept.

Chinese negotiators usually avoid discussing details in the

301

early phase of negotiations. Instead they discuss mutual interest and general principles. When the Westerners commit themselves to these, a commitment that the Westerners may not take very seriously because of the lack of details, Chinese negotiators will appeal to those mutual interests to get the other side to agree to what the details should be. This is consistent with the collectivist culture preference for doing business with partners with whom a trusting and durable relationship has been established. When such a relationship is formed, there are no precise limits on what one party should do for the other. Chinese negotiators are not nearly as legalistic as Westerners and do not completely share the Western view that a contract is a complete, binding, and limiting set of requirements.

Because decisions are usually made through consultation with several levels in a hierarchy, Chinese negotiators may not be free to change their positions during actual face-to-face negotiating sessions. Even if they are free to change their position, they may be unwilling to, because to change a position may be seen as a loss of respect for the person or group that is negotiating. If a negotiating team faces opposition, they are likely to keep on restating their original position. After the formal session the negotiators will discuss the issue with all the important decision-makers and may change their position at that time.

I had to learn this the hard way, through painful experience. When I first came to China and was negotiating terms and working conditions with various units of my university, I expected people to be persuaded by my reasonable arguments. When my Chinese counterparts did not immediately agree to what I was asking, I would continue the discussion and be frustrated by my lack of success. After several years I finally realized that I would get better results by simply stating what I wanted, giving good reasons and then going away to give those involved a chance to consider what I had said. Often the people I was talking to would come back to me several days later with a decision to agree to my request or with a new proposal.

Western negotiators are more likely to change their position in the middle of an argument and may be flexible enough to consult with colleagues in the middle of a session. This flexibility can be explained as a desire to achieve the goal, which is agreement. The details can be changed if that helps to reach the final goal.

Exploring Ideas

Read and discuss the following case of a negotiation between Americans and Chinese.

Case 18 Whose Car Is It?

Whose Car Is It?

A joint venture in Beijing involved Chinese and American partners. American-recruited specialists were working together with Chinese specialists in establishing a factory. The American side of this project had provided most of the material and equipment necessary to start the plant, including a car. The use of this car became the focus of an on-going battle that was regularly raised at each semi-annual management meeting.

The Americans claimed that the car had been provided for project use during working hours and for private use for American project members outside office hours. They claimed that this implied that American team members should be able to drive it. The Chinese felt that the car should only be driven by authorized Chinese drivers, which effectively limited its use by Americans but increased its use by senior Chinese project members.

The conflict centered on the registration. The car first had a registration that prevented its being driven by the Americans. Their aim was to change this registration. The Chinese were apologetic—it could not legally be done. The Americans cited the Memorandum of Understanding that formed the legal basis of the project; they cited Chinese law and precedent. All agreed that it was possible. The Chinese authorities answered with a number of practical difficulties, but conceded that the Americans had the right to drive the car and promised to look into the matter.

Six months later nothing had changed. The matter was again raised at the semi-annual management meeting. The right of the Americans to drive the car was again acknowledged, difficulties again mentioned and action again promised. Six months later, nothing had changed.

1. What does having the car mean to the Chinese group and to the American group?
2. What strategies are the Americans using to get the car?
3. What strategies are the Chinese using to keep the car?
4. How would you explain the situation to the Americans? What more effective strategies can they use to achieve their goal?

Applying for a job

As we might expect, the most effective strategies for persuading a potential employer to offer you a job vary from culture to culture. You should use different strategies when presenting yourself as a candidate for a job in a Western company than for a Chinese company. For instance, Chinese applicants often think they should say that they are hardworking. This may be acceptable to a Chinese employer, but it will not be persuasive to a Western employer. Instead, you should be prepared to state what you have accomplished with your hard work. Referring to your hard work is a statement of your character. This may persuade someone with "being" culture values, but a record of accomplishments is necessary to persuade someone from a "doing" culture. (See page 206.)

Recently the fourth year English majors that I teach participated in a program on preparing for employment. Later they discussed what they had learned in their writing journals.

Students discuss job-seeking strategies

Now I have a general idea how we should behave in interviews. As the Human Resources manager of one company told us, honesty is the best policy. I have a former classmate who on his resume claimed that he could speak English fluently. In fact, his English was rather poor, so when he was interviewed his broken English annoyed the interviewers. He did not get the job and later said, "If I had not claimed that I could speak English very well, then maybe they wouldn't ask me to answer questions in English. If so, then maybe I would have gotten the job."

Liu Hong

A former classmate who studies in another department brought his roommate to me to translate his materials into English for a job fair. To my surprise they were quite poor in both format and ideas. Paragraph after paragraph attesting to the excellence of his school performance, but no information on his precise educational experience. So we had an honest talk. The concepts of being concise, writing a cover letter, and presenting materials in an attractive format were all new to my "client." In his Chinese introduction he used many adjectives to describe his hard work. I told him that in an English cover letter he should first say where he got the information about the company, in what ways he thinks he is better than similar candidates, and the specific qualifications he has for the job.

Yuan Limin

In Chinese resumes we usually include information about our family background and experiences in middle school, which generally are not included in English resumes. Chinese employers want to know your family, hometown, and middle school, because they think these things have a great influence on your personality. If you come from a decent and intellectual family then you are probably a quality person with a good disposition. Westerners pay more attention to your specific experiences and how you used them for personal growth.

Interviewers from state-owned enterprises told us that it would be disadvantageous to ask questions about salary and housing, because it would leave the impression that we pay more attention to payment than to the work we are expected to do. However, when we asked people who work for joint ventures, they said we should not hesitate to ask such questions.

Cheng Xin

In a Chinese resume we list honors, awards, qualifications, and experiences, but it is just a list to show how good we are as students. We don't consciously identify our skills. In an English resume we list our qualifications in a way that identifies skills relevant to our job objective.

Lin Min

Exploring Ideas

1. For each of the differences between Chinese and Western strategies for applying for a job the students describe, identify the cultural characteristic that explains the difference.
2. From your knowledge of cultural differences, identify further strategies that should be used when preparing resumes and participating in interviews in specific cultures.
3. Prepare two resumes and cover letters to present yourself to potential employers, one suitable for a Chinese company and the other for a Western company.
4. Read the following case and answer the questions.

Case 19 The Job Interview

The Job Interview

Jiang Anshi applied for a job as a computer programmer in a large foreign-owned computing company. Because he was very well qualified in computing and had extensive experience, he thought that he had a very good chance of getting the job. Three people interviewed him. They started out by asking him questions about his qualifications and experience. He answered confidently.

Suddenly, however, one of the interviewers asked him whether he could work in a team. Jiang Anshi was rather surprised at the question but said, "Yes." He was then asked why he was interested in this particular job. He explained that the job was very suitable for him as he had done similar work before. He also explained that the salary was better than the salary he was currently receiving. Finally, he was asked if he himself had any questions. He did not.

Jiang Anshi left the interview feeling that he had done well. However, he did not get the job and later found out that the successful applicant had less experience than he had.

1. What mistakes did Jiang Anshi make in his job interview? Why didn't he get the job?

2. Give him advice about how to conduct himself on his next job interview with a similar company.

3. Look for advice from several sources both Chinese and foreign about how to conduct yourself in a job interview. Report your findings to the class and point out differences in the advice depending on the culture of the person or organization that is giving it. Write and perform dialogues for two different job interviews, one for a Western company and one for a Chinese company.

Chapter 16: Adapting to a New Culture

Most people are familiar with the idea of culture shock. People use that term whenever they tell a story about problems Chinese meet when they go abroad or when they want to describe problems foreigners have when they come to China. It is a condition everyone knows is unpleasant, but they may not know exactly what is causing their discomfort. What is it about being in a new culture that causes the condition commonly known as culture shock?

Culture shock: Troublesome feelings such as depression, loneliness, confusion, inadequacy, hostility, frustration, and tension, caused by the loss of familiar cues from the home culture.

When a person is living in his home culture, he knows what people mean when they speak and act. He is able to interpret situations and knows how to respond. The world makes sense. When he leaves that familiar environment, he is deprived of familiar cues, familiar behaviors and meanings that reassure him that he understands the world. Suddenly meanings are not clear, and the person does not know how to respond. He feels disoriented. This is perfectly normal and occurs in situations other than moving to a new culture.

All through life people are confronted with new situations that require them to adjust their thinking and behavior. The most familiar one for university students is moving from home to the university. At one time or another during your first few months as a university student you probably experienced all the feelings listed in the definition of culture shock.

What you had to do when you began your university life was to adapt to a new social situation. Looking back on those days now, you can remember how excited you were to be going. You may also remember the pain of living away from home and adjusting to new circumstances without your family and friends to help you. Looking back, you can recall the pain and discomfort and perhaps the doubt you sometimes felt about whether or not you would succeed. For most university students those memories of their early days at the university fade as they adapt to university life. By the time they finish their studies most students only remember what a wonderful experience attending university was. They typically feel that they gained something that they could not have gained in any other way. In the process of adapting they learned how to cope with a situation that required them to learn new skills and new attitudes. They acquired new understandings of the world and became more mature and stronger people. This is exactly what happens when someone successfully adapts to a new culture.

The "shock" in culture shock emphasizes the pain and doubt that a person experiences when faced with a significantly new experience. These troublesome feelings are characteristic of some stages of the process of adapting to a new culture, but that is only part of the story.

Risks and opportunities

When put into any significantly new and challenging situation, the person faces risks and has opportunities. The risk is that the person will not adapt successfully. If the person is not able to endure the pain and overcome the problems, he may abandon the new situation and return to a life that is more familiar and comfortable. If that is not possible, he may continue to live in the new situation, but in a way that causes continuing difficulties for himself and others. If the person adapts successfully, he changes as a person. He acquires new skills, new attitudes, and a new outlook on the world.

Dangers	Opportunities
Loss of self-confidence	More confidence from meeting new challenges
Job loss	New job opportunities
Retreat into home culture	Ability to function in more than one culture
Negative feelings about other cultures	Appreciation of one's own and other cultures
More rigid personality	More flexible personality
Preference for familiar situations	Readiness to deal with unfamiliar situations

It is not easy to predict who will adapt successfully and who will not. Many factors influence the outcome of the adaptation process. Some factors involve characteristics of the person and others are related to the situation to which the person is trying to adapt. Government agencies and companies around the world have spent much time and money studying the adaptation process. Based on research results, international and national organizations have developed methods for selecting personnel they send abroad. They have also learned what they can do to modify the living and work situations of the staff they send abroad. They do all this to increase the probability that their staff will adapt successfully.

Preparing for a sojourn abroad

Preparing for a trip abroad is one concrete thing anyone can do to increase the chances of adapting to the new culture successfully. Good preparation will not prevent culture shock, but it can help to make it less severe. Taking the time to learn about the new culture helps the newcomer to anticipate what the new experience will be like. Knowing about the culture, including history, geography, social conditions, arts and customs, is one way to increase cultural awareness and to gain an intellectual appreciation for it. Keep in mind that your goal is to achieve Level Three awareness, so choose sources of information with this goal in mind. I have met people who devoted much effort preparing for an extended visit to China who picked up negative attitudes along the way. They came fully prepared for a life of hardship and deprivation, their suitcases full of medicines, clothing, household goods, and many, many other things they thought they would need to survive. Apparently they chose information that was out-of-date or contained biases that encouraged the person to adopt negative expectations of life in China as compared to more developed countries in the West.

In addition to information about the culture as whole, it helps to get specific information about the particular situation you are going to. Conditions vary widely within countries as well as between countries. Perhaps the Westerners who prepared for a life of hardship in China had read accounts written by people who lived in underdeveloped or remote areas of the country. The advice in these accounts may not be very relevant to someone who will be living in Beijing. Similarly a Chinese going to graduate school in a large European city will have a very different set of conditions to deal with than someone who is going as a technical expert to learn a specific technology in a factory in a small town.

Fluency in the local language is an advantage

Oral and written fluency in the language of the host culture helps the newcomer form relationships, get necessary information and communicate their needs and desires. If you do not speak the language of the country you are going to, it is usually not possible to make up for this deficit in the few months of preparation before you leave home. In that case, you must use the time you do have wisely. Concentrate on learning the vocabulary and phrases you are most likely to need in your particular situation. If your English learning stressed mastering grammar in order to pass examinations, then your pre-departure language study should emphasize listening and speaking skills. Watching films that show ordinary life are good for this. Even if you do

311

not understand all the dialogue, you are becoming familiar with the sounds of daily speech and increasing your familiarity with English conversation.

People who are going to a place where a language they have never studied is spoken have special problems. This is the usual situation for Westerners coming to China. They will benefit by learning something about the characteristics of the Chinese language. They can also listen to tapes to familiarize themselves with sounds, and they can learn simple phrases. I do not speak any language but English fluently, but I can ask for basic information and understand numbers and basic phrases in several languages. Local residents usually appreciate even this limited effort to communicate in the local language. People who have learned one or more foreign languages, even if none of these are the language of the country they are going to, have an advantage. The experts tell us that each new foreign language a person learns is easier to master than the previous one. The person who has learned several foreign languages has learned how to learn languages.

Consider motivation and physical and mental health when deciding to go abroad

Each person has to evaluate his own personality and his motivation for choosing to go to a culturally unfamiliar place. People who are attracted to the new culture because it provides something positive will adapt better than someone who is leaving to avoid problems at home. Sponsoring organizations such as companies and governments usually assess the personalities and motivations of those they send abroad. They have learned that professional expertise alone is not enough to assure a successful experience. It requires more energy to adapt to an unfamiliar situation than to cope with a familiar one, so physical and psychological health should also be taken into account when considering an extended stay in a foreign country.

Another important factor is the person's level of cross-cultural awareness in relation to the new culture. It should be Level Three. (See Four levels of cross-cultural awareness, page 28.)

Level One awareness is enough for a tourist going on an organized tour, because group tourists are protected from any unpleasant interaction with the unfamiliar culture. Everything possible is done to preserve or increase their sense that the foreign culture is exotic and entertaining. Unfortunately, some people going abroad have Level Two awareness of the culture they are going to. They expect the experience to be troublesome, difficult or unpleasant. Even so, they may choose to go, typically because a work assignment promises financial or professional rewards.

No one factor determines how well someone will adjust. When I meet the new foreign teachers who arrive at my university every autumn, I try to predict how each one will do. I do not always get it right. The older ones often do better than the younger ones, maybe because their experiences and motivation are more suitable to the teaching they will be doing. Sometimes those who do not seem so well-prepared do well, maybe because they expect to have a wonderful time.

Exploring Ideas

Imagine that you are going to a large urban American university for graduate study. To evaluate your adaptation potential, rate yourself on the adaptation checklist. Give yourself a score for each item according to the following scale:
1. Poor
2. Not as good as most people
3. Average
4. Better than most people
5. Excellent

Score	Adaptation Checklist Adaptation Factors
	Background and Preparation
	Age — youth is an advantage
	Education — the higher the better
	Urban background — city dwellers do better than rural residents
	High level of professional skill
	General knowledge of the new culture, its history, customs, arts, etc.
	Specific knowledge of the new situation; company, city, university, etc.
	Oral and written fluency in the language of the new culture
	Previous out-of-culture experiences
	Similarity of home culture to new culture
	Personality factors
	Tends to be accepting of different ways of doing things
	Likes to meet new people and do new things
	Stays calm in difficult situations
	Pays attention to people and not just to tasks
	Can tolerate ambiguous or uncertain situations
	Has a sense of humor
	Strong but flexible in character
	Willing to take risks; not too concerned about social and psychological security
	Attitudes and motivation
	Voluntarily chooses to be in contact with the new culture
	Attracted to the new situation rather than escaping problems at home
	Admiration and respect for the new culture (Level Three Awareness)
	No sense that one culture is superior or inferior to another
	Few stereotypes (inaccurate broad generalizations) about the new culture
	Health
	Robust good health
	Good health habits
	High energy level
	Total score

After you have completed the checklist, discuss it with your classmates.

1. What are your advantages and disadvantages in adapting to a new culture?

2. What can you do to increase your adaptation potential?

The adaptation process

Adaptation is a process with identifiable stages. Learning about the process will not prevent culture shock, but it will help you to understand what is happening to you. When I am feeling confused, frustrated or tense because of cross-cultural misunderstandings, I remind myself that the feelings are only temporary. If I am patient and choose good coping strategies, I will feel better and cope better eventually. I have already gone through all these stages in my long sojourn in China, but I continue to repeat them in small ways as I become increasingly more involved in my Chinese life.

Typically people experience the following stages as they adapt to a new cultural situation:
1. Excitement about the new situation
2. Confusion when faced with the hidden aspects of culture
3. Frustration when old ways of dealing with situations fail to work
4. Growing effectiveness as new skills are acquired
5. Appreciation as new skills and attitudes enable the person to live more fully in the new situation
6. Increased ability to deal with new and novel situations

Because adaptation is a process that occurs in any new situation, the person who stays at home but has continuous, long-term contact with a new culture also goes through the adaptation process. Chinese who go to work for joint venture or foreign owned corporations also have to adapt to a culturally unfamiliar environment. They and their expatriate colleagues are going through the process in different ways and experience different problems, but the process is the same. When they recognize the similarities in their experience, they can better understand and support one another.

Not everyone completes the process successfully. At the second and third stages the risk of dropping out is high. A Chinese worker in a foreign company may drop out by leaving his job, and the expatriate manager may drop out by returning home prematurely. Even people who stay do not necessarily adapt successfully. Some people who are in a challenging new situation develop attitudes or adopt behaviors that are not constructive. These may be a normal part of learning if they are temporary. If they persist over a longer time, they cause harm to the person and others with whom he lives and works.

With patience and attention to the adaptation process, most people can successfully adapt to a new culture. When they do, they will have learned a great deal about themselves and about how to live in the global village.

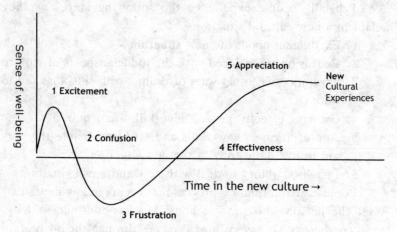

Figure 18 Stages of adaptation to a new culture

Stage One: Excitement

Except for refugees and others who are being pushed to leave home against their will, most people who go abroad to live temporarily or permanently in a new culture do so willingly. They have some specific purpose in mind such as furthering their education, pursuing economic or professional opportunities, or simply experiencing something new. Especially when friends and relatives put a positive value on going abroad, when they give it

316

high prestige or think they will also benefit, then the person who is going usually anticipates the experience with a great deal of excitement. This is especially true if this is to be an entirely new experience. Before leaving or before starting the new job with a foreign company, expectations for the new experience are high and generally positive. The excitement of this stage gives the person more energy than usual. On the chart this is shown as an increase in feelings of well-being above the baseline, above the level that is normal for that person.

The excitement of this stage typically continues through the early period after arriving in the new culture. Everything seems to be wonderful. The expectations the person has for the new experience have not yet been tested. The student might be impressed by the facilities at his new university and the helpfulness of the people he meets. The expatriate manager might be pleasantly surprised by his better-than-expected housing and by the professional attitude of the local staff. The new foreign teacher may find his students and colleagues particularly charming and cooperative. In all these cases the newcomer is using standards from his home culture to evaluate the situation in the new culture.

The newcomer reacts to the new culture

The problem in this initial period of excitement is that the newcomer is responding based on images and expectations of the new culture that were formed at home. These may or may not be accurate or realistic. At first the person sees only those things that are consistent with his expectations. He is likely to notice the ways in which the new culture is like the home culture. For instance, a businessman may notice that the workday and workweek are the same in China as they are at home. Job titles and the jobs to be done appear to be similar to those at home. The newly arrived person does notice what is different about the new culture, but at first these differences seem exotic and entertaining (Level One awareness) or easy enough to deal with. "I have to learn the language," the person says to himself, or "I'll pay attention to how the students study here and do what they do." In both cases the person is underestimating the difficulty of these tasks.

Sometimes suddenly and sometimes gradually, the newcomer starts to recognize that coping with the new situation may be harder than he first thought. At first he responds to problems with behaviors that work well in difficult situations at home. Be polite to the people around; show respect; be patient; work hard; ask questions; keep a sense of humor. This may work for a time, but sooner or later, these strategies fail to produce the desired results. One reason is that the high energy level of the first stage cannot be sustained indefinitely. It takes energy to cope with a new and challenging situation, so over time the person gets tired. This may show itself in minor illnesses or accidents, in a lower energy level, or less patience than the person had when he first arrived. Another factor that contributes to the end of the first stage is trying to live up to unrealistic expectations. Students think they can complete their courses as quickly as at home, and businessmen think they can solve organizational problems as easily as they have solved them at home. The stress of trying to meet unrealistic expectations drains their energy away.

Sooner or later the newcomer encounters cultural differences

Eventually the person will meet a situation in which home culture strategies for dealing with problems not only do not work, but make the problem worse. The student may work hard at his studies, but in the same way that he did at home, not realizing that the teacher is looking for an entirely different kind of response. The businessman may pursue his home culture strategy of bringing disagreements out in the open so they can be solved, without realizing that in the new culture being firm and direct

318

only hardens the resistance of the people he is negotiating with. When this happens, devoting more energy to solving the problem only increases the negative responses of the person receives from people in the host culture. Eventually the person can no longer avoid recognizing that he is not doing well.

This marks the end of the first stage and the beginning of the second.

Exploring Ideas

Two factors that effect the success of adaptation are the expectations the person has for the new culture experience and the support the person receives from the important people and groups in his life.

Great Expectations 1

A European-based joint venture company has just hired Mr. Wang. With his fine university record, English proficiency and good work record, he successfully competed with many other applicants to win the entry-level position. The company has just built a state-of-the-art factory in the outskirts of his hometown, which means that he can go ahead with his plans to marry without delay.

What does this new job mean to him and the people around him?

What will his mother tell the relatives and her friends about her son's new job?

Great Expectations II

For several years Mr. Stevenson has been working at the home office of the same company that just hired Mr. Wang. He has had previous work assignments in Europe, but now he has been asked to go to the company's new factory in China. He has traveled widely in Europe and has visited the US, but he has never been to Asia before. He wants to go but is not sure his wife will be as enthusiastic as he is.

What will Mr. Stevenson say to his wife to convince her that he should take the assignment in China?

---

1. Compare the expectations Mr. Wang has for his new culture experience to Mr. Stevenson's expectations. What support does each man have?
2. What difficulties do you expect each man to experience that

might bring the excitement of the first stage of adaptation to an end?

Stage Two: Confusion

The diagram of the stages of the adaptation process shows a line that rises and falls over time. The line represents the person's sense of well-being. At the beginning of the confusion stage, the line falls sharply, meaning that the person in an unfamiliar culture often experiences a sudden decline in mood or spirit. The person is no longer able to avoid facing the reality of the new situation. Cultural differences appear at every turn.

Doubts

Wu Lian, an English major studying at a university in the US, starts out confidently. She knows that her language skills are better than those of most Chinese studying abroad. At first everything is fine, but gradually she discovers that professors do not always present material in an organized way nor do they always speak clearly. Some are from other countries and speak English with a foreign accent; some talk into their chests; and others talk so fast that she cannot keep up. They expect her to read a whole book every week for each class! Several of her courses require her to write term papers longer than her graduation thesis. The library is so big and complex and lists so many resources on the assigned topics that she wonders how she will manage to do the necessary research.

Wu Lian finds she cannot understand the group conversations of her native speaking classmates. They use a lot of slang, make jokes she does not understand, and convey much of their meaning with subtle gestures she cannot decode. Some treat her kindly but like an incapable child; others expect her to know everything and feel and do as they do. The way they talk about "partying" frightens her. They sometimes invite her to join in their social activities, but she has neither the time nor the money to participate.

In the meantime she gets letters from her family and friends at home, expressing their pride and confidence in her. Her parents tell her to work hard and take care of her health. She is already studying more hours a day than anyone she knows. Fresh fruits and vegetables are so expensive, and the food in the dining hall is so unappetizing. Why don't they have street sellers here? She would like to cut costs by cooking for herself, but the local convenience store does not sell vegetables and it takes too long to get to the supermarket by bus.

Wu Lian writes to her parents, but what she tells them is not what she really feels.

Like most people, Wu Lian is trying very hard to cope with

the difficulties she faces. She is probably using coping strategies she brought with her from home. For instance, she may be trying to read all the books her professors assign as carefully as she read her English textbooks in China. She is looking for a dining room and markets similar to the ones she depended on at home. These strategies are not working, so she is starting to doubt her ability and the wisdom of her decision to attend graduate school abroad.

Typical problems of the second stage

Often at this stage newcomers misread or misinterpret the behavior and speech of the local people. Part of the problem may be limited language skills, but more important is a tendency to interpret meanings according to the home cultural grammar. When she hears her American classmates talk about their parents and teachers in a casual joking way, Wu Lian may think they have no respect for them. They may actually respect their elders, but according to the rules of social interaction among American young people, it is better to assert your emotional independence from such authority figures. She may hear her classmates making fun of elected officials and condemning the policies of the government and conclude that Americans are not patriotic. In fact most Americans think their country is the best in the world. She may overhear young people making sexual comments to one another and conclude that their sexual behavior is freer than it actually is.

A person in a new culture often feels disoriented and unable to predict accurately what people from the new culture will do or say. When a professor calls on her to answer his question in class, Wu Lian may respond by giving an accurate and thorough account of what she read in the book he assigned. He may respond critically saying, "Yes, Miss Wu, I can see you have read the assignment. Now, what do you think the author of the book you read last week would say about that?" She did not anticipate

321

that her teacher would expect her to argue against what she reads or even against what the professor says in class. She starts to feel that she is the only one who does not know what to do. Everyone seems to be more competent than she is. She feels at a disadvantage and strains to understand what is going on and what is expected of her. In this tense state, she redoubles her efforts and may go to the other extreme and overestimate what is expected of her. Quite possibly, Wu Lian is over-reacting to her classmates' wild talk about partying, and she might be overestimating the demands of her professors.

Wu Lian sees fast food restaurants and convenience stores that sell snacks and other packaged food all around her campus. She sees so many people eating "junk food" that she concludes that all Americans are careless about what they eat. In this case she is overgeneralizing. Many Americans are very conscious of eating well and prefer fresh fruits and vegetables just as she does. Because she is making an inaccurate generalization, she may fail to look for and find people whose food preferences are similar to hers. She is responding to her new culture as if everyone living there were alike. She is not able yet to see the many differences that exist within the culture. In this second stage of the adaptation process, all her energies are devoted to reacting to the new culture. She has little energy left over to initiate actions that could make her more comfortable.

Wu Lian's parents are right to worry about her health. If she continues to feel tense and anxious, she is likely to become seriously fatigued or suffer other health problems. They will undoubtedly continue to write their sympathetic and encouraging letters. They may even send her medicine from home. They will do everything they can to help, but they cannot do much, and their attempts to help may actually add to the pressure Wu Lian is feeling. I once watched a Chinese student in America collapse into tears while reading a letter from her parents. They had given her well-intentioned advice that increased her feelings of inadequacy and her fears of disappointing them.

Because of the time pressure she feels, lack of money, and her difficulty communicating with local students, Wu Lian may not develop new social networks that could give her support and help. She is comforted by the letters from home and may live emotionally in her memories of happier times. In her letters she pours out her love for family and friends and as a result feels temporary relief from her distress. If she relies on this too much, she risks becoming emotionally isolated.

Living in an enclave eases the difficulties of the early stages of adaptation

Wu Lian and other Chinese students studying abroad can avoid or postpone many of the problems described above by living in an enclave. These are special communities made up of people from the home culture. Many universities in Western countries have hundreds or even thousands of Chinese students, so it is often possible for a newcomer to find housing and friends from China at the new university. The advantages of enclave living include speaking one's native language, eating and living in a way similar to home, and having many associates who have more experience with the host culture than the newcomer. It is like living on a home culture island in the middle of the new culture. This island of familiarity provides an opportunity for rest and relaxation from the demanding work of adapting to the new culture. Here the newcomer feels understood and can get realistic help in coping with the new culture.

Westerners working in China also have enclaves of Western life. International companies often provide villas or apartments for their staff. Here the housing is similar to that in the home country and the neighbors are likely to be people who work for the same or similar companies. The residents organize activities similar to those they enjoy at home. They eat Western food and celebrate Western holidays. In some cities there are special international schools for the children of foreign workers where the teachers are from Western countries and the instruction is in English.

It sounds wonderful but there are disadvantages to enclave living. The enclave may be so much more comfortable than the host culture that the newcomer spends most of his time there and becomes overly dependent on it. There are Chinese graduate students abroad who are still unable to speak English beyond the minimum needed to complete their academic work even after years of living in an English speaking country. Their social contacts are entirely within the enclave, so except for a few professors and fellow students, they have no relationships with host culture people. The same is true for some Westerners living in enclaves in China. Expatriate workers rely on company employees who speak English, and all their business and social contacts may be with other Westerners and a few English-speaking Chinese. The situation is usually worse for their family members who usually do not even have a job to take them outside the enclave.

A real danger of enclave living is that it may interfere with or delay adaptation to the new culture. Someone living in an enclave usually experiences the host culture from a distance even though it appears that he is living within it. With limited contact with the host culture, the problem of misinterpreting the behavior of local people continues for a longer time than it otherwise would. This makes the newcomer more vulnerable to falling into a Level Two awareness of the host culture. Everyone who lives in the enclave is adapting to the new culture and the more experienced residents are likely to be in the third stage of adaptation in which they are especially conscious of the negative aspects of the new culture. Their opinions are influential within the group, so the newcomer often accepts their negative opinions. What often happens is that enclave residents develop their own subcultures based on the difficulties of living in the host culture. (See

324

Case 21 Practicing English.) At the same time the enclave resident has few if any host culture relationships through which he could gain a more realistic understanding of the new culture.

Living in an enclave is not a solution to cross-cultural adaptation problems. It eases the strain of the early period of life in the new culture, but the newcomer eventually has to move out from the enclave emotionally as well as physically in order to adapt to the new culture successfully.

Retreating into an enclave is only one way in which some newcomers drop out of the adaptation process. International companies report that as many as 20 to 40% of the staff they send overseas return home prematurely. It is in this second stage of confusion that the risk of abandoning the adaptation process is greatest. The costs of adaptation failure are often high. International companies pay a big price when their expatriate workers return home earlier than planned or adapt to the new culture in a negative way. Corporations compute these costs, but we cannot easily estimate the psychological costs to individuals and families when their hopes for their stay abroad are not realized.

While everyone goes through the adjustment process, there are ways to ease discomfort and improve the probability of adapting successfully.

Strategies for coping with adaptation stress

Do what you can to increase your score on the cultural adaptation checklist
- You can't change your age, but you can learn more about your company or city and you can adjust your thinking

Be alert for signs of adaptation stress
- Health problems
- Loss of self-confidence
- Loneliness, sense of loss, severe homesickness
- Withdrawal from social contacts
- Negative feelings
- Behaving more aggressively than usual

Tell people at home what kind of support you really need from them
- You may need freedom to make new decisions and their understanding of the difficulties you face more than you need their advice

---

Use your "retreats" from the new culture constructively
- Find home culture time and friends to refresh yourself and restore your positive feelings (speak your own language, eat familiar food, etc.)
- Look for people from your home country with positive attitudes
- Don't spend time with people from home who reinforce negative feelings

Pay attention to differences within the new culture
- Avoid making broad generalizations about everybody in the host culture
- Notice differences in background, motivation, personality; some people will be more like you than others
- Just as you are not like everyone from your culture, so not everyone from the new culture is alike
- People from the host culture may also be experiencing adaptation stress. When you are sensitive to their adaptation stress, you won't take their responses to you too personally

Try to find two mentors (experienced helpers)
- Look for someone from your home culture who has more experience in the new culture than you do
- Someone from the new culture with much experience with your culture
- Consult your mentors to check your interpretations of cross-cultural events
- Use your mentors to learn about hidden aspects of the new culture

Seek out positive experiences within the new culture
- If you like to watch football, watch football with people from the new culture
- If you enjoy music, enjoy it with people from the new culture
- That is, take your pleasures and relaxing activities into the new culture

Be tolerant of yourself and others
- Keep your sense of humor; misunderstandings can turn into funny stories
- Assume that new culture associates have reasons for their actions even if you do not understand them
- Recognize that you are learning culture as you go through difficult experiences
- If necessary, adjust your goals and time frame to make them more realistic

Use your cross-cultural experience to increase your skills
- Notice and imitate the communication styles of people from the new culture
- Use concepts from cross-cultural communication study to interpret your experience and adjust your behavior

1. Using the list of strategies for coping with adaptation stress, give Wu Lian advice about coping with her situation. Imagine her objections to your advice and try to find good answers for them.

2. Write a letter to Wu Lian's best friend at home explaining Wu Lian's present feelings and giving the friend some suggestions about how she can support Wu Lian while she is going through this difficult time.

3. Talk with a foreigner living in your country about his or her adaptation. Are they aware of the adaptation process? What were their greatest difficulties during the confusion stage? What did they do about it?

4. Talk with a foreigner who lives in an enclave. What does the person report as the advantages and disadvantages of this living arrangement? What is life like living in this special community? Would the person prefer to live elsewhere? What is your opinion about how the person is coping with adaptation stress?

Stage Three: Frustration

At this stage the confusion, self-doubt and depression of the second stage usually decline and are replaced by more negative attitudes about the new culture. Instead of blaming or doubting himself, the newcomer starts to put the blame for his difficulties on the new culture and its people. He may become suspicious and believe that the host country people around him always have negative reasons for doing what they do. The person has much more knowledge of the new culture but what has been learned is judged negatively.

In a way, this is a change for the better, because it shows that the newcomer is paying more attention to what the people around him are actually doing. That he frequently misinterprets what he observes is due to his stress and his incomplete under-standing of the host culture. It is also likely that the newcomer has actually had an experience or two with people who behaved badly for one reason or other and is now over-generalizing from that experience. Everyone living in another culture will meet people who have odd stereotypes and unpleasant prejudices about people from their home culture. The newcomer is still not very skilled at distinguishing one situation from another or pick-ing up more subtle messages that would help him evaluate the in-tentions of the people with whom he is communicating.

The newcomer feels worse but is learning to cope

At this point the person's mood and sense of well-being are at their lowest point as represented by the bottom of the curve on the diagram of the adaptation process. The person may total-ly reject the new culture and want more than anything in the world to escape. If he stays, he will inevitably start to express his frustration. This may take the form of minor irritability or spectacular outbursts of anger. The Westerner in China who sus-pects he is being cheated by a vendor may simply toss his bag of fruit back and walk away, or he might start yelling and accusing in whatever language he is able to manage. The vendor will surely understand. The feeling being expressed is unmistakable.

It takes energy to express frustration and anger. It is a sign that while the newcomer is behaving badly; he has more energy now than he did during the confusion stage. He has decided that he will not allow this new situation to defeat him. He feels terri-ble, but his energy for coping has increased. The Westerner who thinks he is being cheated is taking the first step in learning how to bargain. He has decided he will not pay whatever price is asked, but will do whatever is necessary to get a fair price. He has decided to actively cope with the new challenges he faces, which requires that he learn culturally appropriate skills. At first he is not good at it, and his bad behavior may create a neg-

328

ative impression, but he will get better at it with time. One day he will surprise himself by actually enjoying the bargaining and may even gain some respect from the sellers for his skill and determination. He has started the long climb up toward feeling as positive about himself and the new culture as he did the day he left home.

Exploring Ideas

Work on the next three case studies in small groups. Each group should identify the adaptation stage of each of the participants in the case it is assigned. Remember that people living in their home culture who have contact with people from another culture are also adapting to an unfamiliar culture.

Case 20 Off to a Bad Start

Off to a Bad Start

David Hu had just started working for the foreign owned company. He was sitting at his workstation but had not been given any assignment that he should be doing at this moment. He was relaxing and waiting and then thought he would take the opportunity to have a look around. He poked his head into several offices just to see what there was to be seen.

Suddenly Mr. Parker came up to him and angrily asked him what he was doing. David Hu was embarrassed. He laughed and quickly started to move back toward his workstation. This did not seem to satisfy Mr. Parker who started to talk rapidly and angrily. Hoping to calm him down, Mr. Hu smiled and apologized, trying to explain that he was trying to learn more about the department. However, Mr. Parker got even angrier. Finally, another worker came by and calmed him down, but as Mr. Parker left he still looked angry. Mr. Hu sighed; he knew he had made a bad start, but still didn't understand why.

Case 21 Practicing English

Practicing English

One night a Chinese student majoring in English sat on the steps of the foreign students' residence and talked with two young male foreign students, one German and one American. They did not speak a word to her on their own initiative, but she asked many questions to get a conversation started. Every time they answered her with only one or two words. But she was determined to practice her English so she tried to keep the conversation going.

"How do you spend your weekend?" she asked.

The German boy answered immediately, "Fishing," and the two boys looked at each other meaningfully.

"Fishing?" She was really confused. "But where do you fish?" she asked.

"Fishing has two meanings. One is the literal meaning. The other is just sitting here or walking on the street and waiting for some girls to come up to us." Then they both burst out laughing.

She was annoyed. She sat there silently and then suddenly stood up and walked away without saying good-bye.

Case 22 Fair Price?

> ### Fair Price?
>
> Ken Kopp, an American importer, successfully negoti-
> ated a contract with Zhen Jian garment factory in southern
> Jiangsu Province to purchase 46,000 winter coats in three
> months. The first two months went very smoothly. Ken was
> satisfied with everything from quality control to prompt
> shipping; he was even more surprised with the speed of pro-
> duction. One summer afternoon he decided to drive down
> from his headquarters in a large hotel in a nearby city to in-
> spect some of the factory's workshops. He was pleased to
> find himself cordially greeted by every worker he met.
> Through his interpreter he readily told some inquisitive Chi-
> nese workers that he was paying their company $10 for
> each coat, which he then would sell for $200 in the US.
>
> The following week the American manager unexpected-
> ly noticed a sharp decline of the garments' quality at the
> packing department. He immediately raised his concern to
> the Chinese manager and tightened quality inspection. Noth-
> ing seemed to help. The pile of rejected coats just kept
> growing to the point that it was impossible to finish the con-
> tract in time.

For each case, answer the following questions:
1. At which stage of the cultural adaptation process is each participant?
2. How are adaptation factors influencing their feelings and behavior?
3. What cultural differences are being misunderstood?
4. What negative stereotypes might the participants who are in
   the confusion or the frustration stage of adaptation form of
   the other culture?

Once your group members are satisfied that they understand the adaptation issues and cultural differences that are influencing events in your case, present your case analysis to the class.

Give advice to each of the participating groups and individuals about how they can respond more positively to the challenges of adapting to an unfamiliar culture.

Stage Four: Effectiveness

During the third stage the person is feeling bad but is acting in a more assertive way to deal with the new culture. In time these efforts pay off and the person becomes more effective. The person is gaining cross-cultural skills that lead to more positive experiences. As a result the person starts to have more positive feelings about the new culture and his outlook becomes more optimistic.

The sojourner (no longer a newcomer!) is now a sensitive observer of life in the new culture and uses that ability to observe and to learn new behaviors. The person may improve in their language skills, but equally important is the growing ability to communicate non-verbally. They know what facial expressions and body movements are called for in most situations. They know what they can say or should say and they know what not to say. They are able to make more accurate assessments about what the behavior of the host country people means and they can choose their responses deliberately rather than being overwhelmed by feelings of doubt or anger. These new behaviors bring them some success and this in turn helps them to be more relaxed. Now the person is not spending so much energy defending against the "bad" or "manipulative" behavior of some local people. Now he is more likely to see these situations as opportunities to try out a new strategy for coping with the problem such a person presents.

The Westerner who six months earlier walked away from the street vendor in anger, now confidently enters a Chinese hotel ready to bargain for a reduction in the foreigners' room rate. Wu Lian has learned which of her classmates are worth spending time with and she has learned how to ask them the right questions to learn what she needs to know to manage her study well. One new friend told her that it is not necessary to read all of the books her professors assign page by page. She has learned how to read selectively and how to get the information she needs from each book quickly. She has learned how to evaluate the actual requirements for each course and each teacher and is now getting enough rest.

By this time the person is able to accept both the similarities and the differences between his home culture and the new culture. He is becoming more sensitive to local people and as a result his relationships with them are becoming warmer and more personal. The person has added important new skills to his cultural software and has some confidence that he can deal with new situations as they arise. Life is definitely becoming more comfortable.

Exploring Ideas

1. If possible, find someone who has been living in your culture long enough to have entered the stage of effectiveness. Ask that person what new skills and ways of behaving he or she has adopted to be effective in the new culture.
2. Alternatively, consult someone from your culture that has been living in another culture for a year or more. What new skills and behaviors has he or she adopted in adapting to the new culture?
3. After you have consulted several people who have experienced cross-cultural adaptation, make two lists of advice, one for someone from your culture going abroad and one for someone from abroad coming to live in your culture.
4. Can such advice ease or even prevent adaptation problems?

Stage Five: Appreciation

In this stage the person moves beyond effectiveness in the new culture to an attitude of appreciation. He is developing a more personal understanding of the new culture and values it. The person is able to live a full life, experiencing the full range of human feelings in the new culture. The person can love, trust, laugh and solve problems, just about everything he can do at home. He is becoming more creative, expressive and able to take initiative and responsibility.

In comparing life at home to life in the new culture, the person finds he prefers some things about the new culture. When the person carries this tendency to positively value the new culture while criticizing his home culture to an extreme, some will say that he has gone native. This is an informal way of saying that the person is trying to get rid of his home culture identity in favor of adopting an identity rooted in the new culture. This can become a serious psychological problem, because it is not really possible to do this, as hard as one may try. Such a total rejection of the home culture is essentially a rejection of the self.

A more positive way of moving through this stage is to become a cultural interpreter who helps others bridge the gap between cultures. A more experienced sojourner may become a mentor to someone from his home culture or may take on some responsibility for helping members of the new culture understand his home culture better. Such people can share their own adaptation experiences with people from both cultures and help their organizations find new ways to promote cross-cultural understanding.

From the diagram of the adaptation process, we see that in the appreciation stage the person may be functioning at a higher level and is likely to feel even better than during the excitement stage. The person has grown as a person, not just in terms of skills that may be valuable at home as well as in the new culture, but also as a human being. The cross-cultural experience can be a profound learning experience. What has been happening is that the former more limited personally has crumbled and been replaced by a new one that functions at a higher level of human sensitivity and self-awareness.

This very positive, life transforming outcome is not inevitable. There are pitfalls all along the way, but if the person comes to an appreciation of the new culture without rejecting his home culture, then the adaptation process has been successful.

Exploring Ideas

From your study of adaptation think of ways that organizations can help to support people through the adaptation process. For instance, what should international companies do to:
1. Orient new employees from the local culture who are beginning work with the foreign company;
2. Provide support for the family members of expatriates working for international companies who accompany them abroad;
3. Develop company personnel policies that are responsive to adaptation issues;
4. Provide opportunities for local employees and expatriates to discuss their adaptation issues with each other;
5. Provide appropriate social activities and information to local employees and expatriates that are responsive to adaptation issues;
6. Provide training in cross-cultural communication.

Returning Home

When people return home, they go through another adjustment period called reentry. The evidence indicates that the stressful period of this adaptation process begins sooner, is more

335

severe and lasts longer than the stress of adapting to an unfamiliar culture. It is also clear that those who made the best adjustment when they were overseas have the most difficulty with reentry. Why is this so?

One reason is that those who adapted best are probably the ones who changed the most from their sojourn. They are confident in their ability to adapt and succeed, so they are unlikely to be anxious about returning home. Also in a foreign country the hosts expect the newcomers to make mistakes and be different. Most expect the sojourner to have difficulties and to experience stress and homesickness. Back in the home country, however, everyone expects the one who is returning to fit in quickly. They are less tolerant of mistakes and do not expect the returnee to experience stress.

Another problem is that sojourners often idealize home while they are away. Suddenly they realize that the streets are not as clean as they remembered them and that people are not as warm and friendly as they had thought. Seeing the home culture through the eyes of the new culture to which the person has adapted often leads the returnee to be more critical than before the overseas experience. If returning to a low context culture after a stay in a high context culture, it may seem that people talk too much and are insensitive to the unspoken feelings of others. If returning to a collectivist culture from an individualistic one, the person may resent the burden of social obligations family members assume the returnee will fulfill. If returning to a rich country from a poor one, the returnee may notice the waste of electricity, paper and money that they never noticed before. If returning to a poor country from a relatively rich one, the returnee may have trouble with physical inconveniences and wonder how life was ever enjoyable under such conditions.

As with cultural adaptation, reentry is a process. Anticipating it and adopting good strategies for coping with the return will not make the return trouble free, but it will help to reduce

336

the magnitude of the problems and contribute to a positive readjustment to the home culture. If the person has spent a long time in another culture, he has much to share with the people at home. The problem is that he may share his observations and feelings all at once, and in a way that confuses or offends loved ones and colleagues at home. The returnee is trying to communicate how important the new experience has been, but people at home cannot be expected to understand this all at once.

The same strategies that the sojourner used to adapt to the foreign culture now must be used to cope with the stress of returning home.

Exploring Ideas

1. Review coping strategies for cultural adaptation and apply them to the reentry process. What should the returning person do to ease the adjustment of reentry?
2. Read the following case and answer the questions.

Case 23 The Homecoming

The Homecoming

Hong, a college student from an ordinary family from one of the smaller cities of Jiangsu Province, was wild with joy when her older sister Lan told her she would return home for a two week visit after living in the United States for six years, first as a student and now as an employee of a San Francisco company. Hong remembered all the letters and phone calls from her sister and knew that Lan had been lonely in America.

Even though Lan was only going to be home for two weeks, the whole family regarded this reunion as of prime importance. Lan, too, had been looking forward to returning home for years, but until now lack of funds, rules and regulations about visas and the demands of study and work had kept her away. Even though the expense was considerable, Hong, her parents and several other relatives traveled to Shanghai to meet Lan's plane. Once they returned home, there was a big celebration as this was the Spring Festival season as well as Lan's homecoming.

Soon, however, everyone was not as happy as they had expected. Lan was impatient when her friends and acquaintances came to visit her one after another. They wanted her to tell them story after story about her life in the US. Lan also started to complain about life in China, finding fault with the streets, department stores and television programs, among other things.

"Hong, how can you bear these freezing winter days in this cold house? Only one heater is not enough. Why don't you buy three, one for each room?" She asked as she walked restlessly from one room to the other shivering with cold. Hong forced a smile and said, "We cannot afford that yet, as you surely know." Lan said nothing more but a subtle look of disdain appeared on her face.

Once while cooking with her mother in the kitchen, she became annoyed with the difficulties of preparing a meal. She said, "My goodness. The water is unbearably cold. In every American home, you can make the tap water any temperature you want. I think you should try to make your life better." The mother looked into her daughter's disapproving eyes, said nothing and left the kitchen in a hurry to hide her tears.

Lan's mother and father insisted that Lan buy some small gifts for her old friends and former teachers or at least invite them to a restaurant for dinner. Every time they suggested this, Lan objected. "Why should I spend money on them? That's my money. I earn it and spend it as I choose.

In America no one is forced to spend their money to save face for the family. " As she raised her voice, Hong could hardly believe that she was the same person who had been so kind and considerate years before. What had become of her dear elder sister?

What surprised Hong most, however, was when she heard her sister talking to her American boyfriend on the phone. She knew she should respect Lan's privacy, but she could not resist peeping through the keyhole into the next room. Shivers ran down her spine as she saw and heard her sister weeping and revealing her suffering to that American man over the telephone.

On the day Lan left, Hong had mixed feelings. She was sad because she felt she and Lan now belonged to two different worlds, but she was glad that Lan was able to return to her American life, as it was clear that she now preferred the US to home.

When it was time to say good-bye, Lan was confused. She did not love her family or her motherland any less, so what went wrong?

1. Do you think that something went wrong with Lan's visit? Or is it a matter of Lan and her family having unrealistic expectations for the long-awaited homecoming?
2. What could Lan or members of her family have done to make the visit more successful?
3. How should Lan and her family do things differently when Lan comes home the next time?
4. Do you think that Lan has "gone native" that she is rejecting her home culture identity and trying to adopt an American identity?

Stage Six: More challenging cross-cultural experiences

When a person has successfully adapted to a new culture, he

has learned how to learn culture. That is a valuable attribute for anyone living in the global village. The person is now ready for new cross-cultural experiences. Multi-national and global companies are in need of professional employees who can function effectively and live comfortably in more than one culture.

The person will repeat the adaptation process as he or she moves deeper and deeper into the new culture, returns to the home culture, or enters another new culture. The person will continue to experience the stress of adaptation, but now accepts the ups and downs of adaptation as a part of life. The person is wiser now and is better able to cope with it. If someone remains in one new culture for an extended period of time he may become fully bi-cultural, equally at home in both cultures. If he moves to other new cultures as part of a career, he may become an expert in moving between cultures.

There are losses as well as gains in such a life. The person may feel equally at home in two cultures, but not fully at home in either. No matter where the person is living, he always feels that he has left a part of himself in his other home. He will inevitably form strong personal ties with people from both cultures and is not able to be with all of them at the same time. Family relationships can become complicated when some family members are from one culture and some are from another. Despite the long term difficulties of a multi-cultural life, few who live it would choose to go back to living only in the culture of their birth. This is their life now and it is a life more and more of us will live in the future.

Exploring Ideas

Discuss the satisfactions and difficulties of being a cross-cultural person. What do you gain and what do you lose from this kind of life?

References

Anderson, Walter Truett, *Reality Isn't What it Used to Be*, New York: Harper & Row, 1990

Barber, Benjamin R., "Jihad vs. McWorld", *The Atlantic*, March 1992

Blackman, Carolyn, *Negotiating China: Case Studies and Strategies*, Sydney: Allen and Unwin, 1997

Bond, Michael H, ed., *Handbook of Chinese Psychology*, Hong Kong: Oxford University Press, 1986

Brick, Jean, *China: A Handbook for Intercultural Communication*, Sydney: Allen and Unwin, 1995

Brislin, Richard W., *Applied Cross-Cultural Psychology*, Newbury Park, CA: Sage Publications, 1990

Condon, John C. and Fathi Yousef, "Out of House and Home", in *An Introduction to Intercultural Communication*, Indianapolis: Bobbs-Merrill, 1975

Davies, Rod, "Team Mangement Roles on the Margerison-McCann Team Mangement Index" *Orient Pacific Century*, from the Asia-Pacific Management Forum web site: http://www.mcb.co.us/apmforum/opc/opctea, 1996

Davies, Rod and Paul Temporal, "Team Building in Asia" *Orient Pacific Century* from the Asia Pacific Management Forum website, 1996-98

De Mente, Boye Lafayette, "Chinese Etiquette & Ethics in Business", *Orient Pacific Century* from the Asia Pacific Forum web site: http://www.mcb.co.uk/apmforum, 1997

Garreau, Joel, *The Nine Nations of North America*, New York: Houghton Mifflin, 1981

Gudykunst, William B., Lea P. Stewart and Stella Ting-Toomey, *Communication, Culture and Organizational Processes*, Beverly Hills, CA: Sage, 1985

Hall, Edward. T., *Beyond Culture*, New York: Doubleday &

Company, 1976

Hall, Edward. T., *The Hidden Dimension*, New York: Doubleday & Company, 1966

Hanvey, Robert G., *An Attainable Global Perspective*, New York: Center for Global Perspectives, 1976

Higgs, Malcolm, "Overcoming the Problems of Cultural Differences to Establish Success for International Management Teams", Team Management Systems International, 1996

Hofstede, Geert, *Culture's Consequences: International Differences in Work Related Values*, Newbury Park, CA: Sage Publications, 1980

Hofstede, Geert, *Cultures and Organizations: Software of the Mind*, New York: McGraw Hill, 1991

Holland, Dorothy and Naomi Quinn, *Cultural Models in Language and Thought*, Cambridge: Cambridge University Press, 1987

James, David, *The Executive Guide to Asia-Pacific Communications*, 1997

Kolb, Robert K., *Survival Kit for Overseas Living*, Yarmouth, ME: Intercultural Press, 1976

Kluckholn, Florence and F. Strodtbeck, *Variations in Value Orientations*, Evanston, OH: Row & Peterson, 1961

Li Zehou, *The Path of Light*, London: Oxford University Press, 1994

Stewart, Edward C. and Milton J. Bennett, *American Cultural Patterns: A Cross-Cultural Perspective*, Yarmouth ME: Intercultural Press, 1991

Tannen, Deborah, *The Argument Culture: Moving from Dialogue to Debate*, New York: Harper, Collins, 1998

Tuan, Yi Fu, "Strangers and Strangeness", in *The Georgraphic Review*, 1978

Wu Jian and Cornelius Grove, *Encountering the Chinese*, Yarmouth, ME: Intercultural Press, 1990

342

Suggested Readings

It is not likely that you will find much professional literature on cross-cultural communication in your library or book store. That is because as a professional field of study cross-cultural communication is relatively young. Even if you are lucky enough to find some of the books listed as references for this book, you should keep in mind that you want to "do culture" not simply read about it.

When choosing books to read, look for those that look at your home culture from the perspective of an outsider and those that look at cultures that are unfamiliar to you from the perspective of an insider. In other words, gain some distance from your own culture and try to get closer to the unfamiliar culture. Also, be sensitive to the level of cross-cultural awareness of the authors of books that you choose. Some books with promising titles are written from Level One or Level Two cross-cultural awareness (See chapter 3). Reading such books may be entertaining (Level One Awareness) but they probably will not increase your cross-cultural understanding. Even worse are books that have a negative tone and describe the foreign culture as a knotty problem to be solved (Level Two awareness).

Both China and the West have long traditions of travel writing. This is a good way to travel in your imagination when you cannot travel in reality. You can share others' journeys and learn what it is like to experience a new culture.

Iron and Silk by Mark Salzman (New York: Random House Vintage) tells his story of teaching English and studying the martial arts in China. He has both frustrating and very satisfying experiences as he tries to learn Chinese culture. His book will give you an idea how your culture appears to someone who is unfamiliar with it.

Pico Iyer, a British-American travel writer wrote a series of essays for his book *Video Night in Kathmandu: and Other Tales from the Not-So-Far East* (New York: Random House Vintage). He visited several Asian countries, including China, briefly and makes extensive comments on the influence of Western popular culture on the cultures of Asia.

For books dealing specifically with cross-cultural communication, look for those published by the Intercultural Press in Yarmouth, Maine, USA. Most of these books are written for Westerners who are visiting other cultures for professional purposes such as teaching or business. The many books by Edward T. Hall dealing with cross-cultural communication can also be obtained from this publisher. Their titles include:

From Da to Yes: Understanding the East Europeans
From Nyet to Da: Understanding the Russians
Understanding Cultural Differences: Germans, French, and Americans
American Ways: A Guide for Foreigners in the United States
Developing Intercultural Awareness: A Cross-Cultural Training Handbook
Survival Kit for Overseas Living
Intercultural Negotiation: A Cross-Cultural Perspective
Encountering the Chinese

If you are interested in cross-cultural communication as part of your professional development as a staff person for an international company, there is much new information available, but not necessarily in book form. You should look for materials posted to various web sites such as the Asia-Pacific Management Forum at http://www.mcb.co.uk/apmforum. They have a section on Team Building in Asia that will help you learn more about working on cross-cultural teams.

If you are teaching English as a second language look for the culture section of the TEFL-China Teahouse at http://teflchina.com. It includes materials on how to incorporate the teaching of culture into language teaching and has anecdotal reports of cultural differences observed by Westerners teaching English in China. There are many other ESL web sites. Just type ESL as your search term when using one of the web search sites such as Yahoo!

On the Internet you can also find "The Edge: The E-journal for Intercultural Relations" at http://www. kumo. swcp. com/biz/theedge. This is a new magazine published every month, but only electronically, that contains articles about research in cross-cultural communication. You should also be able to find theoretical articles that discuss some of the concepts introduced in this book more fully.